Toward a Code of Ethics for Management Accountants

by

C. Mike Merz
Professor of Accounting
Boise State University

and

David F. Groebner
Associate Professor of Management
Boise State University

National Association of Accountants
New York, N.Y.

Published by

National Association of Accountants
919 Third Ave., New York, N.Y. 10022

NAA Publication Number 81129
ISBN 0-86641-009-0

Foreword

Technical matters never have been the only concern of the National Association of Accountants. NAA programs and activities traditionally have fostered a sense of quality fellowship characterized by the commitment to high standards of professional conduct. The decision to commission a study on ethics makes the concern more explicit and may take the commitment one step further—toward a code of ethics.

The Association's concern for professional ethics has been reflected in the structure of the Certificate in Management Accounting program. In the current CMA examination outline, the subject matter regarding "ethical considerations" reads: "The role of the management accountant in organizations and society. Commitment to employer, the profession and society. Accounting and information integrity."

An important initiative for this research evolved from the demand related to the CMA examination requirements and the scarcity of published work on ethics. Research support for the CMA program was a major objective of the study. Another major research support objective was to provide a basis for an informed evaluation of the need for a code of ethics and to explore alternative courses of possible action by the Association.

The findings indicate that NAA members tend to favor a code of ethics, although most of the surveyed members have not experienced serious ethical dilemmas in their professional work. The NAA Committee on Research has recommended to the Executive Committee that a task force be established to prepare recommendations regarding a code of ethics.

The research work included a review of the literature on ethics, an examination of codes of ethics in other professions, and a three-phase survey of NAA members. In the course of the survey, 749 NAA members participated: 137 were interviewed—in 30 unstructured and 107 structured interviews—and 612 completed a mail questionnaire. The researchers and the NAA Committee on Research are grateful to all of them.

A final note of gratitude goes to the Project Committee under whose thoughtful guidance the study was conducted and the report prepared:

Patricia P. Douglas, *Chairman*
University of Montana
Missoula, Montana

Robert U. Boehman
Jasper Rubber Products, Inc.
Jasper, Indiana

Homer Figler
Ernst & Whinney
New York, New York

David P. McElvain
Dresser Industries
Dallas, Texas

Henry A. Schwartz
IBM
Armonk, New York

The report reflects the views of the researchers and not necessarily those of the Association, the Committee on Research or the Project Committee.

Stephen Landekich
Research Director
National Association
of Accountants

Table of Contents

List of Tables

Executive Summary

This study was initiated to help NAA decide what posture, if any, to take with respect to ethics for management accountants. One event which stimulated the study was the enactment of the Foreign Corrupt Practices Act, which forces more responsibility for financial information upon management accountants. Very little prior research specifically addressed ethics for management accountants. A vast body of ethical theory has been developed since the writings of the earliest philosophers, and considerable guidance is available from codes of ethics in other professions. No one, however, had ever asked management accountants if they encountered ethical dilemmas in their work. To accomplish the broad objectives of the study, three main research tasks were performed:

- A review was made of the body of ethical theory which underlies contemporary societal and business ethics.
- Other professional codes of ethics were analyzed so that management accountants might benefit from the experiences of other professional business groups.
- Surveys were made of management accountants; 137 personal interviews were conducted in 10 different metropolitan areas; NAA members completed more than 600 questionnaires mailed to a random sample of 1,000 members.

Results of this research suggested the following implications and conclusions with respect to a code of ethics for management accountants.

Ethical Theory

Contemporary societal ethics seems to blend utilitarianism and Kantian ethics. Management accountants, however, will not find specific guidelines for a code of ethics from ethical theory. Ethical theorists really have not addressed ethical issues relevant to a professional business person in the United States in the 1980s. Certain ethical responsibilities of the management accountant have been addressed in the Law of Agency, which specifies, for example, that an employee must follow all reasonable directions of the owner of the business, but that the employee has no obligation to follow directions to perform illegal or unethical acts.

Ethical theorists do not agree on many issues such as whether a code of ethics influences personal behavior. One of the major principles of the so-called Judaic-Christian ethic is that man is able to freely choose between right and wrong. Some psychologists and philosophers, such as Skinner and Freud, however, believe man's actions are determined primarily by environmental conditioning or by subconscious parts of the brain and that man is not able to choose freely between courses of action.

Another issue frequently debated is what role business should play in our society. Classical economists believe that business fulfills its ethical duty to society best by striving to maximize profits. Some contemporary philosophers believe that business also has a responsibility to achieve societal goals. Seeking guidance from ethical theory seems like a necessary first step in developing a professional code of ethics, but ethical theory does not provide much specific guidance for a code of ethics for management accountants.

Other Codes of Ethics

Most people are aware that the established professional groups—CPAs, doctors, engineers and lawyers—have adopted codes of ethics. Not so well known is that the vast majority of other professional groups also have adopted codes. All professional business groups with a certification program, such as the Financial Analysts Federation with its Chartered Financial Analyst and the Institute of Internal Auditors with its Certified Internal Auditor, have adopted codes for their general members and certificate holders. Thus, the absence of a code for its general members and for the holders of Certificates in Management Accounting makes the NAA unusual among profession associations.

Most codes address issues related more to desired professional behavior than to ethics. For example, the Realtor's Code specifies that an offer on a piece of real estate must be in writing and that the offeror must receive a copy of the offer. And the CPA's code specifies that the CPA must plan and supervise an engagement adequately. Therefore, the title of "Code of Ethics" is really a misnomer. "Code of Conduct" or "Standards of Professional Behavior" more aptly describe the issues addressed by most codes.

With respect to the feasibility of a code of ethics, management accounting closely resembles the data processing and internal auditing professions. Data processors and internal auditors usually work as employees, as do management accountants. Little opportunity for public conflict occurs because management usually would deal internally with any disagreements that occur with its data processors or internal auditors. No artificial barriers to entry in the profession exist to prevent a person from working as a data processor or internal auditor. Membership in a professional organization—the IIA or the Data Processing Management Association (DPMA)—has little effect upon seeking employment. Both professional organizations have established certification programs—the Certified Internal Auditor and Certified Data Processor. Because the professions of data processing and internal auditing resemble management accounting in many ways, NAA might benefit from the experiences that IIA and DPMA have had with their codes of ethics.

Both the IIA and the DPMA adopted codes fairly recently—in the 1940s for IIA and in 1967 for DPMA. Both general members of the organizations and their certificate holders have essentially the same codes that specify how the member should conduct his or her professional affairs. The codes fit nicely on one page; many members display the codes in their offices. Both the IIA and DPMA have policy statements about how they will conduct an investigation if a complaint about unethical conduct is received. Neither organization, however, experiences enforcement problems. The rare complaint which does occur seems to "go away" before any official action is required. Even though they do not try to enforce their codes, the IIA and DPMA appear quite satisfied that their codes enhance the professional image of their members and serve as useful educational tools.

Surveys of Management Accountants

Management accountants do face ethical dilemmas in their work. An ethical dilemma occurs when the accountant feels pressure to do something that he or she feels is not right. In the unstructured interviews, respondents gave specific examples of ethical dilemmas they had faced that are shown in Table 3 on page 30. A number of respondents had left former jobs because of these ethical dilemmas.

How the accountant resolves an ethical dilemma depends upon the environment present within the employing organization. Many companies scrupulously follow all rules and regulations. Management accountants working for these companies solve their ethical dilemmas by determining the right course of action and then taking it. In some companies, however, management exerts pressure upon accountants to perform acts that might be considered unethical, such as distorting or manipulating financial data. Resolving ethical dilemmas sometimes imposes severe strains upon the management accountants in these companies.

Most NAA members who responded to mail questionnaires favored a code of ethics. Of the 600 usable responses, 431 (72%) felt that NAA either *definitely* should or *probably* should adopt a code. A smaller number, 296 (49%), thought that a code would help them or other management accountants resolve ethical issues. Similar results occurred during the interviews. Although most respondents favored a code, it was not a "burning" issue to them. The most frequently cited advantages and disadvantages of a code appear on pages 31 and 32. All interview respondents favored a code of ethics for CMA holders.

A detailed search for statistically significant relationships between the mail survey data was made using univariate (Chi Square) and multivariate (discriminant function) analyses. Several statistically significant relationships occurred between demographic variables and whether or not a respondent favored a code. These relationships were not, however, practically significant for prediction purposes. For example, a significantly smaller percent of respondents who were CPAs favored a code than did non-CPAs. Most of the 201 CPAs responding to the mail questionnaire did favor a code though, as shown below.

Percent of CPAs favoring a code	65%
Percent of non-CPAs favoring a code	76%
Percent of all respondents favoring a code	72%

While these results are statistically significant at the .05 level and provide an interesting insight to the data, the results do not permit accurate prediction about whether any one person favors a code. Discriminant analysis yielded insights about what types of persons most frequently tended to favor a code, but, again, the tendencies were not strong enough to permit accurate predictions. For the most part, the statistical analyses showed that a management accountant's personal feelings about ethical issues or about a code of ethics cannot be predicted from the data gathered in the study.

Results of the interviews and mail questionnaires yielded insights to the form and content of a code that most NAA members would find acceptable. The code should be written in general terms and should address ethical issues relevant only to accounting functions; the code should not address management functions. In format, the code should segregate a management accountant's responsibilities to various entities such as: employer, general public, accounting profession, and colleagues. The code should address most of the issues responded to in question 1 of the mail survey, Appendix E.

The researchers believe that results of this study support the conclusions that: (1) NAA should adopt a code of ethics, and (2) the Institute of Management Accounting (IMA) should adopt a similar code for CMA holders.

Chapter 1

Introduction

The NAA Committee on Research initiated this study to determine if management accountants typically encountered ethical dilemmas in their work and if developing a code of ethics for management accountants seemed desirable.

The study included three main stages. In the first stage, the researchers reviewed the development of ethical theory. They decided that ethics for a specific business group, such as management accountants, should be derived somehow from general or societal ethics. The researchers analyzed other professional codes of ethics in the second stage so that NAA might be guided by the experiences of other professions. In the third stage, they surveyed management accountants to determine the ethical dilemmas that they encountered and to determine how they felt about a code of ethics for management accountants. The survey was conducted by unstructured interviews, structured interviews and a mail questionnaire. One surprising result of these surveys was that several interview respondents commented that participating in the study had been enlightening for them. Apparently these persons subconsciously had been concerned about ethical issues but had not had an opportunity to verbalize their concerns in some sort of constructive manner.

A summary of the entire study immediately follows the Foreword. Chapters 2 and 3 present an overview of ethical theories and codes of ethics, respectively. Chapter 4 describes the interview process and presents results of interviews. Chapter 5 covers the mail survey, including lists and analyses of the responses. Chapter 6 contains a summary of the conclusions reached during the study. The appendices contain documentation and detailed results. (Upon request, the authors will gladly provide additional details of the study to all interested researchers.)

Chapter 2

Contemporary Ethics: Societal and Business

To have the deepest possible roots, and the greatest justification, a professional code of ethics should be derived from a general theory of ethics. In addition, the code for a specific professional group, such as management accountants, should be consistent with both contemporary societal and business ethics. That great advocate of the free enterprise system, Milton Friedman, referred to the role that ethical considerations should play in business when he described the role of corporate executives:

> That responsibility is to conduct business in accordance with their desires (. . . the owner's), which generally will be to make as much money as possible while conforming to the basic rules of the society, both those embodied in law and those embodied in ethical custom.[1]

Therefore, the appropriate sequence for establishing the theoretical framework for a code of ethics for management accountants is first to review ethical theory, then examine how this theory has influenced societal and business ethics in the United States.

Contemporary ethical beliefs prevalent in the United States appear to have evolved from "Utilitarian" and "Deontological" ethics. The researchers review these two schools of ethical thought first. Next, contemporary business ethics are examined, starting with a review of what various ethical theorists believe the proper role of business should be. No consensus exists on this issue. A final question is whether man acts in a rational manner. Some psychologists believe that factors such as environmental conditioning are the predominant influence upon man's actions and, therefore, that a code of ethics would have little or no effect. A summary of the implications this review of ethical

---

[1]R. Baun (ed.), *Ethical Arguments for Analysis,* (Holt, Rinehart and Winston: New York, 1975), p. 205.

theory has for management accountants appears in the final section of the chapter.

This attempt to summarize and analyze many centuries of ethical thought suffers from obvious problems of oversimplification. The intent, however, was only to provide the reader with an idea of how various theories of ethics relate to ethical considerations for management accountants.

Utilitarianism—The Ethical Basis of Democracy

Utilitarianism is the ethical theory which asserts that an act or practice is right (when compared to any alternative act or practice) if it leads to the greatest possible balance of good consequences and that the concepts of duty and right are determined by that which is good.[2] Generally speaking, democracy is based upon utilitarian intuitions.[3] When a democratic society votes on an issue and accepts the wishes of the majority, the underlying principle is that society as a group should pursue that course of action which brings the greatest good to the greatest number of people. Much of the debate over social legislation revolves around the issue of whether the greatest good will result if government transfers resources from relatively affluent persons to those who are needy. Thus, the principle of utilitarianism underlies contemporary societal ethics in the United States.

David Hume, Jeremy Bentham and John Stuart Mill developed the modern theories of utilitarianism although utilitarian views appeared in the earliest ethical writings. Two somewhat different theories of utilitarianism have resulted from the attempts of these philosophers to provide guidelines to the person trying to decide the right action: (1) act utilitarianism and (2) rule utilitarianism.

Act utilitarianism requires that in all situations one should perform that act which leads to the greatest good for the greatest number. Rules should be broken in circumstances where following the rules would not lead to the greatest good. Situation ethics is one form of act utilitarianism.[4]

Rule utilitarianism, however, requires that actions must conform to

---

[2]Tom L. Beauchamp and Norman E. Bowie (eds.), *Ethical Theory and Business,* (Prentice-Hall: Englewood Cliffs, 1979), p. 3. Most of this chapter has been synthesized from the papers presented in Beauchamp and Bowie.

[3]Alex C. Michalos, "The Loyal Agent's Argument," in Beauchamp and Bowie, *Ethical Theory and Business,* p. 346.

[4]The term *situation ethics* was originated by Dr. Joseph Fletcher in *Situation Ethics: The New Morality,* (Westminister: Philadelphia, 1966).

firm and publicly advocated moral rules.[5] Proponents of rule utilitarianism believe that this ethical principle saves us from the temptation to view each situation as a special case for which breaking the established rules is legitimate.

Both act utilitarianism and rule utilitarianism have strengths and weaknesses which are continually debated by ethical theorists. The central issues revolve around whether the greatest good will result when people act as they see fit in each situation or whether the greatest good will result in the long run when all people follow the rules consistently.

Deontological Ethics

Although the underlying principle of our contemporary societal ethics is utilitarianism, deontological theories also have an influence. In contrast to utilitarianism, which places primary concern upon the consequence of an act, deontological ethics asserts that a variety of relationships among persons have a significance independent of the consequences of these relationships.[6]

A person's position in life or society creates certain duties. Deontologism is derived from the Greek term meaning duty. For example, parents have duties or obligations to their children which are not directly related to the consequences of their performing these duties. Deontologists place considerable emphasis upon the motives accompanying an act. For example, one parent might care lovingly for a sick child because of natural paternal instincts, while another parent, who actually might resent having to care for the child, does so purely from a sense of duty. The 18th Century deontologist, Immanuel Kant, argued that a person who acted according to sense of duty was morally superior to the person who acted from natural instincts.[7] Kant developed his "categorical imperative" to provide universal principles of ethics which were independent of each person's conscience.

Kant's Categorical Imperative vs. Conscience as a Guide

Even though the notion "let your conscience be your guide" has a certain intuitive appeal, recent moral philosophers do not trust conscience as a dependable guide to action. Rather, these philosophers

---

[5]Beauchamp and Bowie, *Ethical Theory and Business*, p. 7.

[6]*Ibid.*, p. 15.

[7]*Ibid.*, p. 19.

seek universal ethical principles. Conscience is not considered a sufficient guide to ethical action. It is easy to cite examples of a person who follows his or her conscience to an immoral act—for instance, the political terrorist or assassin. Some psychologists even believe that there is no rational basis for conscience.

Kant, in an effort to define universal principles of ethics which were not dependent upon each person's conscience, developed a categorical imperative: "One ought never to act except in such a way that one can also will that one's maxim should become universal law."[8] The categorical imperative requires consistent actions in all situations and thus helps solve certain ethical dilemmas. For example, a businessman's conscience might permit him to bribe someone in a situation where the bribe would lead to the greatest good and therefore be desirable, according to utilitarianism. Kant's categorical imperative would dictate that bribery always is unethical because if everyone were permitted to bribe, then the entire business system might break down.

Another important aspect of Kant's philosophy is the notion that human rights are important. While utilitarianism would permit the exploitation of the human rights of laborers if this would lead to the greatest good, Kant would condemn such exploitation as unethical. Thus, Kant's philosophy of a categorical imperative which leads to universal principles of ethics is helpful in avoiding undesirable outcomes which utilitarianism could condone. Both Kant and utilitarianism appear to influence contemporary societal ethics.

Contemporary Societal Ethics—a Blend of Several Theories

Contemporary societal ethics existing in the United States in the 1980s contain guides to action which blend each of the ethical theories previously discussed. As mentioned earlier, act utilitarianism forms the underlying principle of our democratic system. "The majority rules," which determines the action to be taken in many situations, embodies the principle of act utilitarianism—choose the act which results in the greatest good to the greatest number.

Rule utilitarianism also plays an important role. The correct act to choose is dictated in many circumstances by laws or unwritten rules of society. We are a "law-abiding society"—people generally respect and follow the rules. Thus, our societal ethics do not condone breaking rules against lying, cheating, stealing, inflicting physical harm on another person, and the like.

---

[8]*Ibid.*, p. 8.

Immanuel Kant's philosophy also has had a strong influence on our societal ethics. We tend to expect that persons will fulfill the duty of their position in society. Doctors, police officers, elected public officials (and perhaps management accountants) perform duties which society expects them to fulfill, independent of the consequences, or good, which results from fulfilling those duties. The influence of Kant's belief that human beings have certain inherent rights is found in our country's Bill of Rights, which contradicts utilitarian principles. The movements in recent years to end discrimination and to provide equal opportunity for all persons in our country have a strong basis in Kant's categorical imperative which sought universal principles of ethics. Thus, contemporary societal ethics are predicated primarily upon utilitarian ethics although other ethical theories also have had a strong influence.

The Role of Business—Conflicting Views

Business ethics generally depend upon the role granted to business by society. A certain amount of conflict currently exists over business' proper role in society. The classical position developed by early philosophers and economists now is attacked as inadequate by various contemporary groups sometimes called moralists. An understanding of the conflicting views of the proper role of business is necessary because a code of ethics for a professional business group might reflect either the classical or moralist position.

The Classical Theory of the Role of Business

The so-called classical view of the proper role of business within society was developed first by the early Greek philosophers Plato and Aristotle. Adam Smith reached similar conclusions based upon his economic analysis. Smith's "invisible hand" principle still finds strong support from many proponents of the free enterprise system. Each of these theorists believed that business should not establish specific social goals or try to achieve social objectives.

Plato and Aristotle sought answers to the general question, "What constitutes goodness?" In considering the make-up of a good state or good society, Plato analyzed the roles of the business and labor community, the armed forces, and the rulers. Business, which Plato relegated to the lowest status of the three classes, was to provide for the material needs of the citizens of the state in an efficient manner.[9] It

[9] *Ibid.*, p. 26.

would be wrong for any class to aspire to the functions of a different class, and thus it would be wrong for business leaders to determine the policies of society since that is a proper function for the rulers. Aristotle's view was similar because he believed that each individual owes a great debt to social institutions, including the state. Aristotle would reject the popular notion of the "self-made man" as impossible because no person can be truly independent of his or her society.

Adam Smith's "invisible hand" principle embodies the ethical theory of utilitarianism. The public good is promoted by individuals pursuing their individual interests. Pursuing a profit is ethical primarily because this profit leads to the public good. Thus Smith used economic analysis to arrive at the same conclusion as Plato and Aristotle. Because the greatest good for the greatest number results when business persons selfishly try to maximize their own profit, it would be wrong to impose any social objectives upon business. Many proponents of the free enterprise system still subscribe to Smith's theories. Milton Friedman, probably the best-known American advocate of free enterprise, succinctly stated that: "The purpose of business is business," meaning that it is wrong for businesses to attempt to accomplish any goal other than making a profit.

The Ethical Egoist

A popular view of business ethics, which agrees with the philosophical views discussed above, is that the business person should act as an "ethical egoist," one who strives to achieve his or her egoistical desires but who ethically follows established rules. By pursuing his or her own best interests, the business person is not being selfish or indifferent to the interests of others. Rather, this pursuit is good business practice because it leads to the greatest good by creating jobs and increasing the overall standard of living. The established rules of competition, however, regulate how the business game is to be played, and the business person acts as a restrained, or ethical, egoist. As the business person follows the established rules, he or she conforms to the principles of rule utilitarianism.

Thus, the classical view of business ethics combines conflicting ethical theories. Utilitarianism provides the ethical rationale for our business system, which should operate to provide the greatest good. Each business person, however, should act as an egoist because pursuing one's best interests leads to the greatest good for the greatest number. Each business person also must follow the established rules of business, so the term "ethical egoist" aptly describes the overall ethical role of the business person. In recent years, however, many persons have challenged this classical view.

The Social Responsibility of Business

Many persons believe that the classical view of the role of business is no longer appropriate for a business community dominated by large corporations. These persons, who sometimes are labeled "moralists," believe that business should assume responsibility for accomplishing desirable social goals. Modern business has immense social power in such areas as minority employment and environmental pollution, and major business decisions affect the entire social system. Keith Davis and Robert Blomstrom developed their "Iron Law of Responsibility," which states that, in the long run, those who do not use power in a manner which society considers responsible will tend to lose their power.[10] Therefore, in order to preserve its position in society, business must attend to important social issues.

A more "Kantian" view is that business institutions have a duty to act as good citizens and accept responsibility to improve society in areas where they have special competence and influence. Just as each individual citizen bears certain social responsibilities, so does the corporation. If an individual has a duty not to litter the highway, then the corporation also has a duty not to pollute the environment.

Both utilitarianism and deontological ethics underlie the view that business has social responsibility beyond the objective of making a profit. The view that society may disenfranchise business if business fails to use its power to help achieve societal goals appears utilitarian in nature. Both the classical theorists and the moralists seek the utilitarian goal of the greatest good for the greatest number. Classical economists believe this goal is achieved best when business tries only to maximize profits, while the moralists believe that the greatest good results if business also pursues social objectives. Some moralists also believe that business has a citizen's duty to pursue social goals. The conflict between the classical economists' views and the moralists' views has not been resolved in our society.

Unresolved Conflict Over Business Ethics

Debate continues concerning the proper role of business in our society and whether business has an ethical responsibility to accomplish general societal goals. Many business persons, corporate executives and classical economists decry increasing government regulation, such as the Fair Employment Practices Act, which imposes social objectives upon businesses. Others criticize the rising influence of multina-

---

[10] Keith Davis and Robert L. Blomstrom, *Business and Society: Environment and Responsibility* (3rd ed.) (McGraw-Hill: New York, 1975), p. 50.

tional corporations which seem to operate beyond the bounds of government regulation. The same philosophical conflict is debated in current political campaigns, with some candidates arguing for restricting government powers and others citing the need to enact new government regulations of business.

Ethical Position of the Employee—the Law of Agency

Most management accountants work as employees. The employer-employee relationship might generate certain ethical pressures upon both the employee and the employer. Several ethical dilemmas that might occur in employer-employee relationships already have been addressed in the law of agency. Established laws represent accepted societal ethics in accord with the principle of rule utilitarianism. The *Restatement of Agency* specifies agent and employee duties and the limitations on those duties in several areas.[11]

1. *The duty of obedience.* An employee has the duty to obey all reasonable directions, although business or professional ethics should be considered in determining if an order is reasonable. In no event is it implied that an employee has a duty to perform illegal or unethical acts.[12]

2. *The duty of loyalty.* The agent (or employee) should act solely for the benefit of the principle in all matters connected with his agency. When not acting as an employee, however, a person may in good faith act in a manner injurious to his employer. For example, an employee of a cigarette manufacturer could campaign for legislation restricting advertisements for cigarettes during nonworking hours.

3. *The duty of confidentiality.* An employee may not use information acquired through relations with his employer to further his own interests or interests of another unless the information is a matter of general knowledge. An employee may, however, reveal confidential information about an employer's illegal acts. Thus, agency law permits, but does not require, an employee to "blow the whistle" on an employer.

Although some professional codes of ethics address the issues of obedience, loyalty and confidentiality, the law of agency already prescribes an employee's duties, and the limitations on duty, in those areas.

---

[11]In 1958, the American Law Institute compiled all of the common law principles of agency into its Restatement (second) of Agency. This Restatement is considered the most authoritative source of agency law.

[12]Phillip I. Blumberg, "Corporate Responsibility and the Employee's Duty of Loyalty and Obedience," *Oklahoma Law Review,* Vol. 25, No. 3, August 1971, reprinted in Beauchamp and Bowie, *Ethical Theory and Business,* pp. 304–317.

Are People Always Rational?

The final ethical issue to be considered is whether people are controlled primarily by their intellect or reason or by some other force such as environmental conditioning. The majority of moral philosophers have been ethical rationalists. Starting with Socrates, who believed that to *know* the good is to *do* it, through Aristotle, Thomas Aquinas, Dewey, and others, this group believed that correct action can be determined by an intellectual process. One of the major principles of the so-called Judaic-Christian ethic is that man is able to choose freely between right and wrong.

The feeling that the right act can be determined by reasoning is by no means universal. For example, one of the leading contemporary psychologists, B.F. Skinner, claimed that regardless of what we think, our actions are determined primarily by our environment. Skinner's idea is shared, to some extent, by a number of ethical philosophers, many of them living long before Skinner. Rousseau, for instance, thought that man basically was good and that all evil acts were a result of social conditioning. To a certain extent Bergson shared his feeling. Another group to question the rational choice school has been the psychologists and psychiatrists influenced by Freud. Freud formulated the theory that much human behavior is caused by parts of the mind that the rational intellect cannot control. To the extent he is right, much human action must be classified as irrational. Many Christian writers, including Augustine and Calvin, found difficulty in reconciling freedom of choice with the concept of an all-powerful and all-knowing God.

Therefore, while most ethical theory assumes that the rational man chooses whether to act rightly or wrongly in any situation, serious doubt exists concerning man's ability to make a conscious choice about how to act. Thus, the influence of a professional code of ethics upon behavior is uncertain. Some current writers believe that while a code cannot legislate behavior, it serves the useful purpose of allowing a profession to evict unethical members.

Summary and Implications for Management Accountants

This analysis has attempted to review the principal theories of ethical thought which influence contemporary societal and business ethics. Reading the works of ethical theorists and attempting to reconcile the various theories tends to be quite frustrating. More questions seem to be asked than are answered. This review of societal and business ethics, however, suggests the following implications concerning ethical considerations for management accountants.

1. Ethical theory does not specify what action is correct in each situation. Because ethical theory must be applied continually to new issues as they arise, considerable debate usually occurs before the applicable ethical priorities seem to emerge. For example, prior to the Foreign Corrupt Practices Act (FCPA), how corporations conducted business in foreign countries received little attention.

2. By definition, professional codes of ethics embody the ethical principle of rule utilitarianism. Although act utilitarianism seems to be the main ethical basis for democracy and business, many ethical dilemmas have been resolved by applying rule utilitarianism, which asserts that the greatest good results when people consistently follow established rules. Thus, a firm precedent exists in ethical theory for establishing a code of ethics.

3. A code of ethics might or might not impose increased ethical responsibilities upon management accountants. Many ethical issues a management accountant might face already have been addressed by societal or business ethics. For example, agency law clearly removes an employee's obligation to follow an employer's directions to perform an illegal or unethical act. Most of the provisions of a professional code of ethics would simply compile existing ethical responsibilities.

A code for management accountants might, however, specify new ethical responsibilities. One major issue is whether management accountants have duties beyond those of managers and employees in general. For example, while agency law permits an employee to "blow the whistle," it does not impose a duty to do so. If the management accountants' code specified such a duty, it would impose a new ethical burden upon them. The recently enacted FCPA may require management accountants to assume new ethical burdens or duties. Developing a code that encompasses existing ethical principles applicable to management accountants should be relatively simple. Deciding which new ethical responsibilities, if any, should be included and securing acceptance of the new responsibilities by management accountants pose considerable difficulty.

4. No consensus currently exists concerning whether business institutions have any responsibility to accomplish general societal goals. Because most management accountants are employed by business institutions, it will be difficult to adopt an explicit position with respect to social responsibility in a code of ethics that will be acceptable to most management accountants and their employers.

In this review of ethical theories, the researchers have attempted to provide the broad insight required for the development of a code of ethics for a specific professional group. Many professional groups in the United States developed and adopted codes of ethics a long time ago. The next chapter examines how these professional codes work.

Chapter 3

Codes of Ethics in Other Professions

Even a casual survey reveals a bewildering number of professional codes of ethics. In addition to the well-known professionals such as doctors, lawyers, engineers, and public accountants that have codes, most other professional associations have adopted a code of ethics for their members. In fact, the only prominent "professional" organization without a code of ethics appears to be the National Association of Accountants. In order to benefit from the experience of other professional groups, the researchers conducted a general survey of how professional codes have developed and investigated the workings of a number of codes of ethics which are considered relevant for management accountants.

Historical Development of Professional Codes

Probably the first attempt at a set of standards or ethics for professional conduct would be the Code of Hammurabi. Of course much more than professional standards of behavior were specified in this code, which attempted to lay down the rules necessary to govern a complex society in 2000 B.C. The Hippocratic Oath, setting standards of behavior for physicians, was formulated about 500 B.C. Neither of these sets of standards, however, appears to be closely related to present professional ethical codes.

The basis for most of the modern professional ethical codes appears to be the code developed by barristers in Medieval England. This code has had the greatest influence on the code of the legal profession in the United States and that of the medical, dental, and other professions as well. To understand this first attempt at a "modern" code of professional behavior requires understanding the conditions in the legal profession in England during the Middle Ages.

Henry S. Drinker, in his book about legal ethics, points out that the barristers in Medieval England traditionally were members of the landed gentry.[1] They were sons of the wealthy who really had no need to work to earn a living. Because of their high social position, they looked down on those who had to work and consequently set themselves above persons engaged in business activities. In addition, the legal profession was a close-knit group with almost nightly social contacts.

Because of these factors, the early legal code of ethics developed by the barristers really was a statement of professional etiquette within the profession rather than a statement of ethics as we now define it. The code attempted to set the legal profession above persons who had to advertise and compete for business, as none of the early barristers had to worry about generating business. Also, it became more important to maintain good relations with a social companion than to represent a client vigorously.

As with so many other traditions, the United States' professions tended to look to England when considering codes of ethics. As such, therefore, many of the earlier codes were more or less statements of correct behavior among members of the profession. Only recently has concern for the consumer of professional services become a major concern in ethical codes. Even today in most of the professional codes we find discussion of the responsibilities of correct behavior toward fellow members of the profession.

In the process of reviewing professional codes of ethics, it became apparent that hundreds of codes exist. Thus, the researchers limited the study to two types of codes considered relevant for management accountants: 1) codes of the commonly known professionals including doctors, lawyers, engineers and public accountants and 2) codes for business professionals somewhat related to management accountants such as internal auditors, financial analysts and insurance agents. As the study progressed, it also became apparent that the codes of certain groups were similar. For example, the code for dentists closely resembles the code for medical doctors, and the code for property and casualty underwriters resembles the code for life underwriters. When duplication occurred, a detailed summary of only one group was prepared. The codes of ethics of the following 12 professions or professional groups appeared to illustrate all of the important variables possible in a professional code:

1. American Bar Association
2. American Marketing Association
3. American Medical Association
4. Certificate in Data Processing holders

---

[1]Henry S. Drinker, *Legal Ethics,* (New York: Columbia University Press, 1953).

5. Certified Internal Auditor
6. Certified Property Manager
7. Certified Public Accountant
8. Chartered Bank Auditor
9. Chartered Financial Analyst
10. Life Insurance Agent
11. National Association of Purchasing Managers
12. National Society of Professional Engineers

A detailed summary of each of these codes is contained in Appendix B. It did not seem practical to make a detailed examination of each of the 35 professional codes for the known certification programs in business disciplines which are listed in Appendix A.

Important Variables

As the researchers reviewed the various professional groups and their codes of ethics, certain patterns emerged. To permit analysis of how a code is structured and how the code works, six important variables were identified:

1. Ethical issues addressed by the code
2. Complexity of the code
3. Structure of the profession
4. Barriers to entry in the profession
5. Enforcement of the code of ethics
6. Opportunity for conflict

Analysis of these six variables permits understanding of the similarities and differences among the codes. A potential code for management accountants should be considered in terms of these variables.

Ethical Issues Addressed by the Code

Four general types of issues or ethical concerns seem to be addressed by the various codes:

a) *Technical.* Many codes specify that the professional person should provide services in a technically competent manner. For example, the AICPA's code states that "a member shall exercise due professional care in the performance of an engagement," and the Realtors' code specifies that realtors "shall see that financial obligations regarding real estate obligations are in writing. A copy of each agreement shall be furnished to each party upon his signing such agreement." These examples typify the nature of technical issues contained in the various codes. Some codes are written in general terms, and some codes are very specific.

b) *Responsibility to Clients*. All of the codes for professionals who serve specific clients, such as doctors, clearly call out the professional person's responsibility to those clients. Most codes give responsibilities to clients the highest priority.

c) *Etiquette*. All the codes deal, at least in part, with maintaining good relations among members of the profession. The feeling always seems to be that professional behavior requires respect and courtesy among members of the profession. Enforcing these etiquette clauses has led many professional organizations into conflict with the federal government, which now asserts that the codes serve to protect the members of the profession from competition.

d) *Responsibility to the Profession and Society*. All of the codes contain provisions which specify that the professional person must consider society in general and try to enhance the public image of the profession. These provisions usually are written in general terms that would be difficult, if not impossible, to enforce. The code for professional engineers is unique in that it gives highest priority to the needs of the general public, which seems appropriate for an engineer designing a public facility.

Complexity

The codes of ethics ranged from the complex, taking up a small book, to the simple, consisting of 10 or more short statements. The most complex codes belong to the doctors and the lawyers, both of whom have very extensive codes. The simplest are those of the purchasing managers and the market researchers. Although it seems as though the longer a code has been in existence, the more complex it becomes, this is not a fixed rule. The purchasing managers' code has been in existence for almost 60 years, yet it remains one of the simplest. No evidence exists to suggest that a complex code ensures more ethical behavior than a simple code, although many organizations feel that a complex code is more effective.

Structure of the Profession

Professions and professional groups have organized into a bewildering array of combinations. In some professions, each of the entities listed on the next page plays a role and has its own code of ethics.

- State licensing boards
- Local and state chapters of professional associations
- National professional associations
- Organizations which award and administer the professional certification program

As each entity usually has adopted its own code of ethics and also may play a role in enforcing the code, understanding how the profession is structured is important in understanding how the code works.

Internal auditors appear to have the simplest organizational structure. An internal auditor has only one organization to join, the Institute of Internal Auditors (IIA). The IIA awards the Certified Internal Auditor (CIA) designation to qualified members. Membership in the IIA is voluntary; a CIA has no legal status. General members of IIA and CIAs have adopted the same code of ethics.

The most complex professional organizational structure occurs in the life insurance business. An agent first must obtain a license from the state. The agent then would join a local or state association of life underwriters that belongs to the National Association of Life Underwriters, a federation of the state and local associations. If the agent wishes to become certified, he or she enrolls in the American College of Life Underwriters, which conducts training courses and awards the Chartered Life Underwriter (CLU) designation. Having achieved a CLU, the agent then joins the American Society of CLUs, which administers all affairs of CLUs who have been awarded the designation by the American College. Thus an insurance agent may be subject to as many as five different codes of ethics during his or her career.

Because of the unique characteristics of their professions, doctors and lawyers are organized somewhat differently. The summary outlines in Appendix B for the American Bar Association and American Medical Association describe how codes work in each of these professions which differ from management accounting in many ways.

Barriers to Entry

Professions, in general, and their professional organizations have widely different barriers to entry. Although some organizations accept anyone working in the field as a member, other organizations have extensive educational, experience, and/or licensing requirements for members. For the established professions, the required license to practice represents an ultimate barrier to the profession. For the less established professions, such as market researchers and internal auditors, one easily can practice as a professional without being a member of the professional association. As the professional association becomes a stronger force in the profession, the requirements for membership become more difficult. Recent actions of two groups appear relevant to management accounting and the National Association of Accountants (NAA).

- Financial Analysts—When the Chartered Financial Analyst (CFA) program was started in 1962, a code of ethics was adopted. However no attempts to enforce the code were made for eight years. Then a fairly strong enforcement program was initiated. The Financial Analysts Federation (FAF), which is the professional organization for all financial analysts including non-CFAs, recently made passing one portion of the CFA exam a requirement for membership.
- Life Insurance Agents—The National Association of Life Underwriters (NALU), the professional association for all life insurance agents, recently started requiring that new members complete certain training programs within four years of joining NALU.

As it now operates, NAA seems to accept all applicants for membership and even recruits new members through the chapter competition system. If NAA wishes to increase its professional status and adopt an enforceable code of ethics, then establishing criteria for membership, such as the FAF and NALU have done, might be appropriate.

Enforcement of the Code of Ethics

The enforcement structure of the professional organizations varies from nonexistent to very complicated. Perhaps the most complex is that of the state bar associations. Because they are part of the legal system in most states, many parts of their codes of ethics are contained in the state legal codes. A violation of ethical standards may lead to a sanction, or even disbarment, by the state Supreme Court. On the other hand, the National Association of Purchasing Managers has no procedure to enforce the provisions of its code; neither does the American Marketing Association. Some organizations, such as the American Medical Association and the American Institute of Architects, have stopped enforcing many provisions of their codes.

When the codes are being enforced, the mechanism varies greatly. In some organizations, such as the data processors, all violations and enforcements are handled at the national level. Other organizations, such as the professional engineers, tend to handle their enforcement at the local level. In fact, only after the contracting scandals in Maryland did the National Association of Professional Engineers set up any form of national enforcement mechanism. Many organizations, such as the state societies of CPAs and the American Institute of CPAs (AICPA), initiate ethics investigations at the local level and then institute regional or national trial boards for those cases which cannot be disposed of informally. Due process has become important during all phases of ethics investigations to protect the professional group from legal suits claiming infringement of civil rights.

Definitive statistics describing the number of alleged violations of codes of ethics are practically nonexistent. Only the AICPA and the Institute of Chartered Financial Analysts (ICFA) provide information about the number and disposition of cases. Appendix B includes detailed summaries of the number of investigations initiated and the disposition of cases for both organizations. Between 0.3 and 0.4% of CPAs and CFAs become involved in ethics investigations each year. Most investigations are dismissed without the alleged violation being substantiated. Formal hearings rarely occur. An informal agreement is reached in the vast majority of investigations.

Opportunity for Conflict

In professions that provide a well-defined service, more alleged ethical violations occur. For example, if the patient dies or the bridge falls down, the doctor's or engineer's technical competence and professional conduct may be attacked. Professions that handle clients' money, such as real estate, also provide many opportunities for alleged ethical violations. Intense competition for clients by life insurance agents also leads to frequent alleged violations.

Less opportunity for conflict occurs, however, in professions where the professional serves as an employee of an organization. Thus, relatively few ethics cases occur for the data processors, purchasing agents, and internal auditors who usually practice as employees rather than serving independent clients.

Recent Federal Action

Recent actions by the Supreme Court and the Federal Trade Commission (FTC) appear to signal that the evolution of professional codes of ethics has entered a new stage. Present confusion caused by these actions recently forced the American Medical Association to announce that it will not enforce its code of ethics. Any organization that is considering adoption of a code should be aware of the current federal attacks upon professional codes of ethics.

As discussed previously, most professional codes contain clauses relating to etiquette among members. Generally these clauses forbid actions such as advertising, engaging in competitive bids and soliciting for business. The feeling within the professions is that these actions are undignified and demeaning to members of the profession. Such undignified actions tend to undermine the public's confidence in the profession in general. The counter argument, of course, is that restricting such actions also tends to reduce competition and raises the prices paid by the public for professional services. In any event, these professional etiquette clauses are the ones that have been under attack.

The first volley was fired by the United States Supreme Court in 1975 when it decided, in *Goldfarb* vs. *Virginia State Bar Association,* that the minimum fee schedules circulated by the state bar were a form of illegal price fixing. Perhaps more important, the Court decided that the professions were not automatically exempted from federal antitrust laws. Even though the Court generally has held that states were exempt from federal antitrust laws, in 1977 the Court found, in *Bates* vs. *Arizona State Bar,* that states may not prohibit attorneys from advertising their routine fees and services. In 1978 the Court, in *National Society of Professional Engineers* vs. *United States,* ruled that the professions are fully subject to the antitrust laws, and, even though the conditions would vary from profession to profession, no profession could adopt rules that would clearly restrict competition. It thus outlawed the professional engineers' ban on competitive bidding.

The Federal Trade Commission, following up on these rulings, seems to be questioning any code of ethics clauses that would tend to discipline organization members for competitive behavior. In general, any clauses requiring a reasonable degree of technical competence seem to be acceptable. The etiquette clauses, however, are being severely attacked. This is particularly true if membership in the organization is important for a professional and if a violation of an etiquette clause permits the organization to discipline a member.

Implications for Management Accountants

The review of how codes of ethics operate in other professions suggests the following implications for management accounting and for NAA:

1. Almost all professional organizations in business-related disciplines have adopted a code of ethics. Except for the Certificate in Management Accounting (CMA), all of the certification programs require that certificate holders abide by a code of ethics. Thus, the absence of a code for general members of NAA and a code for CMAs is unusual.

2. The nature of the profession in which most management accountants serve as employees does not provide much opportunity for alleged

ethical violations. If NAA were to adopt a code of ethics, few enforcement problems should occur.

3. A strong code of ethics with specific provisions probably is inappropriate for NAA, which actively recruits members and accepts virtually all applicants for membership.

4. Certificate programs do not require stricter ethics than are required of noncertified members of the profession. For example, CIAs have the same code as general members of IIA, and CFAs have the same code as general members of the FAF.

5. No new code should be adopted without strongly considering the recent Supreme Court rulings and actions of federal agencies that have been attacking the professional etiquette clauses in other codes. Because management accountants usually do not compete for clients, complying with the emerging federal regulations should not pose a difficult problem.

If management accountants were to adopt a code of ethics, the implications that apply mostly to structuring of the code should be considered. To what ethical issues a code for management accountants should be addressed will be discussed in the next chapter that reports on the personal interviews of management accountants to determine what ethical conflicts they face.

Chapter 4

Personal Interviews of Management Accountants

To discover the opinions that management accountants have about ethical issues, the researchers conducted a three-phase survey:

1. Thirty unstructured interviews were conducted with a "convenience-judgment" sample of management accountants in three different cities.
2. Structured interviews were conducted with a "stratified-judgment" sample of 107 management accountants in seven different cities.
3. A mail questionnaire was sent to a random sample of 1,000 NAA members.

Because no one ever had systematically asked management accountants about ethical dilemmas they encountered in their work, this three-phase plan enabled the researchers to obtain a good understanding of some key issues during the personal interviews. Experience gained during the interviews permitted the researchers to design a meaningful mail questionnaire to ask the opinions of a broad representation of NAA members. Because the interviews were conducted with relatively small samples selected judgmentally, the researchers' conclusions must be considered tentative.

General Research Methodology

Because there seemed to be no prior research concerning the types of ethical conflicts faced by management accountants, unstructured interviews were conducted first. During an unstructured interview, the respondent was encouraged to take the initiative and lead the discussion into areas which the respondent felt were important. Thus, the unstructured interviews were intended to reveal those areas of ethical concerns which would be researched more thoroughly in the structured interviews and mail questionnaires.

Researchers in the social sciences have identified the three conditions which must be satisfied in order to conduct a successful interview:

1. *Data Accessibility*—The respondent must have, in an accessible form, the data sought by the interviewer. The respondent must be able to relate the information in terms familiar to both the respondent and the interviewer.[1]

2. *Respondent Cognition*—The respondent must understand the role he or she must play. The respondent also must understand enough about the research task so that he or she will know what constitutes successful completion of the interview.

3. *Motivation*—Respondent motivation, or willingness to report, is a prime condition for successful data collection.

To make sure that these conditions were met and that the information gathered from each interview was measured reliably, a seven-step interview process was followed for the unstructured interviews.

Interview Process—Unstructured Interviews

Step 1—Identify Prospective Interviewees

To avoid the bias which might occur if all interviews were conducted in one geographical location, three cities were selected for the unstructured interviewing: one in the West, one in the Northeast, and one in the South.

The researchers asked the NAA chapter presidents in the three selected cities to suggest management accountants in their city who could make a meaningful contribution to the study and who would be willing to participate. The chapter presidents were quite willing to help. Because the study plan called for 30 unstructured interviews, approximately 60 prospective respondents were identified by the chapter presidents. An attempt was made to select a judgmental sample of prospec-

[1]For a thorough discussion of research methodology see: Charles F. Cannel and Robert L. Kahn, "Interviewing," in *The Handbook of Social Psychology* (2nd ed.) Vol. II, edited by Gardner Lindzey and Elliot Aronson, (Reading, Mass.: Addison-Wesley, 1968), pp. 526–595, or Charles F. Cannel and Robert L. Kahn, "The Collection of Data by Interviewing," in *Research Methods in the Behavioral Sciences,* edited by Leon Festinger and Daniel Katz, (New York: Holt, Rinehart, and Winston, 1953), pp. 327–380.

tive respondents with a broad coverage of demographic variables such as age, education, and management level in the organization.

Step 2—Letter Requesting Help

The one-page letter appearing first in Appendix C was sent to each prospective respondent.

Step 3—Phone Call

Several days after receiving the request letter, each prospective respondent was called by one researcher to ask whether he or she would be available for an interview during the week when the researcher planned to visit that city. From the list of about 60 prospective respondents, the researchers were barely able to arrange the 30 required interviews; almost half the people suggested had moved, changed jobs, or were unavailable. The demographic variables of the 30 persons who agreed to an unstructured interview and were subsequently interviewed are summarized in Table 1.

Step 4—Information Letter

About one week before the interview, the three-page letter appearing second in Appendix C was sent to each person who agreed to be interviewed. This letter attempted to help the respondent conceptualize his or her experiences and opinions before the interview occurred and thus satisfy the data accessibility condition for a successful interview.

Step 5—Conduct Interviews

One or both researchers conducted each unstructured interview, usually at the respondent's work location. Each interview was conducted informally, with the respondent being encouraged to take the initiative and lead the discussion as much as possible. Some respondents obviously had clarified their ideas prior to the interview and revealed ethical conflict situations they had faced along with strong opinions about what should be in a code of ethics for management accountants. Other respondents had to be asked leading questions to start the discussion.

Step 6—Summary Letter

Each respondent was sent a letter summarizing the main points discussed during the unstructured interview. One of these letters (with the respondent's name disguised) appears as the third item in Appendix C.

TABLE 1
Demographic Variables of the Respondents in the Unstructured Interviews

Characteristic	Classification—Number of Respondents
Sex	Male—24 Female—6
Age	20s—2 30s—13 40s—10 50+—5
CPA	Yes—15* No—15
CMA	Yes—3 No—27
College	No Degree—5 Bachelor's—19 Master's—6
Supervisory Level	Top Management—5 Middle Management—17 Lower Management—4 Staff Accountant—4
Organization Type	Profit Oriented—25 Not-for-Profit and Public Sector—5
Organization Ownership	Public Corporation—16 Privately Held Corporation—7 Not a Corporation—7
Organization Size**	Small—8 Medium—9 Large—13
Level in the Organization	Corporate Office or Single Entity Organization—20 Division or Subdivision—7 Operating Plant—3

*These CPAs were currently employed as management accountants.
**Size of the parent organization, approximately, including divisions and subdivisions.

Step 7—Follow-up Phone Call

To make sure that the respondent's ideas had been recorded reliably in the interview summaries, the researchers called each respondent to ask if he or she agreed with the summary. A few significant changes in the summaries were made as a result of these calls.

Interview Process—Structured Interviews

The process followed for the 107 structured interviews generally was the same as for the unstructured interviews. An attempt was made to stratify the sample demographically. The demographic characteristics of respondents are presented in Table 2. The initial request letter and the information letter sent to respondents are presented in Appendix D. Respondents were selected from seven different metropolitan locations in the United States to eliminate any possible geographical bias.

In the structured interview, the respondent answered a series of specific questions designed to provide more information about issues covered in the unstructured interviews. The "Structured Interview Format," contained in Appendix D, lists each question asked each respondent. For those questions with specific response categories, the number of responses to each question has been added to the questionnaire in Appendix D. Because respondents were asked questions that permitted fairly specific answers during the structured interviews, little opportunity existed for a misunderstanding between the respondent and the interviewer.

As previously discussed, a successful interview requires that the desired data are accessible by the respondent, the respondent understands his or her role, and the respondent is motivated to cooperate. The interview processes were carefully designed to meet these conditions, and the researchers believe that both the unstructured and structured interviews achieved the desired results.

Interview Results

The unstructured interviews, somewhat exploratory in nature, were intended to reveal which ethical issues seemed important to management accountants. In the structured interviews, those important issues were explored in more depth. The combined results of both unstructured and structured interviews can be understood best as providing insights to the following key issues:

1. Do management accountants typically face ethical dilemmas in their work? If so, what specific types of ethical dilemmas do they encounter?

TABLE 2
Demographic Variables of the Respondents in the Structured Interviews

Characteristic	Classification—Number of Respondents
Sex	Male—93 Female—14
Age	20s—17 30s—37 40s—31 50+—22
CPA	Yes—34 No—73
CMA	Yes—11 No—96
College	No Degree—9 Bachelor's—80 Master's—18
Supervisory Level	Top Management—23 Middle Management—31 Lower Management—26 Staff Accountant—27
Organization Type	Profit Oriented—98 Not-for-Profit and Public Sector—9
Organization Ownership	Public Corporation—76 Privately Held Corporation—16 Not a Corporation—15
Organization Size	Small—18 Medium—20 Large—69
Level in the Organization	Corporate Office or Single Entity Organization—52 Division or Subdivision—40 Operating Plant—15

2. Should management accountants have a code of ethics?
3. If a code is appropriate, what should its form and content be?
4. To whom should a code of ethics for management accountants apply?

In the following discussion, the results of the interviews with respect to each of these issues is presented.

Issue 1: Do management accountants typically face ethical dilemmas in their work? If so, what specific types of ethical dilemmas do they encounter?

Most respondents discussed any ethical dilemmas or conflicts that they faced in terms of the ethical climate present in their work environment. In general terms, respondents described three different types of ethical climate:

1. *Ethically Pure*—In many companies, top management apparently has conditioned employees to take the ethically correct action in all cases. All laws and regulations are to be followed scrupulously. External auditors receive complete cooperation. Many companies have adopted their own corporate code of ethics. Such companies usually adopt this ethically pure posture because they believe that it makes the most business sense. Respondents made statements such as "our company just can't afford the bad publicity that would result if we got caught doing something wrong."
2. *Ethical within Reason*—With respect to ethics, some companies emphasize making the best business decision rather than being ethically pure. These companies attempt to conduct their business in an ethical and responsible manner. In a specific instance, however, a minor infraction of a law might be condoned if breaking the law led to the best business decision.
3. *Ethically Questionable*—In a small number of companies, management accountants had been pressured to manipulate financial information to mislead certain users of that information. Several respondents cited such pressures as the principal reason that they had quit former jobs.

The ethical climate existing within the organization strongly influenced how respondents resolved any ethical dilemmas that occurred.

Each respondent in the unstructured interviews was asked to describe specific ethical dilemmas that he or she had encountered. Some respondents did not choose to verbalize specific ethical dilemmas although several did provide explicit descriptions of dilemma situations. Many respondents alluded that dilemmas occurred, but they did not provide specific details. Table 3 summarizes the types of ethical dilemmas mentioned by the respondents. While no precise definition of what constituted an ethical dilemma was provided to respondents, a working definition seemed to emerge. An ethical dilemma occurred when the management accountant felt pressure to do something that he or she felt was not right. A simple choice between two acceptable accounting methods was not considered an ethical dilemma.

Thus, the interviews revealed that some management accountants do face ethical dilemmas in their work and provided specific examples of these ethical dilemmas.

TABLE 3
Summary of Ethical Dilemma Situations Described by Respondents in the Unstructured Interviews

- Management actually changed the management accountant's determination of profit or otherwise manipulated or distorted data.
- Management accountants had to decide what and how much to tell outside auditors.
- The owner-managers of small businesses pressured their management accountants to perform acts which might be unethical.
- Management accountants had to keep client and contractor data confidential by refusing requests for access to these data.
- Management accountants had to reconcile goal conflicts and organization conflicts between the corporation and its operating divisions or plants.
- How to account for items such as cost allocations or certain contract costs presented management accountants with dilemmas of deciding what was the fairest method.
- Management accountants had difficulty trading off their fiduciary responsibility to control costs and preserve assets with their desire to treat other employees, clients and the general public in a responsible manner.
- Management directed the management accountant to shift expenses between two periods for the purpose of smoothing income.

Issue 2: Should management accountants have a Code of Ethics?

Respondents gave three types of answers to this question: strong yes, yes with qualifications, or no or not sure. The number of these responses was as follows:

	Number of Responses	
Responses	Structured Interviews	Unstructured Interviews
Strong Yes	44	13
Qualified Yes	39	10
No or Not Sure	24	2
TOTALS*	107	25

*Although 30 unstructured interviews and 107 structured interviews were conducted, the number of responses to any question did not always conform to the total number of interviews because each respondent did not provide a clear answer to each question.

Interviewees offered the following kinds of reasons for their answers:

- **Strong Yes**
  "A code would improve our professional image."
  "A professional group such as NAA should be expected to have a code for its members."
  "I'm scandalized that management accountants don't already have a code."
  "If we had a code, ethics for management accountants could be taught in colleges."
- **Qualified Yes**
  "Seems like a good idea, but I don't know how a code could be enforced."
  "A code would really be window dressing; it wouldn't change anyone's behavior."
  "With NAA's diverse membership, how could a code apply to all members?"
- **No**
  "NAA is not a professional organization; it's really more of a social club. A code is not appropriate."

"There's no reason to have a code since it can't be enforced."
"My industry is already overregulated; I don't need more regulations to live up to."
"Unless NAA decides to limit its membership to professional accountants, a code would be meaningless."

Although the "Strong Yes" and "Qualified Yes" types of answers comprised 80% of all responses (106 of 132), a significant minority expressed clearly formulated, strong opinions why NAA should not adopt a code. *All* respondents, including those who did not want a code for NAA members, believed that Certificate in Management Accounting holders should have a code.

Issue 3: If a code of ethics is appropriate for management accountants, what should be the form and content of the code?

A number of questions asked during the unstructured and structured interviews related to the format and content of a code of ethics for management accountants. How respondents replied to these questions provided considerable insight as to how a code should be written to be acceptable to most NAA members.

One question referred to whether the code should be written in general or specific terms. Some codes, such as the code for medical doctors, addresses such specific issues as whether doctors may accept credit card payment (they may). Other codes, such as the internal auditors' code, specify ethical behavior in very general terms. A majority of the respondents favored a code written in general terms for management accountants.

	Number of Responses	
Responses	**Structured Interviews**	**Unstructured Interviews**
Code should be written in general terms	68	15
Code should be written in specific terms	34	2
Not sure	2	0
Totals	104	17

Another important question referred to whether the code should address management behavior as well as accounting behavior. Many management accountants perform both management functions and technical accounting functions. To explore this question, researchers sent respondents in the unstructured interviews a description of the various roles which managers must assume along with the information letter they received prior to the interview (Appendix C). No real consensus emerged to this question as shown by the following table:

Responses	**Number**
Yes, the general management functions are important to address.	1
Only a general statement should be in the code because management functions are difficult to describe.	9
No	8
Totals	18

This diversity of responses apparently resulted from the manner in which the researcher brought up the subject. Few respondents raised the issue of management roles by themselves. Because ethical behavior in the management roles did not seem to be nearly as important to respondents as ethical accounting behavior, the researchers concluded that the remainder of the study should focus primarily upon ethical issues relevant to accountants.

If management accountants were to adopt a code of ethics, in what format should the code be written? Other professional codes of ethics have been written in a variety of forms. To address this question, the information letter sent to structured interview respondents contained the three sample formats appearing in Appendix D. Format 1 specified obligations to various groups, such as employers and the general public, similar to the format of the CPAs' and architects' codes. Format 2 was written in the form of ethical canons similar to the format of the internal auditors' code. Format 3 resembled the code of the Data Processing Management Association that first specifies a code of absolute conduct and then specifies a code of specific ethics derived from the code of conduct. Respondents in the structured interviews generally preferred Format 1, the "Obligations To" format as shown in the table on the next page at the top.

To determine what specific types of behavior a code of ethics should address, respondents in the structured interviews were asked if each of

Code Format Preferred by Respondents in Structured Interviews	Number
1. "Obligations To" Format	51
2. "Canon" Format	17
3. "Absolute Conduct—Specific Ethics" Format	17
4. No preference	20
Total	105

20 different ethical responsibility clauses should be contained in a code. The frequency of responses for each of the 20 clauses appears next to each clause on Question 2 of the Structured Interview Format in Appendix D. As the frequency shows, a large majority believed that every clause should be in the code. The one exception was "Responsibility to report a violation of the code by other management accountants," i.e., blow the whistle on your colleague, which was favored by only 42% of the respondents. Most clauses require conduct that any professional accountant should be expected to conform to under existing business ethics, so majority approval of these ethical provisions is not surprising.

Issue 4: To whom should a code of ethics for management accountants apply?

Management accountants perform a wide range of services for their employers. NAA, the only professional organization representing management accountants, has great diversity in its current membership. If a code of ethics were to be developed by NAA, to whom should the code apply? During the structured interviews, respondents answered this question as follows:

Response	Number
Code of ethics should apply to:	
All members of NAA	21
Only to CMA holders	22
Only to NAA members performing management accounting work	61
Total	104

Although the frequency of responses indicated a preference for having a code apply only to NAA members performing management accounting work, most respondents were uncertain about their response. All respondents believed that CMAs should have a code. Many respondents also recognized that all management accountants are not NAA members and that all NAA members are not management accountants. Thus, the interview results did not provide clear guidance on the question of to whom a code should apply.

Conclusions from Interviewing

The results of 30 unstructured interviews and 107 structured interviews with management accountants in 10 different metropolitan areas in the United States suggest the following conclusions:

1. Some management accountants do face ethical dilemmas in their work. The interviews provided specific examples of these ethical dilemmas that occurred. How severe these dilemmas become depends upon the ethical climate present in the accountant's employing organization. In some companies, the management accountant felt pressure to perform unethical acts. Several respondents cited such pressure as the principal reason why they quit former jobs.

2. About 80% of the respondents believed that management accountants should have a code of ethics. Therefore, strong support seems to exist for a code. All respondents felt that CMAs need a code of ethics. The feelings recorded during the interviews conform to the results of an earlier mail survey of NAA members.[2] Eighty-three percent of the more than 1,200 respondents in that survey favored a code.

A code is not a "burning" issue with most management accountants. Many respondents felt that while a code generally was desirable, the code would not really help them personally or affect their behavior. Also, some respondents provided clearly thought-out answers why NAA should not develop a code of ethics.

3. The unstructured interview results suggest that ethical conflicts become more complex and more severe as the management accountant rises in the organization. The results also suggest that management accountants employed in government or regulated industries recognize more responsibility to the general public than do management accountants employed in the private sector.

4. Many management accountants seem to feel their ultimate responsibility is to do a good technical job of preparing accounting information. This suggests that management accounting is truly a profession

---

[2]Joyce Capagna Lambert, "A Code of Professional Conduct for Accountants in Industry," Unpublished Doctoral Dissertation, Louisiana State University, 1973.

according to Gouldner's "Cosmopolitan-Local" model and that a code of ethics would be appropriate for management accountants.[3]

5. The interviews provided some insight about the content and form of a code that would be most acceptable to management accountants, should it be developed. The code should be written in general terms and should address issues relevant only to accountants. The code's format should differentiate between obligations to employers, the general public, the profession, and other items similar to the format of the CPAs' code. Many management accountants also are CPAs, and the CPAs' code has strongly influenced their feelings about professional ethics.

These conclusions must be considered tentative because of the manner in which respondents were selected. Although attempts were made to stratify demographically, respondents for both the unstructured and structured interviews were selected primarily because of their interest in NAA and willingness to participate. Thus, significant sample bias might be present since the responses may not be representative of all NAA members or all management accountants. In order to measure the feelings of a representative sample of management accountants, a mail survey was made of a large, random sample of NAA members. The next chapter reports the results of the mail survey.

[3]A.W. Gouldner, "Cosmopolitans and Locals: Towards an Analysis of Latent Social Values," *Administrative Science Quarterly,* No. 3, 1957, pp. 281–306.

Chapter 5

Mail Survey

A mail survey was conducted of a large random sample of NAA members to determine if the findings of the personal interviews could be validated. The questionnaire asked respondents if they thought certain ethical issues were important to management accountants and if they thought NAA should adopt a code of ethics. The researchers carefully selected a research design to ensure a relatively high response rate; 59% responded.

Survey Process

A fairly elaborate research process was designed to ensure a high response rate. The survey process included the following six steps:

1. Design and pretest questionnaire—The four-page questionnaire appearing in Appendix E was designed and pretested.
2. Select random sample—A random sample of slightly more than 1,000 NAA members in the United States was selected from the file of all NAA members. The few interview respondents that appeared in the sample were deleted from the survey list.
3. Request letter—The researchers sent the first letter in Appendix E to each person. The letter described the study and alerted the person that he or she would receive a questionnaire in one week. Each person's name and address on the letter and mailing envelope were typed individually to avoid the appearance that the survey was an impersonal mass mailing.
4. Approximately one week after receiving the initial request letter, each person received a second letter and the questionnaire, both appearing in Appendix E, along with a return envelope.
5. Follow-up on nonrespondents—About two weeks after sending the questionnaire, a follow-up letter and another questionnaire were sent to a random sample of about 200 of those who had not yet responded. Although respondents were promised confidentiality, a con-

trol number appeared on each questionnaire so that the researchers could record who had responded.

6. Tabulate and analyze responses—All answers were coded for computer tabulation using the Statistical Package for the Social Sciences (SPSS) programs. To search for statistical relationships among the data, Chi Square and discriminant analyses were made using available SPSS programs.

Response Rate

The researchers received 612 responses from the 1,037 persons who were mailed questionnaires, and the U.S. Postal Service returned six questionnaires as nondeliverable. Therefore, the overall response rate was 59% (612 responses from an effective mailing of 1,031). For various reasons, 12 of the responses were unusable, so the results reported below pertain to 600 valid responses. As shown in Table 4, the random sample resulted in a broad demographic distribution.

Survey Results

The questionnaire was designed to provide information on four different issues:

1. Which areas of ethical concern seem important? (Question 1 on the questionnaire)
2. Would a code of ethics help management accountants resolve their ethical concerns? (Questions 2 and 3)
3. Should NAA adopt a code of ethics? (Questions 4 and 5)
4. If a code were adopted, to whom should it apply? (Question 6)

The 14 areas of ethical concern which seemed most important to the interviewees were included in the mail questionnaire. Therefore, the researchers expected a high percentage of respondents to believe that each of these was very important or somewhat important. The responses in each category appear next to each question on the questionnaire in Appendix E. Between 73% and 99% of the respondents believed that each area of ethical concern in Question 1 was either very or somewhat important. The rank order listing of very important responses, shown in Table 5, probably is the best indicator of the relative importance of each issue. Because at least 73% of the respondents believed that each area of ethical concern was either very or somewhat important, the mail survey results confirmed the findings of the interviews.

TABLE 4
Demographic Variables of Respondents to the Mail Survey

Characteristic	Classification—Percent of Respondents
Sex	Male—89% Female—11%
Age	20s—17% 30s—38% 40s—20% 50+—25%
Certification	CPA—34% CMA—2.1%
Supervisory Level	Top Management—30% Middle Management—18% Lower Management—28% Staff Accountant—24% (Inferred by researchers from job title)
Nature of Current Work	Substantially Involved with Management Accounting—68% Public Accounting—16% Teacher—2% General Management—11% Other—3%
Organization Type	Public Corporation for Profit—34% Private Corporation for Profit—40% Proprietor or Partnership for Profit—17% Not-for-Profit—5% Governmental—4%
Size of Employer	Large—47% Medium—28% Small—25%
Membership in NAA, Years	0–2 Years—17% 2–5 Years—31% 6–10 Years—23% Over 10 Years—29%
Ever on Board of Directors in a Local NAA Chapter	Yes—30% No—70%

TABLE 5
Areas of Ethical Concern Listed by Rank Order of "Very Important" Responses

Area of Ethical Concern	Percent "Very Important" Responses
1. Maintaining your professional competence.	89.9
2. Presenting information in the most reasonable manner so as not to deceive the primary user of the information.	78.4
3. Recognizing that the management accountant's primary responsibility is to the owners of the firm or the trustees of the organization, while refusing to follow orders to perform illegal or unethical acts.	78.1
4. Maintaining the appropriate degree of confidentiality for information about your employer.	77.7
5. Deciding whether to report a significant violation of law to someone within the business organization and then what to do if the report is ignored.	71.8
6. Following Generally Accepted Accounting Principles even if asked to use other methods.	60.8
7. Being asked to recalculate certain financial figures to make a division or organization look more profitable this year.	57.3
8. Deciding how much to cooperate with external auditors in informing them of items which might materially affect the entity's financial statements.	55.7

TABLE 5 (continued)

Area of Ethical Concern	Percent "Very Important" Responses
9. Treating other management accountants with professional courtesy.	51.1
10. Balancing your fiduciary responsibility to control costs and preserve assets with the necessity to treat employees fairly.	45.0
11. Not being given sufficient time to become technically competent for work which you must undertake.	41.3
12. Deciding which external activities will cause a significant conflict of interest with your employer.	36.8
13. Being directed to undertake work for which you are not technically competent.	34.0
14. Deciding which organizational level to attach your primary loyalty to—for example, corporate headquarters or to a division or plant.	25.1

Note: A total of 600 usable responses were received; therefore, each percentage point represents six actual responses.

Questions 2 and 3 asked if respondents thought that a code of ethics would help them personally or would help other NAA members resolve ethical concerns they might have. Thirty-eight percent thought a code would help them personally, and 49% thought the code would help others. These results provide one rationale for NAA adopting a code. Apparently a code would benefit a significant number of members.

Question 4 listed the major advantages and disadvantages of having a code as cited by interviewees. This list was intended to force each person to balance these advantages and disadvantages before he or she answered Question 5: "Do you believe that NAA should adopt a code?" The frequency of responses to this critical question is tabulated in the example below.

Frequency of Responses to Question 5

"Do you believe that NAA should adopt a code of ethics for management accountants?"

Response	Frequency
Definitely Yes	18%
Probably Yes	54
Not Sure	7
Probably Not	18
Definitely Not	3
	100%

Thus, 72% of the mail survey respondents favored adoption of a code by NAA. In the interviews, 80% of the respondents favored adoption of a code, so the mail survey generally confirmed the results of the interviews. Persons who favored a code would be expected to agree with the purported advantages of a code and disagree with purported disadvantages. Responses to Question 4 tended to support this expectation although certain purported advantages did not achieve much agreement, as shown in the following examples:

Percent of Mail Respondents Who Strongly Agreed with Purported Advantages of a Code of Ethics

Purported Advantage	Percent
1. Would enhance professional image	70%
2. Would have public relations benefits	58
3. Would encourage the teaching of ethics in college curricula	54
4. Would help the management accountant to resist unethical pressures by management	52
5. Would forestall government regulation	29

Percent of Mail Respondents Who Strongly Agreed with Purported Disadvantages of a Code of Ethics

Purported Disadvantage	Percent
1. Would be "window dressing;" each person acts according to own personal convictions	41%
2. Code would be meaningless since NAA has no means to enforce	33
3. Many NAA members are not really professionals; code not appropriate unless membership is limited	32
4. Management accounting differs from public accounting; management accountant must follow directions; therefore code not needed	8

Responses to Questions 4 and 5 indicate that, after considering the major advantages and disadvantages of a code, a substantial majority of respondents favor a code of ethics for management accountants.

Responses to Question 6, "To whom should a code apply?", are difficult to interpret. A slight majority, 53%, favored a code which would apply to all management accountants, not just NAA members. Limiting the code only to NAA members who are practicing management accountants or only to CMAs did not receive much support. Therefore, if a code were adopted, respondents seemed to favor broad application of the code.

Statistical Analysis

A detailed statistical test of the data from the mail questionnaire was made using the Chi Square and discriminant analysis programs in the Statistical Package for the Social Sciences (SPSS). Both analyses permit using the data gathered to test a null hypothesis that there is no statistical relationship among answers to different question sets and that random chance was responsible for the frequency distributions. Chi Square was used to test the relationships between two variables or question responses. Discriminant analysis was used to attempt to predict the answer to one question from prior knowledge about the answers to other questions. Both tests indicate the probability that the frequency of responses resulted from random chance. For this study, levels of significance below .05 were considered critical. This statement means that the researchers rejected the null hypothesis of no statistical relationship whenever the level of significance was less than .05

or a probability of only one out of 20 that random chance could explain the data adequately.

Two types of relationships were sought:

1. Does a statistically significant relationship exist between whether a person feels an ethical issue is important and other variables?
2. Do a person's demographic characteristics influence whether that person favors a code of ethics for management accountants?

Relationships with Ethical Issues

Question 1 asked whether each of 14 ethical issues was: very important, somewhat important, or not important. A Chi Square analysis was made between how each respondent replied to Question 1 and if the respondent believed that a code would be helpful in resolving ethical issues as indicated by his or her responses to Questions 2 and 3. Knowing that relationships exist between these answers might help in deciding what issues a code should address. A Chi Square contingency table test was made of each of the 14 issues in Question 1 and answers to Questions 2 and 3 (28 separate tests). Table 8, Appendix F, shows the contingency table for Question 1h: "Is following Generally Accepted Accounting Principles important?" versus Question 2: "Do you think a code of ethics would help you resolve any of the ethical concerns listed above?" The raw Chi Square significance of .0001 indicates an extremely strong statistical relationship between how a person answered Question 1h and how he or she answered Question 2. Significant relationships were found between most of the issues in Question 1 and the answer to Question 2 (see Table 6). The direction of change in the percents of very important answers indicates that persons who feel a code would be helpful also tend to attach more importance to almost all of the ethical issues. Similar results occurred from the tests of answers to Question 1 versus Question 3, "Would a code help other NAA members resolve their ethical concerns?" These results imply that most of the issues contained in the questions should be addressed in a code because persons who felt that a code would be helpful tended to believe that the issues were more important.

Next, researchers sought significant relationships between demographic variables and whether a person felt that the ethical issues in Question 1 were important. With 14 separate issues and nine demographic variables for each person, interpreting the results of the 126 necessary contingency tables (9 x 14) becomes quite difficult. The significance levels of each of the 126 tests are listed in Table 9, Appendix F. For the four most important demographic variables—age, sex, certification and supervisory level in the organization—the researchers in-

TABLE 6
Summary of Tests for Relationships Between Responses to Questions 1 and 2

Question 1 Areas	Overall Percent of "Very Important" Answers to Question 1	Percent Answering Yes to Question 2 and "Very Important" to Question 1	Chi Square Significance
a. Maintaining your technical competence	89.9%	92.8%	.060
b. Undertaking work for which not competent	34.0	38.6	.001
c. Not time to become competent	41.3	46.2	.009
d. Primary responsibility to management	78.1	79.4	.691
e. Professional courtesy	51.1	56.5	.001
f. Conflict of interest	36.8	39.2	.046
g. Confidentiality	77.7	78.0	.156
h. Following GAAP	60.6	72.6	.000
i. Present information in most reasonable manner	78.4	82.1	.054
j. Report violations of laws	71.8	77.5	.066
k. Cooperate with auditors	55.7	63.3	.001
l. Recalculate profit	57.3	65.0	.001
m. Balance fiduciary responsibility	45.0	52.7	.018
n. Loyalty to corporation or to plant	25.1	31.7	.001

TABLE 7
Relationship of Demographic Variables Upon Feelings That Ethical Issues Are Important

Demographic Variable	Relationships of Statistical Significance
Sex	1. Women tend to believe that issue 1b, "being directed to undertake work for which you are not technically competent" was more important than did men.
	2. Women tend to believe that issue 1c, "not having sufficient time to become technically competent" is more important.
	3. Women tend to believe that issue 1k, "deciding how much to cooperate with external auditors" is more important.
Age	1. Older people tend to believe issue 1f, "conflicts of interest" more important.
	2. Older people tend to believe issue 1m, "balancing fiduciary responsibility with necessity to treat employees fairly" more important.
Certification[1]	1. CPAs tend to believe that issue 1b, "being directed to undertake work for which you are not technically competent," more important than non-CPAs.
	2. CPAs tend to believe that each of the following issues was less important than non-CPAs: Issue 1e. "professional courtesy" Issue 1k. "cooperation with auditors" Issue 1m. "balancing fiduciary responsibility" Issue 1n. "loyalty to corporate headquarters or to the plant
Supervisory[2] Level in the Organization	1. Top management thought issue 1e "professional courtesy" less important.
	2. Top management and middle management thought issue 1m, "balancing fiduciary responsibility," less important.
	3. Staff accountants and lower management thought issue 1n, "loyalty to corporate headquarters or to plant," more important.

Notes: 1. The effect of a CMA was not tested because there were only 13 CMAs in the sample and 5 of those were also CPAs.
2. The supervisory level was inferred by the researchers from the job title.

Table Comparing Men's and Women's Responses to Question 1b

"Is being directed to undertake work for which you are not technically competent important?"

Percent of women in the sample answering very or somewhat important	96.9%
Percent of men in the sample answering very or somewhat important	85.0%
Overall percent of very or somewhat important answers	86.3%

ferred the relationships shown in Table 7. While some of these relationships are intriguing, none of them is very useful for prediction. For example, a statistical significance of .0126 was found between the way men and women felt about the importance of technical competence for work undertaken. Most women and most men thought this issue was important as shown in the above table comparing their responses.

While a statistically significant difference occurred between men's and women's answers, the difference has little practical significance since most men and women believed that being technically competent for work undertaken was important. Thus, the relationships among demographics yield interesting insights regarding general tendencies, but they do not have practical significance for prediction purposes.

A final analysis with respect to ethical issues was made by searching for relationships between how respondents felt about the importance of the ethical issues contained in Question 1 and whether they favored a code of ethics for management accountants, Question 5. As with the previous analyses, Chi Square contingency table analysis was used. The results generally showed that persons who favored a code tended to believe each issue was more important than persons who did not favor a code.

Discriminant Analysis of Demographics

Discriminant analysis was used to determine if one could predict from knowledge about the demographic characteristics of a person whether that person favored a code of ethics for management accountants. For example, would a financial vice president of a large public corporation who was in his or her 50s and who was a CPA favor a code as much as a younger staff accountant, not a CPA, who worked for a medium-size, not-for-profit organization? Knowledge of how the nine demographic variables, Table 4, were related to feelings about a code might be very helpful in deciding upon the content of a code.

The stepwise discriminant analysis continued to enter demographic variables into the analysis as long as they were useful in explaining variation in the response to Question 5. Best results were obtained by collapsing the five category responses to Question 5, "Should NAA adopt a code?", into three categories as shown below:

Five Category Responses to Question 5	Three Categories Used in Discriminant Analysis
Definitely Yes Probably Yes	Yes
Not Sure	Not Sure
Probably Not Definitely Not	No

The discriminant functions selected, as shown on the computer printout, Table 10, Appendix F, included only five demographic variables: age, type of employer, certification, nature of work, and supervisory level. Although its interpretation presents some difficulties, the discriminant analysis suggests the following relationships:

Demographic Variable	Type of Relationship
Age	More persons who were older did not favor a code.
Nature of Work	Persons who work in public accounting tended to favor a code less; persons who work in other functions not closely related to management accounting tended to favor a code more.
Certification	Persons who were not certified tended to favor a code more.
Type of Employer	Persons employed by partnerships and proprietorships tended to favor a code more; persons employed by not-for-profits favored a code less.
Supervisory Level	More members of top management did not favor a code.

How useful these relationships are for prediction can be understood best from the so-called "confusion matrix" in Table 11, Appendix F. This matrix shows that 50% of responses favoring a code could be predicted from the five demographic variables included in the discriminant function. With only three categories of response, however—yes, not sure, or no—random chance would result in correct prediction 33% of the time. Therefore, while the discriminant function was highly significant in a statistical sense, it only improved the chance of correct prediction from 33% to 50%. Thus, the discriminant analysis yielded certain insights to the effects of demographics but had little significance for predicting whether or not any person would favor a code for management accountants.

Summary of Statistical Analysis

Good research methodology requires a rigorous search of all available data for any underlying relationships. The many combinations of Chi Square analysis and discriminant analysis used by the researchers led to two general conclusions.

1. How important a person feels about the various ethical issues is strongly related to how he or she feels about a code. Persons who feel that the ethical issues are very important also: (a) believe that a code would help them or other NAA members, (b) agree with the advantages of a code and disagree with the disadvantages, and (c) favor a code more than do persons who don't feel the ethical issues are important. The researchers expected these relationships.

2. How any person feels about the ethical issues and a code of ethics cannot be predicted accurately from that person's demographic characteristics. The researchers expected demographic variables to have a greater influence.

Nonresponse Bias

In a large mail survey, a possibility exists that nonrespondents hold different feelings from respondents. Although this study experienced a fairly high response rate, 59%, no data were available on the 41% who did not respond. To search for nonresponse bias, a second request was sent to about 200 persons who had not returned the questionnaire; 69 responses resulted from the second mailing. A series of Chi Square tests between the 531 usable responses to the first mailing and 69 responses to the second mailing showed that there were no significant differences (at the .05 level) with respect to: the importance attributed to ethical issues, whether a code would be helpful in resolving ethical conflicts, or whether NAA should adopt a code. While not conclusive, the results of the second mailing suggested an absence of any strong nonresponse bias.

Comparison with Prior Research

The results of two prior surveys of management accountants concerning ethics complement the results of this study (Merz-Groebner). In 1973, Joyce Lambert conducted a survey of a stratified random sample of 2,885 NAA members as part of her doctoral dissertation at Louisiana State University.[1] She achieved a response rate of 44%. Her questionnaire asked respondents if they favored a code and if they agreed with a code that she had prepared which contained 41 specific clauses. Many clauses in her proposed code addressed issues contained in Merz-Groebner's questionnaire, and she also received very high percents of agreement. Eighty-three percent of Lambert's respondents favored a code of ethics for industrial accountants, and 79% said that they would vote to accept her code if a vote were taken. Thus, Lambert's results were similar in many ways to the results of the Merz-Groebner study.

In 1979, Terry Sheldahl developed a normative theory of codified professional ethics and then applied this theory to management accounting in his doctoral dissertation at the University of Alabama.[2] His research included a mail survey of 573 CMA holders and members of the Financial Executives Institute. He received only 140 responses (24%) to his complex questionnaire. Sheldahl's questionnaire addressed 15 hypothetical dilemma situations. He did not ask specifically if the respondent favored a code for management accountants even though a majority of his respondents thought a code should govern some of his hypothetical dilemmas. Sheldahl was concerned more with the broader field of normative ethics than with developing a specific code of ethics for management accountants. Because he addressed different issues from Lambert or Merz-Groebner, Sheldahl's results cannot be compared directly with these other studies.

The Merz-Groebner study differs from the two prior studies in one very significant way. Merz and Groebner conducted extensive personal interviewing first to determine which ethical issues seemed impor-

[1]Joyce Campagna Lambert, "A Code of Professional Conduct for Accountants in Industry," Unpublished Ph.D. dissertation, Louisiana State University, 1973.

[2]Terry Kent Sheldahl, "Development of a Code of Professional Ethics for Management Accountants," Unpublished Ph.D. dissertation, University of Alabama, 1979.

tant; their mail questionnaire addressed issues that the interviewees thought were important. Neither Lambert nor Sheldahl devoted nearly as much effort to selecting the issues to be included in his mail survey. Therefore, the Merz-Groebner results should reflect the opinions of a broad cross section of NAA members more accurately than either of the other two studies.

Conclusions from Mail Survey

A questionnaire was mailed to a random sample of 1,031 NAA members. A total of 612 responses (59%) was returned, of which 600 contained usable data. The researchers made detailed analyses of the data. Those analyses, both descriptive and statistical, support the following conclusions:

1. Most NAA members who responded believed that the 14 ethical issues mentioned in the questionnaire were important to management accountants. This response rate confirmed results of the interviews because the ethical issues asked about in the mail questionnaire had been culled from interview results.

2. Many respondents (38%) thought that a code of ethics for management accountants would help them personally to resolve ethical concerns; about half of the respondents (49%) believed that a code would help other NAA members resolve their ethical concerns. These results imply that a code indeed would be helpful to many management accountants.

3. Most respondents (72%) favored a code, confirming the results of the interviews conducted in this study and a previous mail survey made in 1973. The interview samples were comprised primarily of practicing management accountants, most of whom were active members in their local NAA chapters. The random sample for the mail survey contained CPAs in public accounting, teachers, personnel recruiters, and the like, as well as practicing management accountants. Only 30% of the mail survey respondents had been active in NAA, as indicated by their ever having been a board member in a local chapter. Therefore, the mail survey confirmed a much broader-based support for a code than did the interviews.

4. The effects of demographic variables were not strong enough to predict, for example, that an older woman who is a CPA in public accounting feels differently about ethical issues from a younger man, not a CPA, working as the controller of a not-for-profit corporation. The absence of strong demographic effects implies that if a code is devel-

oped for management accountants, the code will not have to be oriented specifically to the needs of any demographic group.

These conclusions from the mail survey combined with conclusions drawn from earlier phases of the study led the researchers to the overall conclusions presented in the next, and final, chapter.

Chapter 6

Conclusions

The researchers believe that the overall study results support the conclusions that:

- NAA should adopt a code of ethics for management accountants.
- IMA should adopt a similar code for CMA holders.

The summaries at the end of each of the preceding four chapters presented the implications of each phase of the research for management accounting. This short, final chapter summarizes why the researchers reached the conclusions that NAA and IMA should adopt codes.

1. *A code would help some management accountants.* The overriding reason for adopting a code is that apparently it would help some management accountants resolve ethical dilemmas they face in their work. The unstructured interviews revealed that ethical dilemmas do occur. Most management accountants work for employers who maintain very high ethical standards; these accountants may not need a code of ethics. But some management accountants revealed that their managements exerted pressure on them to act unethically. About one-half of the mail survey respondents said that a code would be helpful to them or to their colleagues.

2. *Most NAA members favor a code.* Although it apparently is not a burning issue to them, 72% of the mail survey respondents answered that NAA definitely should or probably should adopt a code of ethics. The research showed that a code could be developed easily so that its form and content would be acceptable to most members. As such, the code would specify behavior normally expected of a professional person. The code probably would not impose any additional ethical responsibilities upon management accountants.

3. *Low cost—high benefit to NAA.* Adopting and administering a code of ethics should be a relatively low-cost program for NAA. The experiences of the Institute of Internal Auditors and Data Processing Management Association indicate that essentially there would be no

problems or costs associated with enforcement. With respect to benefits, a code of ethics seems to be a normal trapping of a profession and of a professional association. Most members surveyed in this study agreed that a code would enhance the professional image of management accountants. While adopting a code of ethics does not appear critical to NAA's continued survival and success, the researchers believe that the potential benefits of a code outweigh its costs.

Appendix A

List of Known Certification Programs in Business

1. Accredited Personnel Diplomate
2. Accredited Personnel Manager
3. Accredited Personnel Specialist
4. Certificate in Management Accounting
5. Certified Administrative Manager
6. Certified Commercial Lender
7. Certified Data Processor
8. Certified Financial Planner
9. Certified Industrial Developer
10. Certified Internal Auditor
11. Certified Management Consultant
12. Certified Manager of Patient Accounts
13. Certified Manufacturing Engineer
14. Certified Member, American Society of Traffic and Transportation, Inc.
15. Certified Property Manager
16. Certified Public Accountant
17. Certified Purchasing Manager
18. Certified Quality Engineer
19. Certified Records Manager
20. Certified Reliability Engineer
21. Certified Shopping Center Manager
22. Certified Tax Consultant
23. Chartered Bank Auditor
24. Chartered Financial Analyst
25. Chartered Life Underwriter
26. Chartered Property Casualty Underwriter
27. Diplomate, American Academy of Environmental Engineers
28. Fellow, American College of Hospital Administrators
29. Fellow, American Production and Inventory Control Society

30. Fellow, Casualty Actuarial Society
31. Fellow, Hospital Financial Management Association
32. Fellow, Life Management Institute
33. Fellow, Society of Actuaries
34. Member, Appraisal Institute
35. Registered Professional Engineer

Appendix B

Summary Outlines of Twelve Codes of Ethics

Summary Outline of the Code of Professional Responsibility of the American Bar Association

Description of the Code

The Code of Professional Responsibility of the American Bar Association (ABA) is, as one may expect, one of the most extensive codes surveyed. The original Canons of Professional Ethics were adopted by the American Bar Association in 1908. These canons were based primarily on the code adopted by the Alabama Bar Association in 1887. The original Canons were revised, and the present code became effective in 1970. The present nine canons deal with the general issues of providing competent legal counsel to members of the public needing such counsel. They also address the issue of maintaining technical competence.

The code is unusual in that it not only lists a series of ethical considerations, but it follows them by a listing of disciplinary rules. These rules become quite specific in spelling out the actions a lawyer should or should not take in carrying out the provisions of each canon.

Structure of the Profession

A lawyer receives his or her license to practice from each state or states where employed. In most, but not all, cases the licensing agency is the State Bar Association. This situation makes most state bar associations a quasi-legal organization because the entire state legal profession is headed by the state Supreme Court. In most cases the bar association acts as the administrative arm of the Supreme Court for directing the lawyers in the state. Each lawyer is able to join the state Bar upon graduating from an accredited law school and passing the state bar examination.

The ABA Code of Professional Responsibility is published only as a guide; each state bar association adopts its own code. In large part these state codes follow the national guidelines. In addition, some provisions of the code, and issues not in the code, are contained in the laws of each state regulating the conduct of the legal profession. Therefore, a lawyer violating a section of the code also may be violating a law of the state.

Legal Status

As mentioned, the bar association in many states is different from the other professional organizations examined because it is a partial branch of the state Supreme Court. Since the United States Supreme Court ruled in the *Parker* vs. *Brown* case that state governments are exempt from the Sherman Anti-Trust Act, the state bar associations may be able to enforce some provisions of their codes more than other organizations. However, this ruling did not prevent the same Supreme Court from ruling that states could not entirely ban advertising by their members.

In addition to the bar association's legal standing, and perhaps more important, is the fact that a constitutional right of all citizens is legal representation in court cases. Hence lawyers, and in many cases the state bar associations, are very involved in constitutionally guaranteed rights.

Constituencies Addressed by the Code

The majority of the Code of Professional Responsibility deals with the lawyer-client relationship. The code also addresses, however, a lawyer's relation with other lawyers, the public in general, and the overall legal system.

Enforcement of the Code

The enforcement system in the legal profession rests with the state court system. In most cases this means the state Supreme Court. In those cases in which the state bar association is the administrative arm of the Supreme Court, those provisions of the Code of Professional Responsibility that are also contained in state statutes are enforced by the Supreme Court.

The enforcement procedure follows strict due process procedures. Discipline may range from an informal sanction to suspension or disbarment. The lesser disciplines, such as a sanction, remain confidential. More severe disciplines, such as suspension or disbarment, are made public both in professional and local news publications.

Enforcement History

At present, there is no official mechanism to tabulate and report the number of cases under investigation and those having been settled. As such, there is no way to trace the enforcement history either on a national or local level. There is a move among the Association of State Bars, however, to tabulate these data. At present, no one knows whether this tabulation actually will occur.

Analysis of Effectiveness

Analyzing the effectiveness of the Bar Association Code of Professional Responsibility involves an apparent contradiction. On the one hand, the code is one of the most thorough and concise professional codes. It emphasizes the relationship between the lawyer and client, certainly much more than do most other codes. The enforcement mechanism is well defined and operational. Unfortunately, the code apparently has not ensured ethical behavior on the part of the individual members. In fact, a long series of opinion polls shows public esteem for the legal profession falling lower and lower.

Perhaps the legal profession, more than any other, points up the prime difficulty of any code of ethics, at least in a free society. While the code clearly can point out the actions a person should take to be an ethical member of a profession, it is difficult to ensure that all members behave according to the code. Also there appears to be little relationship between the complexity of a code and the degree to which the public views the performance of that profession as ethical.

Sources

1. American Bar Association, Code of Professional Responsibility.
2. Idaho Legal Code, Rules of Disciplinary Enforcement and Withdrawal of Right to Practice Law.
3. Idaho State Bar, Code of Professional Responsibility.
4. Mark Downing, Bar Counsel, Idaho State Bar.

Summary Outline of the Market Research Code of Ethics of the American Marketing Association

Description of the Code

The American Marketing Association is the best known of the marketing associations. The Association adopted its first Marketing Research Code of Ethics in 1962 and revised and updated it in 1972. The code outlines quite specific responsibilities for research practitioners, research users, and field interviewers. While the guidelines are quite specific, they generally deal with areas involving honest representation and privacy for the sponsor of the research, the user of the research, and the supplier of information. While the code defines some concrete guidelines for personal behavior, it does not deal with the issue of technical competence.

Structure of the Profession

The American Marketing Association is a society of marketing managers, marketing research executives, sales managers, advertising specialists, teachers and others interested in marketing. Therefore, membership in the organization is open to anyone. While the Association has more than 300 local groups, it has no certification program. The certification issue is raised periodically, but at this time the certification committee has been disbanded and there is now no movement toward certification.

Constituencies Addressed by the Code

The Marketing Research Code of Ethics specifically mentions responsibilities to the users of market research and the public participants in the research.

Enforcement of the Code

The American Marketing Association presently has no method to enforce its code. The feeling exists, at least on the part of some members of the Association, that a certification program would be necessary before enforcement would be possible. The apparent major problem with certification is the difficulty in defining "good" research as opposed to "bad" research. The feeling is that what is good in one situation when performed by one person may well be bad if performed by another person. The American Marketing Association at present feels no certification test would adequately identify persons able to do "good" research.

Analysis of Effectiveness

Because the code has no enforcement mechanism, it cannot be used to ensure a uniform set of actions or technical competence. (The enforcement problems of organizations which do have an enforcement mechanism have already been discussed.) Therefore, the code cannot be used to prevent "bad" actions although the Marketing Research Code is quite specific in those areas it addresses and would likely be a help for persons seeking guidance on what is the correct action.

Sources

1. Gerald Zaltman and Philip C. Burger, *Marketing Research: Fundamentals and Dynamics,* The Dryden Press, Hinsdale, Ill. 1975.
2. American Marketing Association: The Market Research Code of Ethics.
3. Alice M. Tybout and Gerald Zaltman, "Ethics in Marketing Research: Their Practical Relevance," *Journal of Marketing Research,* November 1974, pp. 357–368.
4. O.C. Ferrell and K. Mark Weaver, "Ethical Beliefs of Marketing Managers," *Journal of Marketing,* July 1978, pp. 68–73.
5. Loraine Caliendo, staff of the National Office of the American Marketing Association.

Summary Outline of the Code of Ethics of the American Medical Association

Description of the Code

The Principles of Medical Ethics of the American Medical Association is one of the most extensive codes of ethics we examined. In addition, the medical profession has one of the most complicated structures of all the professional organizations. Not only does the American Medical Association have its code, but so does the American College of Surgeons and the American Osteopathic Association. This situation is complicated by the fact that most physicians practice in a hospital which also has its own code. Here we will be concerned primarily with the AMA's code.

The medical profession has had a code of ethics perhaps longer than any other profession. Certainly the Oath of Hippocrates, developed in Greece in the Fifth Century B.C., remains perhaps the best-known statement of physician-patient relationships in the world. The AMA adopted its first code of ethics at its first national meeting in 1847. These ethics were based primarily on a set of ethical principles developed by Thomas Percival, an Englishman, in 1803. In general the concepts developed in 1847 have remained the same over the years. The language has been changed, of course, and somewhat major revisions have taken place, the most recent in the 1950s.

The code contains 10 major sections, each starting with a general summary of the principle addressed in that section. This summary is followed by a detailed discussion of the practical issues that fall under that section. For instance, in the section discussing patient fees, a specific segment discussed that it is ethical to accept bank cards. The specific points addressed in each section seem to cover most of the issues a practicing physician would be faced with, which, of course, is the point.

Structure of the Profession

A physician receives his or her license to practice from a board of medical examiners in each state. While a physician must be licensed to practice medicine in a state, he or she does not have to belong to the American Medical Association. Thus the AMA is a voluntary professional organization, and a significant number of physicians do not belong to the AMA.

Each state has a branch of the AMA. The state units may decide not to be bound by the national code. In fact, because of the Federal Trade Commission problems discussed earlier, the Idaho Medical Association said it will not be bound by the tenets of the AMA's Code of Professional Responsibility.

Legal Status

The medical profession in each state is controlled and defined, to a certain extent, by the laws of that state. A physician must be licensed to practice medicine in the state, and it is against the law to practice medicine without a license. This legal status applies to the profession and the state board of medical examiners, however, not to the AMA. The AMA also has no certification that will aid a physician in practicing. For example, a person may become an accountant and then a Certified Public Accountant, but a physician does not become certified further by the AMA. There is, therefore, no legal necessity for a physician to either join or obtain a certification from the AMA.

The Federal Trade Commission now is challenging, in the form of several major lawsuits, the ability of the AMA to enforce its code of ethics. We hope the legal status of professional organizations will be clarified soon.

Constituencies Addressed by the Code

The Principles of Medical Ethics deals primarily with the physician-patient relationship. The code also addresses the relationship between physicians and their responsibility to remain current in medical knowledge.

Enforcement of the Code

Enforcement of the Principles of Medical Ethics is a complicated process that seems to vary from case to case. Right now, however, the AMA is undertaking no enforcement proceedings as the Federal Trade Commission is claiming that such enforcement may be a restraint of trade and hence illegal under the Sherman Anti-Trust Act. Therefore, our discussion will be of the enforcement system as it once was practiced.

Many of the acts defined as unethical by the AMA also would be illegal under the laws of the various states, so much of the enforcement was handled by the state boards of medical examiners or the state attorney general offices or some other state agency. If the discrepancy took place in a hospital, the unethical practice probably would be handled by a predetermined hospital procedure. In all these cases, the enforcement procedure primarily was a peer review process. If the process was not handled by the state or hospital, or perhaps even if it were, it also could be handled by the AMA. Local issues were addressed locally, while issues with more than local impact would be considered by a committee appointed by the Judicial Council of the AMA. If the issue were handled at the national level, an extensive procedure to ensure due process would be followed.

Enforcement History

At present, there is no official mechanism to tabulate or report the number of cases under investigation or those having been settled. As such, there is no way to trace the enforcement history either on a national or local level. Because the whole enforcement policy is now being challenged, this point may well become moot.

Analysis of Effectiveness

Analyzing the effectiveness of the American Medical Association's Principles of Medical Ethics would depend on a person's perspective. Certainly the AMA is cited as being the most effective professional association. Because the public holds physicians in greater esteem than almost any other professional organization, the code apparently has been effective in ensuring ethical conduct. The AMA is certainly not without its critics, however, who contend that the AMA is primarily concerned with preserving the position of the AMA and not concerned with the health care of the nation.

The effectiveness of the code, in fact the code itself, is likely to be changed severely by the recent federal challenges. The AMA is trying to put together a code and enforcement mechanism that will meet these challenges.

Sources

1. American Medical Association, Judicial Council Opinions and Reports, including the Principles of Medical Ethics and Rules of the Judicial Council.
2. Don Sower, Executive Director, Idaho Medical Association.
3. American College Health Association, Recommended Standards and Practices for a College Health Program.
4. Bylaws of the Medical and Dental Staff of St. Lukes Hospital, Boise, Idaho.

Summary Outline of Code of Ethics for Holders of the Certificate in Data Processing

Description of the Code

The Certificate in Data Processing (CDP) program was started by the Data Processing Management Association. The Certificate now is presented by the Institute for Certification of Computer Professionals (ICCP), a separate organization with a board of directors containing a member from the Data Processing Management Association and members from seven other data processing organizations. The Code of Ethics was adopted by the Certification Council in 1967 and is accompanied by the Codes of Conduct and Good Practice which were adopted in 1973. The Code of Ethics is a short, concise statement giving the certificate holder responsibility to serve the interests of the employer and clients and responsibility to have high ideals and knowledge. The Codes of Conduct and Good Practice are more extensive and are meant to be changed periodically. They deal more specifically with such issues as disclosure, conflict of interest, privacy, competence and other areas of personal and technical concern. The issues covered in the Codes of Conduct and Good Practice are dealt with in quite specific terms. While the Codes are written specifically for holders of the Certificate, they also apply to all members of the Data Processing Management Association.

Structure of the Profession

The Data Processing Management Association is an organization of data processing managers, researchers, educators and others with a direct interest in data processing. Again, the Certificate in Data Processing is presented by the Institute for the Certification of Computer Professionals. While the certification program has no educational requirement, it does have a five-year experience requirement. An academic degree can count for some, but not all, of this experience requirement. The Codes are adopted by the national organizations and are adhered to by the state and local chapters.

Constituencies Addressed by the Code

The Code of Ethics cites, in general terms, obligations to the public, the data processing profession, and employers and clients. The Codes of Conduct and Good Practice again mention these groups and add fellow professionals.

Legal Status of CDPs

At present, holders of the Certificate in Data Processing are not licensed legally and hence have no legal responsibility. With the increasing concern with confidentiality of computerized data sources, however, many people see a future legal licensing requirement so some group can certify this confidentiality.

Enforcement of the Code

The Certification Council of the ICCP enforces the provisions of the Code of Ethics. There is no enforcement mechanism at the local or state level. The enforcement provisions have clauses designed to ensure the rights of the accused, including the right to have the decision reviewed.

Enforcement History

The enforcement history is rather vague. Charges have been brought against members based on alleged violations of provisions of the code and rules of conduct, but these cases have not been summarized in a public report.

Analysis of Effectiveness

The Code of Ethics for CDP holders is one of the newest codes we examined. As such, it is particularly important from the context of this study. The similarity between the information supplied by data processing managers and managerial accountants also is obvious. The fact that the first CDP test was given in 1962 and the initial code of ethics was adopted in 1967 has timing similarities with the NAA and the Certificate in Management Accounting. The Data Processing Management Association, and now the Institute for Certification of Computer Professionals, obviously has taken the subject of ethics seriously. Their Codes of Conduct and Good Practice are quite explicit in describing acceptable behavior, yet they are not nearly as definite and formal as the older codes. If computer professionals become licensed, a likely possibility, the codes of conduct and ethics may become more explicit in describing behavior.

Sources

1. The Institute for Certification of Computer Professionals: Codes of Ethics, Conduct and Good Practice for Holders of the Certificate in Data Processing.
2. Allen H. Seed, III, "The Current Financial Certification Programs: What They Are and What They Entail!" *The Practical Accountant,* March/April, 1976, pp. 67–69.
3. Emerson Maxson, Idaho Director of Certification, ICCP.

Summary Outline of Code of Ethics for a Certified Internal Auditor (CIA)

Description of the Code

The CIA's Code of Ethics is a simple, one-page code containing seven articles. Four of these articles relate to the CIA's responsibility to his or her employer, while the other three articles require the CIA to use professional auditing standards such as obtaining sufficient factual evidence when he or she expresses an opinion. Although the code clearly gives highest priority to the interests of the CIA's employer, it also addresses the interests of stockholders and the general public in two of the articles. Article II calls for loyalty to the employer in all matters, but it prohibits the CIA from knowingly being a party to an illegal or improper act. Article VI requires the CIA to reveal material facts which, if not revealed, would distort result of operations or conceal unlawful practice.

In addition to the Code of Ethics, the Institute of Internal Auditors, which is the parent organization, has adopted a "Statement of Responsibilities" and "Standards for the Professional Practice" for internal auditors. These two documents describe how internal auditing *should be* performed and organized, however, and do not appear to bind the CIA in any way.

Structure of the Profession

The CIA program is administered by the Institute of Internal Auditors (IIA), a professional organization similar to NAA with 16,000 members and 136 chapters. All members of IIA must subscribe to a Code of Ethics which is almost identical to the code for CIAs. All aspects of the CIA program are administered at the national level except that local IIA chapters sometimes administer the CIA exams.

Since 1973 when the program started, 5,600 internal auditors have registered for the CIA program, and about 1,100 have successfully completed the exam and received certificates. Most CIAs work as regular employees of large organizations.

Legal Status of CIAs

The CIA indicates professional achievement, but there are no services that legally require a CIA.

Constituencies Addressed by the Code

The CIA's code recognizes an obligation to the profession, management, stockholders, and the general public. The specific articles of the code emphasize the CIA's responsibility to his or her employer.

Enforcement of the Code

A Professional Standards and Responsibilities Committee of the IIA is empowered to receive and hear complaints that the Code of Ethics has been violated. Almost identical procedures are to be followed for a CIA or a general member of the IIA. The disciplinary procedures have been designed carefully to provide due process to the person accused.

Enforcement History

Essentially there has been no requirement to enforce the CIA code since the program began in 1973. One person who was about to receive the CIA under a grandfather clause apparently forged a letter, so the IIA simply destroyed his certificate before it was sent to him. One or two other problems "went away" before the Board had to take any action.

Year When Code Enacted and Enforced

The CIA program began in 1963, and the code became effective then. Essentially the same code was adopted for all IIA members in the early 1940s.

Analysis of Effectiveness

Because there have been virtually no complaints against CIAs or general members of the IIA for alleged violations of the Code of Ethics, it is difficult to assess how effective the code is in regulating behavior of internal auditors. The nature of the internal auditors' code combined with the auditors' positions as employees naturally would tend to make complaints to the IIA or the Board of Regents for the CIA rare. As an employee, the internal auditor has his or her prime responsibility to and working relations with management. The Code of Ethics, which is the same for CIAs and general members of IIA, dictates behavior which management naturally would expect from a professional employee. Therefore, if management becomes dissatisfied with the conduct of an internal auditor, then management probably would terminate that employee rather than file a complaint with an external organization such as the IIA.

Thus, while the codes of ethics for CIAs and IIA may serve a useful purpose to enhance the image of the profession, these codes do not regulate professional behavior effectively.

Sources

1. Robert Rivers, CIA Program Director, Institute of Internal Auditors.
2. Ed Dooley, Assistant Manager of Internal Audit, Boise Cascade Corporation and President of the Boise Chapter of IIA.
3. Institute of Internal Auditors, "Certified Internal Auditor Program Information and Study Guide," IIA, Orlando, Fla., 1978.
4. Institute of Internal Auditors, "Code of Ethics," "Statement of Responsibilities," and "Standards for the Professional Practice of Internal Auditing," IIA, Orlando, Fla., undated.
5. "Facts and Figures About CIA Program," *The Internal Auditor,* December, 1978, pp. 15–17.
6. Victor C. Brink, CIA, "Internal Auditing: A Historical Perspective and Future Directions," *Internal Auditor,* December, 1978, pp. 23–35.
7. Institute of Internal Auditors, *Bylaws and Rules of Eligibility for Membership,* IIA, Altamonte Springs, Fla., 1978.

Summary Outline of Code of Ethics for a Certified Property Manager (CPM)

Description of the Code

The major thrust of the CPM's Code of Professional Ethics is to protect the property interests of clients or employees. Sections of the code require very specific behavior. For example, the CPM cannot receive any rebate or commission which has not been disclosed to and approved by the client. One section of the code regulates relationships between CPMs, but this section is very general and would be difficult to enforce. Two sections of the code require that the CPM continue his or her professional education and maintain a knowledge of applicable laws, which attempts to ensure a high level of technical proficiency by the CPM.

A CPM also must subscribe to the Code of Ethics of the National Association of Realtors (NAR). The NAR code contains many specific requirements for a realtor's handling of a sales transaction such as maintaining a special account in which to keep client deposits. In addition, the NAR code requires realtors to consider the interests of the general public and act in a professional manner toward other realtors.

Structure of the Profession

Most CPMs act as agents for property owners. In this capacity the CPM collects rents, makes disbursements for expenses and manages all aspects of the property for the owner. A few CPMs act as employees to manage property owned by their employer.

The CPM designation is granted by the Institute of Real Estate Management (IREM), which is one of the many divisions of the National Association of Realtors (NAR). A CPM must maintain membership in both IREM and NAR and must subscribe to the codes of ethics of both organizations.

Legal Status of CPMs

A few properties which receive federal subsidies must be managed by a CPM according to the terms of the subsidy agreement. Thus, the CPM has achieved some legal status.

Constituencies Addressed by the Code

Most provisions of the CPM's code and the NAR's code protect clients. Also addressed are the general public, the real estate profession, other CPMs and the CPM's employer.

Enforcement of the Code

An ethics committee at the national level of IREM receives and decides all ethics complaints against CPMs. The decision of the ethics committee is to be final and binding upon the CPM who agrees not to seek recourse against IREM.

Enforcement of the code for general members of NAR has the unique provision that if a controversy arises between realtors, they agree to submit the dispute to the local board rather than litigate. All disputes are arbitrated by a local committee whose decision is binding.

Enforcement History

Relatively few complaints, three or four per year, are received by IREM against CPMs. Embezzlement occasionally occurs, as apparently is typical in cases where agents, such as CPMs, handle other people's money. The IREM has revoked a few certificates for such blatant offenses. In other instances, the IREM has suspended a member for less serious violations which the member could correct. Currently, there are about 4,500 CPMs with another 2,300 candidates seeking the certificate. Thus, less than 0.1 percent of CPMs become involved in ethics complaints in any year.

Year When Code Enacted and Enforced

The CPM code was adopted in 1934 when the IREM was established.

Analysis of Effectiveness

Little incentive exists for a CPM's client to complain about the ethical behavior of a CPM. In cases involving a dispute about money, the client naturally would litigate to seek redress. In other cases, the client probably would cancel the contract with the CPM. Thus, it is concluded that the CPM's code does not effectively regulate professional behavior, but it may effectively educate the CPM as to his or her professional responsibilities.

Sources

1. Kathlyn Andler, Admissions Director, Institute of Real Estate Management.
2. Institute of Real Estate Management, *1979 Catalog,* IREM, 1979.
3. Institute of Real Estate Mangement, "Code of Professional Ethics of the CPM," IREM, date unknown.
4. National Association of Realtors, "Code of Ethics," NAR, date unknown.
5. Norman J. Zuckerman, CPM, Boise, Idaho.

Summary Outline of Code of Ethics for a Certified Public Accountant (CPA)

Description of the Code

CPAs have adopted a code of ethics which regulates their behavior related to the practice of public accounting in five areas: (1) independence, integrity, and objectivity, with respect to financial statements being attested to, (2) competence and technical standards to be employed by the public accountant, (3) responsibilities of the CPA to clients, (4) responsibilities of the CPA to other CPAs, and (5) other responsibilities to act like a true professional in the best public interest. The code generally is quite specific, although Rule 501 of the AICPA code states that: "A member (CPA) shall not commit an act discreditable to the profession." In addition to the actual rules of conduct, the code contains a philosophical description of the practice of public accounting and prior interpretations of the various rules.

Structure of the Profession

A CPA receives his or her license from the State Board of Accountancy, which is a state agency in the state or states where employed. The state boards have formed their own National Association of State Boards of Accountancy (NASBA). After receiving the license, the CPA becomes eligible to join the state society of CPAs, the American Institute of CPAs, and CPA firms. The state boards, the state societies, and the AICPA essentially have adopted identical codes of ethics. The AICPA appears to be the driving force for continued development and modification of the codes.

Legal Status of CPAs

The Securities Acts of 1933 and 1934 require public corporations to issue financial statements that are audited by a CPA. Thus, a CPA certificate represents a legally required license to provide a certain type of service.

Constituencies Addressed by the Code

The CPA code specifically mentions the following constituencies: (a) management, (b) investors, (c) creditors, (d) government agencies, (e) taxing authorities, and (f) others.

Enforcement of the Code

A CPA who violates the code of ethics may be sanctioned by either the state board or the state society or the AICPA. Suspension or revocation of the CPA license by the state automatically brings the same sanction by the state society and the AICPA. State boards generally are empowered to conduct hearings to suspend or revoke a CPA's license for alleged violations of the code of ethics. Due process to the accused and appeal procedures have been included in the hearing process by the states. Most state societies have entered into a Joint Ethics Enforcement Program in which an alleged violation is reviewed first by the AICPA's ethics division or the state society's ethics committee. Either of the groups may dismiss this case or refer it to a joint trial board of the AICPA which conducts formal hearings that provide due process. Findings of the joint trial board are reviewed by the AICPA's national review board.

Enforcement History

The AICPA, which has about 140,000 members, recently began publishing statistical summaries of its ethics investigations in *The CPA Letter*. For 1978, the number of cases is summarized as follows:

Open Investigations, January 1, 1978	592
Investigations Opened during 1978	444
	1,036
Less Investigations Completed during 1978	484
Open Investigations, December 31, 1978	552

Very few investigations reach the trial board. During 1978, 14 cases were approved to go to the trial board which heard only six cases during the year. The AICPA keeps all details of ethics cases confidential unless public release of a sanction against a member is agreed to as part of the settlement, in which case the nature of the violation, the sanction, and sometimes the CPA's name are published in *The CPA Letter*. Such public releases result in only a small number of cases. The AIC-

PA's staff member for professional ethics would say only that most of the ethics cases involve technical standards.

With about 1,000 active CPA licenses in the state, the Idaho State Board of Accountancy usually has "several" ethics investigations going on. Thus, the frequency of alleged ethics violations both in Idaho and for the AICPA seems to involve between 0.3 and 0.4% of all CPAs each year.

Year When Code Enacted and Enforced

The AICPA adopted its first formal code in 1917 in the form of eight rules of professional conduct. During that first year, a trial board suspended two members for violating these rules.

Analysis of Effectiveness

In the area of technical standards, the CPA's code of ethics seems to promote a high level of professional work, and many CPAs have been sanctioned for substandard work. The encroachment and solicitation provisions of the code, however, tend to protect a CPA from competition with other CPAs. The AICPA deleted both these provisions from its code, but most of the state boards still enforce the encroachment and solicitation codes. Thus, in addition to protecting the CPA's constituents, the CPA's code is partly self-serving because it also restricts competition between CPAs.

Sources

1. Herb Finkston, AICPA staff member for professional ethics.
2. Jeanette Drury, Executive Secretary of the Idaho State Board of Accountancy.
3. John L. Carey, *The Rise of the Accounting Profession* (2 vols.), New York: AICPA, 1970.
4. *The CPA Letter,* semi-monthly newsletter published by the AICPA.
5. *Idaho Accountancy Act* (as amended July 1, 1976).
6. AICPA, *Rules of Conduct of the Code of Professional Ethics,* as amended March 31, 1978.

Summary Outline of Code of Ethics for a Chartered Bank Auditor (CBA)

Description of the Code

The code of ethics adopted for the CBA program is very similar in scope and content to the code for CIAs.

Structure of the Profession

The Bank Administration Institute (BAI) administers the CBA program as one of its many programs of research, education and training for all aspects of bank operations. There appears to be no structure of local chapters of CBAs; all affairs are directed from the national headquarters of BAI.

In a manner very similar to a CIA, each CBA provides professional services as an employee. Thus the position of bank auditors and internal auditors closely resembles that of the management accountant in that each type of professional serves primarily as an employee answering to management rather than providing a service to a client outside the professional's organization.

Legal Status of CBAs

The CBA indicates professional achievement, but there are no services which legally require a CBA. One large bank in Idaho now requires a CBA or CPA designation for promotion to senior bank auditor, so the CBA program has achieved a prominent status in at least one organization.

Constituencies Addressed by the Code

"The CBA has professional obligations to his bank, its customers, stockholders, directors, and the general public." (direct quote from the CBA code)

Enforcement of the Code

A Board of Regents has been empowered to hear alleged ethics violations.

Enforcement History

Alleged ethics violations by a CBA rarely are reported to national headquarters. The person contacted could remember only one case in prior years, and there were no active cases. This pattern of no enforcement problems is consistent with the position of the CBA as an employee. As the CBA's code requires conduct which management naturally should expect from a professional employee, conflicts between a CBA and his or her employer normally would be settled directly; no motivation would exist for complaining to the Board of Regents.

Year When Code Enacted and Enforced

The CBA program began in 1966; the first exams were given in 1968. The Code of Ethics in its present form apparently was adopted when the program was initiated.

Analysis of Effectiveness

It is concluded that the CBA's code does not regulate professional behavior effectively for the same reasons discussed in the summary outline of the CIA's code.

Sources

1. Bank Administration Institute, *The Chartered Bank Auditor Program* (information pamphlet), Bank Administration Institute, Park Ridge, Ill., undated.
2. Unnamed staff member, Bank Administration Institute.
3. Jim Hogan, CPA, Internal Audit Manager, Idaho First National Bank, Boise, Idaho.

Summary Outline of Code of Ethics for a Chartered Financial Analyst (CFA)

Description of Code of Ethics

The CFA's Code of Ethics and Standards of Professional Conduct address two main areas: (1) The CFA must comply with and maintain knowledge of all applicable laws and regulations relating to securities markets, and (2) the CFA must give highest priority to the interests of investors receiving the CFA's advice and use a high standard of technical competence in arriving at advice given to investors. Most of the standards are fairly specific. Two of the standards which were so general that they would be difficult to enforce recently were made more specific.

Structure of the Profession

The CFA program is administered at the national level by the Institute of Chartered Financial Analysts (ICFA), which is closely affiliated with the Financial Analysts Federation (FAF). The CFA certification originated with the FAF in a manner similar to the one in which the CMA was originated by the NAA. Although most CFAs work for clients through investment advisory firms, a number of CFAs work as employees in the trust departments of banks and insurance companies.

In their quest for professional recognition, the financial analysts took two unique actions:

(1) When the FAF started the ICFA and the CFA designation, a one-time CFA exam was prepared for FAF members who were over 35 years old and who had at least ten years of professional experience. A large number of older FAF members received their CFA by passing this exam. After this one-time exam, all new candidates were required to pass Level I, Level II, and Level III exams with at least one year's time between each exam.

The one-time exam solved the dilemma of how to get the professional designation started without using a grandfather clause that would reduce credibility.

(2) In 1976, the FAF required new members to pass the CFA Level I exam. This rule would be analogous to the NAA requiring that new members join the IMA and pass one or two parts of the CMA exam.

The FAF and the ICFA have adopted identical codes of ethics.

Legal Status of CFA

The CFA indicates a high level of professional competency, but there are no services which legally require a CFA.

Constituencies Addressed by the Code

The CFA code addresses mainly the three groups to which the CFA provides services: customers, clients and employers. In a more general way, the code calls for the CFA to act in a highly ethical manner with the public, employees, associates, and fellow analysts.

Enforcement of the Code

The enforcement structure for the CFA code has three distinct stages:

(1) The executive director of the ICFA makes a somewhat informal investigation upon receipt of a written complaint against any CFA.

(2) If the executive director decides that it is appropriate, he refers the investigation to a regional committee which decides that (a) sufficient evidence exists of a possible violation, or (b) the investigation should be dismissed.

(3) A regional hearing panel hears the charges of those cases which the regional committee believes show evidence of a possible ethics violation. The hearing panel is conducted in an elaborate and formal process to ensure due process to the accused. For example, a court reporter makes a complete transcript of the proceedings, and the accused may be represented by his or her counsel. If the hearing panel decides that an ethics violation has occurred, it makes recommendations to the ICFA Board of Trustees who, in turn, decide how to sanction the member.

Since the ICFA began enforcing its code in 1972, only two cases out of almost 100 cases went to a hearing panel. Most cases in which the violation appears certain are settled through a "Stipulation of Facts and Offer of Consent to Disciplinary Sanction" between the accused member and either the executive director or the regional committee.

Most ethics investigations begin when a CFA returns the "Annual Professional Conduct Questionnaire," which each CFA is required to return to the ICFA. This questionnaire simply asks if the CFA's professional or business conduct has been complained about or has been the subject of investigation by any of the groups which regulate investments such as the Securities & Exchange Commission or the National Association of Securities Dealers.

Enforcement History

Although the Code was adopted when the CFA designation was granted in 1964, the ICFA had no active enforcement procedure for the Code of Ethics until 1972. Thus, the profession had a full eight years to consider and change its code before it had to worry about the implications of enforcing any of the specific provisions.

From 1973, when the first case was investigated, through 1978, 99 cases were initiated by the ICFA and disposed of approximately as follows:

Cases Pending, 12/31/78	14
Dismissed with No Sanction	60
Violation Upheld and Member Sanctioned	15
Total	99

For the sustained violations, the sanction was reached by the stipulation and consent process in twelve cases, two cases were tried by the hearing panel, and one sanction became automatic because the member had been found guilty of a felony.

In 1976, 1977 and 1978, the ICFA started 19, 26, and nine cases, respectively—an average of about 18 per year. Therefore, an average of about 0.4% of the 4,800 current holders of the CFA are involved in ethics investigations in any year.

Years When Code Enacted and Enforced

The CFA code became effective in 1964 when the first CFAs were granted. Enforcement of the code began in 1972, eight years later.

Analysis of Effectiveness

In the opinions of the executive director and the former executive director of the ICFA, most CFAs take their code seriously. Financial analysts fear that if they do not regulate themselves, then increased government regulation will occur. Thus the CFA code appears structured in such a manner as to protect only the constituency served by the profession.

Sources

1. O. Whitfield Broome, Jr., CPA, the Executive Director of ICFA. (Mr. Broome also is an active NAA member.)
2. W. Scott Bauman, CFA, Professor of Business Administration, University of Virginia. Dr. Bauman is the former Executive Director of ICFA.
3. Institute of Chartered Financial Analysts, *The ICFA Code of Ethics and Standards of Professional Conduct,* Charlottesville, Va.: ICFA, as revised January 15, 1976.
4. M.H. Earp, CFA, and John G. Gillis, Esq. (eds.) *Professional Standards of Practice,* Financial Analysts Research Foundation, 1978.

Summary Outline of Code of Ethics for a Life Insurance Agent and a Chartered Life Underwriter (CLU)

Description of the Code

A life insurance agent who has achieved the Chartered Life Underwriter (CLU) designation is subject to ethical standards of: 1) the state licensing department which licenses all insurance agents, 2) the National Association of Life Underwriters (NALU), to which almost all CLUs belong, and 3) the American Society of CLUs, which is the professional association for CLUs. These ethical standards address three areas of professional conduct: service to the client, enhancement of the profession, and personal integrity. When an insurance agent receives a license from the state, he or she must conform to the standards of personal integrity specified by the state licensing code. Both the NALU and the American Society of CLUs have adopted codes which emphasize service to clients and to the profession and which require a higher standard of ethical conduct than required by the state licensing department. Although the NALU's code and the CLU's code are written and organized differently, both codes appear to address the same issues. Thus, achieving the CLU designation does not seem to impose higher ethical standards upon an insurance agent than does general membership in NALU.

Structure of the Profession

The basic structure of the life insurance business consists of an agent who sells life insurance from a specific company to a client. Four entities participate in organizing and regulating the industry.

State Insurance Department

Each agent must obtain a license to sell insurance from his or her state. Most states require the applicant to pass a relatively simple test (compared to the CMA exam) and to have a personal background free from felony convictions, bankruptcy, and the like.

Associations of Life Underwriters

Most life insurance agents join the professional association organization consisting of local, state, and national associations. The national association, NALU and state associations actually are federations of the local associations. An agent "belongs" only to a local association. All the associations have adopted codes of ethics.

The American College

An applicant for the CLU designation actually enrolls in a study program of the American College's S.S. Huebner School of CLU studies. The American College grants the CLU designation, which is more similar to a college degree than to a license.

The American Society of CLUs

After an agent receives the CLU designation, he or she joins the American Society—the professional society for holders of the CLU. Thus the American College grants the designation, but the American Society regulates CLUs after they achieve the designation.

Legal Status of CLUs

To sell life insurance, an agent needs only a license from the state; the CLU designation indicates professional achievement only. In some states, a CLU does not have to take the state exam to obtain a license.

Constituencies Addressed by the Code

The codes for CLUs address responsibilities to: clients, the insurance company, other insurance agents, and the insurance business and profession.

Enforcement of the Code

The nature of the life insurance business seems to generate intense competition between agents and therefore lends itself to numerous complaints about the behavior of certain agents. Thus, each of the organizational entities has become organized to process complaints about unethical behavior.

The state insurance departments receive many complaints which usually are investigated under state administrative procedures to ensure due process to the accused. The only way to stop an agent from continuing to sell insurance is to revoke his or her state license; thus the state licensing department holds the ultimate censuring power.

A considerable amount of ethics enforcement activity occurs in the system of the local, state and national life underwriters associations. To avoid compromising legal positions if the local association violates the rights of an accused agent, the NALU prepared a detailed instruction booklet, "Keep It Legal," which tells local associations how to conduct ethics investigations. The NALU occasionally gathers evidence of wrongdoing by an agent to present to the state licensing department.

Until last year, the American Society of CLUs had no formal system for investigating ethics complaints against members. Several instances of unethical conduct by a CLU apparently occurred in prior years, but the local CLU chapters "bungled" the investigations so much that the American Society was afraid to sanction the member whose rights to due process had been violated. Thus, to avoid legal liability, the American Society has never sanctioned a member. Last year, the American Society instituted a new procedure for investigating ethics violations. It provides for an initial investigation by the chapter's ethical guidance committee, a formal hearing by a local tribunal board, and a review hearing by a national tribunal board. The accused member will receive due process in these procedures.

In summary, ethics enforcement in the life insurance profession is unique in that the professional association, NALU, has been more aggressive than the association of certificate holders, the American Society of CLUs.

Enforcement History

As previously noted, the American Society of CLUs has never enforced its code of ethics even though the number of complaints has been growing. In the past, emphasis has been on guidance rather than punitive action, and most cases have been resolved informally. Members having obviously unethical behavior seem to resign or fail to pay their next year's dues. The NALU does not keep any statistics on the number of ethics investigations in which it is involved although its Director of Public Relations said the number of cases was relatively small.

Most of the action apparently occurs at the state licensing department. In Idaho, for example, about 500 investigations into alleged wrongdoings by life insurance agents are initiated each year, and there are only about 6,000 licensees in the state. Many of these investigations involve cases such as simple fraud or embezzlement rather than matters of ethics.

Year When Codes Enacted and Enforced

The NALU adopted its first code of ethics in 1918; the American Society adopted its first code in 1928 when the society was founded.

Analysis of Effectiveness

Many of the provisions of the various codes of ethics to which an insurance agent must conform protect the interests of specific clients and the general public. These provisions are enforced, so the codes of ethics are at least partially effective. Leaders of the professional organizations stressed that much of their ethics enforcement focuses upon education and advice rather than policing. Thus, the professional organizations operate programs to inform members about their ethical responsibilities.

Sources

1. George Conradi, Idaho Insurance Department, Head of Investigations.
2. Marvin A. Kobel, CLU, National Association of Life Underwriters, Director of Public Relations.
3. Robert J. Lowder, CLU, President, Boise Chapter of the American Society of CLUs.
4. James J. Chastain, Ph.D., Director of the Center for Insurance Education, Howard University.
5. Tom Klein, Director of Field Relations, American Society of CLUs.
6. Jerry Burke, former President of Idaho's Society of Life Underwriters.
7. State of Idaho, "Instructions for Obtaining a Life Insurance Agent's License," 1979.
8. American Society of CLUs, *CLU Chapter Guide,* 1979–80.
9. National Association of Life Underwriters, *NALU* (booklet of general information), 1978.
10. National Association of Life Underwriters, *Keep It Legal,* February 1976.

Summary Outline of the Code of Ethics of the National Association of Purchasing Managers

Description of the Code

The Principles and Standards of Purchasing Practice, the code advocated by the National Association of Purchasing Management (NAPM), has been in existence since the early 1920s. As such, it is one of the older professional codes. Despite its age, however, it has not followed the common trend of becoming more specific and detailed over time. The code contains ten rather general statements requiring the member to receive and be guided by competent counsel, for instance, and to first consider the interests of his company in all transactions. This code appeared to be the least specific studied.

Structure of the Profession

The National Association of Purchasing Managers is an organization of purchasing managers and buyers in all types of organizations. Five years ago the Association began issuing a Certified Purchasing Manager (CPM) designation. The certificate is issued to those passing the certification test and accumulating a fixed number of other points for qualifying activities and education. While there is no educational requirement for the certificate, college degrees do give a member some of the points needed for certification. The certificate is issued for a five-year period during which the member must accumulate additional points for recertification.

The code of ethics applies equally to all members of the NAPM whether they have a certification or not.

Constituencies Addressed by the Code

The NAPM code mentions, in general terms, responsibilities to: the member's employer, suppliers, and fellow purchasing managers.

Enforcement of the Code

At present there is no mechanism for enforcing the provisions of the NAPM code. The Ethical Standards Committee presently is considering the enforcement issue. The Committee's findings, however, have not been finalized.

Analysis of Effectiveness

The effectiveness of this code depends on a person's perspective. If the purpose of a code is to prevent bad behavior, then the code has not been particularly effective. A recent survey of purchasing agents conducted in the East shows 10% of 192 respondents violating the current code of ethical standards. In addition, 21% practice reciprocity (pressuring suppliers to buy your products), a practice outlawed by the Supreme Court ten years ago. If the purpose of a code is to show people how to behave well, however, then the code may well be effective for it does contain general principles for desirable professional behavior.

Sources

1. "Purchasers Consider Ethics Code with Teeth," *Industry Week,* July 24, 1978, pp. 31–32.
2. Ed Bierman, Director of Certification, National Headquarters of the NAPM.
3. National Association of Purchasing Managers, "Principles and Standards of Purchasing Practice."
4. Rogene Buchholz and William Rudelius, "Purchasing Standards Revisited," *Journal of Purchasing and Materials Management,* Fall 1978, pp. 23–26.
5. NAPM Certification Program Study Guide, Dan Roman, ed.

Summary Outline of the Code of Ethics of the National Society of Professional Engineers

Description of the Code

The engineers, along with the lawyers, physicians and accountants, form the four recognized professions. Like the other three, the engineers have a firmly developed code of ethics. The engineers are somewhat different in that each of the engineering specialities, such as civil, mechanical, electrical, has a code of ethics. In addition, the Society of Professional Engineers has a code. While these codes are all quite similar, there are differences. For the purposes of this report, it is adequate to consider only the code of the National Society of Professional Engineers.

The Professional Engineers' Code of Ethics, while much less extensive than the codes of either the American Medical Association or the American Bar Association, is much more formal than the codes of the Purchasing Managers, Data Processors or Internal Auditors.

The code consists of 15 sections, each stating in a few sentences a specific responsibility of the engineer. These statements then are followed by from one to seven more specific statements clarifying the general points made in the section. The professional engineers' code fits quite nicely on one sheet of paper.

Structure of the Profession

A person becomes an engineer upon graduating from an engineering school, but a person cannot become a professional engineer until he or she has passed two tests and worked for a time as an engineer. The first test is the Engineer in Training test (EIT), which covers the academic technical knowledge an engineer will need. After passing the EIT test, the engineer is required to work as an engineer before taking the Professional Engineer (PE) test.

Both tests are given by state licensing boards, not the national society. The engineer then is licensed to practice by the state in which the test was passed. In all states but Iowa, once the license is granted it is good for life. Iowa recently has enacted a continuing education requirement for maintaining an engineering license.

Legal Status of Professional Engineers

Because he is licensed by the states, the Professional Engineer (P.E.) is a legal creation of the state. The P.E. certification is legally required for an engineer to perform specific engineering jobs in that state. These jobs are generally those that have to do with public health or safety. Therefore, the engineer designing a highway bridge will have to be licensed to do that job. The engineer designing a computer for a major electronics firm probably will not have to be licensed.

Constituencies Addressed by the Code

The P.E. Code of Ethics specifically addresses the engineer's relationship with the public, the employer or client, fellow engineers and the individual engineer's professional dignity. The code specifically establishes that the engineer's paramount duty is to the public.

Enforcement of the Code

Because many of the acts that would be judged unethical by the P.E. code also are covered by the laws governing the state licensing agency, an engineer might be sanctioned by both the licensing board and the state Society of Professional Engineers. If such a circumstance occurred, the issue probably would be addressed by the state licensing board rather than the state society, but the board would form a review panel that probably would contain many state society members.

In general, discipline is considered primarily at the state level. In fact, this discipline often is done on an informal basis, although each state society maintains the ability to sanction its members and even ask that their state licenses be revoked. The National Society of Professional Engineers, however, has recognized that in some cases local societies may not be able to address a discipline issue adequately. This fact was brought out by the bribery problems in Maryland in the early 1970s involving, among others, Spiro Agnew. Therefore, in cases where there may be severe local pressure on the state society, the national society will form a committee to investigate any allegation.

The enforcement problems of professional societies is illustrated again by the recent Supreme Court decision against the P.E. code. The code had contained a clause stating that bidding for engineering work was unprofessional and hence should not be done. The court found that this clause is illegal under the Sherman Anti-Trust Act, although the Court also stated that no engineer could be required to bid on a contract.

Enforcement History

While the state chapters and licensing boards have an active history of enforcement, there is no agency compiling enforcement figures on either a state or national basis. Much of the enforcement seems to be on an informal basis although for serious issues it can be rigorous, despite care taken to follow rules of due process.

Analysis of Effectiveness

To a large extent, the engineer's code seems to have struck a happy medium between the rather loose codes of some organizations and the very extensive codes of other organizations. The code seems concerned with setting some general standards of "good" behavior rather than addressing all possible contingencies. The code appears to have been rather effective as there apparently is a general feeling that engineers have done a good job in maintaining the ethics of their profession. The code does address itself to relations between engineers, however, and this concern has been attacked by federal agencies as detrimental to the public welfare.

The engineers seem to be addressing ethical issues actively, and their journal, *Professional Engineer,* contains frequent articles on the subject.

Sources

1. National Society of Professional Engineers, Code of Ethics.
2. American Society of Civil Engineers, Code of Ethics.
3. James L. Pline, President, Idaho Society of Professional Engineers.
4. Supreme Court ruling in National Society of Professional Engineers vs. United States.
5. Numerous issues of *Professional Engineer* including: May 1979, October 1978, December 1977, August 1977, October 1976, June 1976. Most of these issues have more than one article dealing with ethics.

Appendix C

Unstructured Interview Documents

Page

BOISE STATE UNIVERSITY • 1910 UNIVERSITY DRIVE • BOISE, IDAHO 83725

DEPARTMENT OF ACCOUNTING AND DATA PROCESSING
SCHOOL OF BUSINESS

Date

Mr. John L. Doe
Controller
ABC Corporation
City, State 99999

Dear Mr. Doe:

We are writing to seek your help in a research study we are conducting for the National Association of Accountants (NAA).

In order to determine if management accountants need a code of ethics, NAA commissioned our study last summer. One portion of the study requires that we interview a sample of management accountants. Your city was selected as one of three cities to conduct interviews in because of its geographical location and the wide diversity of its business community. Jim Smith, the President of NAA's chapter in your city, suggested that you could make a valuable contribution to the study.

Specifically, we would like to interview you, in your office, about any ethical problems you feel are important to management accountants. The interview should last from one to one and one-half hours. Results of the interviews may be published, but your name, your company's name and industry and the specific location will remain confidential.

Mike Merz will conduct interviews in your city between December 4 and 7; he will call you soon to try to arrange an appointment. If you agree to help, we will send you more information about the study and types of information we want before the interview.

Sincerely,

David F. Groebner	C. Mike Merz
Associate Professor	Associate Professor

BOISE STATE UNIVERSITY • 1910 UNIVERSITY DRIVE • BOISE, IDAHO 83725

DEPARTMENT OF ACCOUNTING AND DATA PROCESSING
SCHOOL OF BUSINESS

Date

Mr. John L. Doe
Controller
ABC Corporation
City, State 00000

Dear John:

Thank you for agreeing to help with our research into a code of ethics for management accountants. We believe you can make a valuable contribution to our study which the National Association of Accountants (NAA) initiated.

Our research so far has revealed that most professional business groups have adopted a code of ethics to help guide personal decisions on ethical issues. For example, the professional associations of Internal Auditors, Chartered Financial Analysts, Certified Public Accountants, Purchasing Agents, Data Processors and many others have codes of ethics. However, no code has been adopted by NAA or any other group of management accountants. Thus, the major purpose of our study is to help NAA determine if management accountants need a code of ethics, and if so, what the code should contain.

Specifically, the purpose of the interview is to determine if you believe that management accountants encounter ethical conflicts in:

- Their professional role as management accountants, or
- Their role as managers.

Most professional codes of ethics specify that a professional has responsibilities in four different areas:

1. Responsibility to be technically competent in issues related to the theory and practice of accounting.

2. Responsibility to protect the interests of clients or employers.
3. Responsibility to treat colleagues who are management accountants in a professional, courteous manner.
4. Responsibility to act in a manner for the general benefit of society and the accounting profession.

Many management accountants also act as managers. The best description of management roles for our purposes was developed by the management scholar, Henry Mintzberg, who actually watched managers at work. Mintzberg observed managers acting in the following roles.

1. Figurehead Roles—Those actions a manager is obligated to take just because of his or her position within the organization. Any ceremonial actions, actions involving status or representation at events.
2. Leader Roles—Most actions involving subordinates, such as staffing, training, etc.
3. Liaison Roles—Maintaining outside contacts and sources of information through correspondence and membership on mixed committees and boards.
4. Monitor Roles—Searching out and receiving information needed to understand the changing environment of the organization. Acting as the nerve center of both internal and external information in the work group.
5. Disseminator Roles—Transmitting both information and interpretation to individuals in the organization that need the information. Often giving personal opinion of the value of the information to the organization.
6. Spokesman Roles—Transmitting information on the organization to outside sources, often with an expert's opinion on the organization or industry role.
7. Entrepreneur Roles—Searching the environment for opportunities for the organization and initiating change in the organization to take advantage of opportunities found.
8. Disturbance Handler Roles—Responsible for identifying problems in the organization and implementing corrective courses of action.
9. Resource Allocator Roles—Giving the final approval or

disapproval of almost all major organizational changes that affect resources.

10. Negotiator Roles—Representing the organization in situations that require negotiations for contract terms, work agreements, etc.

If you consider ethical conflicts within the framework of either the professional roles or the managerial roles as described, our discussions can start from the same reference point.

Since no one has ever asked management accountants about ethical conflicts they encounter, we do not know what your ethical concerns are. Just as an example, we believe that the following ethical conflicts might occur for a management accountant.

- Company management directs you to complete a complicated cost analysis in two working days. You know that you, or the management accountants that you supervise, cannot do an adequate technical job in such a short time. (Technical Issue)
- You are working with the public accountants who are auditing your firm. You are trying to decide whether to disclose to them a piece of information which might result in an exception on the audit report. (Conflict as Disseminator)
- An operating manager incurred an expense for an activity clearly against company policy. You are directed to hide the expense in the account. (Technical Conflict in Role as Disturbance Handler)

These examples are provided only to stimulate your thinking. Once again, our purpose is to gather information about your ideas on professional codes of ethics. Thank you for your help and we look forward to personally meeting with you.

David F. Groebner	C. M. Merz
Associate Professor	Associate Professor

BOISE STATE UNIVERSITY • 1910 UNIVERSITY DRIVE • BOISE, IDAHO 83725

DEPARTMENT OF ACCOUNTING AND DATA PROCESSING
SCHOOL OF BUSINESS

Date

Mr. John L. Doe
Controller
ABC Corporation
City, State 00000

Dear Mr. Doe:

Thank you for providing us with your thoughts about ethical problems faced by management accountants. During our interview with you I recorded the following main points.

SUMMARY OF INTERVIEW 26

- The big problem you see for a code is how the management accountant, as an employee, could tell the boss that the accountant couldn't do something because it was against the code of ethics.
- You feel that a code might be a helpful tool to resist management direction to do something unethical.
- Your biggest ethical conflicts occurred in a privately held, smaller company that you once worked for. When that company was engaged in a big tax problem, you had to prepare data for banks and lawyers in such a hurry that the final job was somewhat of a farce.
- In that company, when one accountant concluded that internal control of certain expenses was adequate, he was told to change the report to say that someone was cheating on his expenses.
- Also in that company, a feasibility study was changed until a positive cash flow was forecast so that the owner could substantiate the answer he wanted.
- In your current company, there is a strong motivation to avoid taxes in ethical manners but not to cheat.

- You have heard tales within your company of gifts and political contributions made by certain managers. In these instances, a management accountant somewhere in the company must have been told to code the gift or contribution to some expense account like maintenance and repair. However, you have not had to face this type of ethical conflict.
- An education process would be needed to teach people about the code of ethics to counteract the big motivation for management accountants to change numbers to help the company get loans, improve cash flow, reduce taxes, etc.
- Your value system with respect to taxes is first to ask if it's criminal; if not criminal, then you ask how severely would a third party such as a state be injured by the company's action to avoid taxes. Your current employer's philosophy is to prepare tax returns correctly and to lay everything out for the auditors. Your values tend to be derived from the company's values. In ethical situations you tend to cover yourself by forcing a decision by another person in the company.
- You feel a responsibility to cooperate with the outside auditors. You feel such cooperation actually saves money in the long run because if you establish credibility with the auditors, they accept your reports at face value.
- It might be valuable for a code of ethics to remind people of their responsibility to promote the profession, but such a clause would not be enforceable.
- If the code were too general in nature, each person would interpret to suit himself. Some specific provisions such as "responsibility to prepare financial statements to fairly present, etc." would be desirable, but the code shouldn't get into very technical areas like the FASB's.
- If you pass an ethical problem, such as an illegal contribution, up to a higher level in the organization, but you are still aware of the illegal contribution, are you a "party to the act?"
- You see a problem in structuring a code of ethics to address the many levels of financial responsibility that different NAA members have, i.e., from bookkeeper up to financial V.P. Throwing a member out of NAA for violating the code might be an effective enforcing mechanism; the violation could be published in the NAA literature. However, a long and careful investigation would have to be made first and solid evidence would have to be presented. A

censure should occur only for "really bad" violations. Informal investigation of complaints, such as the CPAs and Professional Engineers do, would be effective.

I will call you in several days to make sure that we validly recorded your ideas and opinions. As we promised earlier, your name and your company's identity will be held strictly confidential by the two researchers.

Sincerely,

C. Mike Merz
Associate Professor

Appendix D

Structured Interview Documents

BOISE STATE UNIVERSITY • 1910 UNIVERSITY DRIVE • BOISE, IDAHO 83725

DEPARTMENT OF ACCOUNTING AND DATA PROCESSING
SCHOOL OF BUSINESS

Date

Mr. John Doe
ABC Corp.
1234 Main Street
City, State 00000

Dear Mr. Doe:

We are writing to seek your help in a research study we are conducting for the National Association of Accountants.

The NAA commissioned our study last summer in order to determine if management accountants need a code of ethics, and if so, what form the code should take. Lee Brummett, NAA's President for 1979–80, mentioned this effort to develop a code of ethics in the March, 1980 issue of *Management Accounting,* page 4. Our background research and a series of unstructured interviews of NAA members already conducted at three locations in the United States have revealed substantial interest concerning ethics for management accountants. In the present phase of our study we will conduct a series of structured interviews at six or seven separate locations across the nation. Your city was selected because of its geographic location and wide diversity of its business community. The president of your NAA chapter suggested that you could make a valuable contribution to our study.

Specifically, we would like to interview you, in your office, about whether you think NAA should develop a code of ethics, and if so, what issues should be covered and what format the code should follow. The interview should last about one-half hour and will be "structured" in that we will ask you a series of specific questions. Results from the interviews may be published, but your name, that of your company, your location and industry will remain confidential.

Mike Merz will conduct interviews in your city between June 24 and June 27; he will call you soon to try to arrange an appointment. If you agree to help, and are available, we will send you some pre-interview information we would like you to consider.

Sincerely,

David F. Groebner Associate Professor	C. Mike Merz Professor

BOISE STATE UNIVERSITY • 1910 UNIVERSITY DRIVE • BOISE, IDAHO 83725

DEPARTMENT OF ACCOUNTING AND DATA PROCESSING
SCHOOL OF BUSINESS

Date

Mr. John Doe
ABC Corp.
1234 Main Street
City, State 00000

Dear John:

Thank you for agreeing to help with our research into a code of ethics for management accountants. We believe that you can make a valuable contribution to our study which the National Association of Accountants (NAA) initiated.

You will be participating in the structured interviews of the second stage of the study which has the following three principal stages:

1. Background Research—We reviewed ethical theory in general and examined many other codes of ethics for professional persons. As you are probably aware, many professional business groups such as the Internal Auditors, Chartered Financial Analysts, CPAs, etc., have adopted codes.

2. Surveys of Management Accountants—In a series of "unstructured" interviews, we asked a small sample (30) of management accountants how they felt about a code of ethics. Now, "structured" interviews are being conducted with a larger sample to seek specific answers to the issues raised in the unstructured interviews. Finally, a large sample will be asked to respond to a mail questionnaire.

3. Recommendation—We will analyze results of the surveys of management accountants to recommend whether or not NAA should adopt a code of ethics and if so, what the code should contain.

We have, at this point, completed the series of unstructured interviews with NAA members at three locations in the nation. These interviews gave us good insight into ethical issues facing management accountants and greatly aided our thinking about which issues are important and which are not important to NAA members. In addition, we found substantial interest concerning ethics for management accountants.

During the structured interview we will ask you specific questions about issues such as:

- Should NAA adopt a code of ethics?
- If a code is desirable, what ethical issues should the code contain?
- To whom should the code apply?
- Should the code have an enforcement mechanism?
- What other issues do you think are important concerning ethics for management accountants?

To stimulate your thinking about issues which might appear in a code, we prepared the three sample codes in the attachment which were patterned after the codes for other business groups. If a code appears desirable for management accountants (and this is a big if), it could be structured similar to one of these three samples.

We look forward to meeting you to obtain your ideas and feelings about a code of ethics for management accountants.

Sincerely,

David F. Groebner
Associate Professor

C. Mike Merz
Professor

ch

Attachment

Attachment

Sample Code of Ethics Formats

1. The "Obligations To" Format
2. The "Canon" Format
3. The "Absolute Conduct - Contemporary Ethics" Format

Explanatory Note

Each attached code of ethics format resembles one or more of existing codes in other business professions. As written, these sample codes contain a few clauses which might be appropriate in a code for management accountants. The sample formats are not intended to be all-inclusive or necessarily representative of a code of ethics which may be recommended for the National Association of Accountants as a result of this research project.

In addition, codes typically contain introductory procedure sections covering: the code's purpose, enforcement procedures, governing bodies, and a change mechanism. These sections tend to be standard and are not included in the following samples.

Sample Code of Ethics Format #1 "Obligations To"

Obligations to Employer

1. The management accountant's first responsibility is to the owners or trustees of the organization which employs him or her.
2. The management accountant will not engage in activities which represent a significant conflict of interest with his or her employer without first obtaining the employer's approval.
3. Etc.

Obligations to the Public

1. The management accountant will obey all applicable laws and regulations which influence his or her activities as a management accountant.

2. The management accountant recognizes that public trust in the business system is built upon the belief that information presented about an organization is reliable and reasonable. The management accountant will not prepare or present information in a manner which would deceive the general public.
3. Etc.

Obligations to the Profession

1. A senior management accountant accepts responsibility to promote and encourage the professional growth of management accountants under his or her supervision.
2. A management accountant will continue his or her professional development so as to stay reasonably current in the disciplines of management accounting.
3. Etc.

Note: This code format is similar to the CPA's code and the architect's code which have been structured into different sections specifying the professional's obligation or responsibilities to various groups.

Sample Code of Ethics Format #2 "Canons"

Canons

1. A management accountant's first responsibility is to the organization which employs him or her.
2. A management accountant will not knowingly engage in any illegal or unethical act, even if directed to do so by his or her employer.
3. A management accountant shall continue his or her professional development so as to remain reasonably current in the field of management accounting.
4. A management accountant will obtain his or her employer's permission before engaging in an activity which represents a significant conflict of interest with the employer.
5. A management accountant will not prepare information for or present information to the general public which will be deceiving.

6. A management accountant will not act in a manner which would discredit the management accounting profession.
7. Etc.

Note: This code format resembles the code of the Institute of Internal Auditors. Each ethical issue is addressed with an independent canon.

Sample Code of Ethics Format #3 "Absolute Conduct—Contemporary Ethics"

Code of Conduct

A management accountant will conduct himself or herself in accordance with the general provisions of the following code of conduct. These provisions are considered absolute and rarely will be changed.

1. The management accountant accepts that his or her first responsibility is to his or her employer.
2. The management accountant also accepts responsibilities to the profession of management accounting and to the general public.
3. The management accountant will practice management accounting with a high degree of technical competence.
4. The management accountant will not knowingly engage in an illegal or unethical act.
5. Etc.

Code of Ethics

A management accountant shall abide by the following specific rules which have been derived from the Code of Conduct and which occasionally may be modified to reflect changes in the business environment.

1. Before engaging in any activity which will significantly conflict with his or her employer's interests, the management accountant shall obtain the employer's approval.
2. A management accountant shall ensure his or her continued professional development by devoting at least 40 hours (or 20 or 50) each year to appropriate professional development activities.

3. The management accountant shall perform his or her work in accordance with those generally accepted accounting principles which are relevant to the task being performed.
4. Etc.

Note: This code format resembles the code of the Data Processing Management Association. The Code of Conduct contains a relatively small number of concise provisions which are considered absolute. The Code of Ethics deals with very specific issues such as confidentiality and conflict of interest. Occasional modification of the Code of Ethics is anticipated as the business environment changes.

Structured Interview Format*
for Code of Ethics Study

This interview format outline will serve as a guide to the interviewers. Interviewees will be asked a series of questions in person by the interviewer, but the interviewee will not receive a copy of the questions.

I. Description of Project

The interviewer will tell the interviewee how the structured interviews fit into the overall project. The interviewees will be told that there are no "right" answers and that their own personal opinions are being sought.

II. Interviewee's Job Description

To get the interviewee to feel comfortable and to start talking, he or she first will be asked to describe his or her job. Much of the desired demographic data about the interviewee usually is disclosed along with the person's job description.

III. Questions (to be read to the Interviewee)

Question 1.

Although most professional business groups have adopted some form of a code of ethics, NAA has not. However, there is really no reason for NAA to copy other organizations. Do you think that a code of ethics would be appropriate for NAA? What are your reasons? What do you see as the major benefits and drawbacks for a code?

Strong Yes __44__; Qualified Yes __39__; No __24__.

---

*NOTE: The frequency of responses of the 107 structured interviews has been entered next to each question. For various reasons, the total number of responses to each question does not always sum to 107.

Question 2.

The other codes of ethics that we reviewed covered a wide variety of topics, with certain topics being found in almost every code and other topics rarely found. Here is a list of about 20 topics. Please indicate whether you think that a code for management accountants should include each topic. Please answer: 1) SHOULD BE CONSIDERED, 2) NOT SURE, or 3) SHOULD NOT BE CONSIDERED.

		Should Be	Not Sure	Not
a)	Responsibility for professional development of junior accountants.	72	8	22
b)	Responsibility to further the public image of the profession.	88	7	8
c)	Responsibility to continue your education and to remain current in the field.	93	6	4
d)	Responsibility not to undertake work for which you are not technically competent.	80	10	13
e)	Obligation toward the general public.	84	5	14
f)	Obligation to be of good moral character (whatever that means).	89	9	5
g)	Responsibility to avoid conduct which would discredit the profession.	100	1	2
h)	Responsibility to treat other management accountants with professional courtesy.	85	7	11

The next set of topics appears to be legal obligations of any employee under Agency law or other laws. Therefore, an employee must abide by these legal and/or ethical responsibilities whether or not a code of ethics contains them. Do you think these also should be in a code for management accountants?

		Should Be	Not Sure	Not
i)	Responsibility not to discriminate for any reason.	66	8	30
j)	Recognition that the management accountant's primary responsibility is to the			

	Should Be	Not Sure	Not
owners of the firm or to the trustees of the organization.	84	5	13
k) Responsibility not to perform an illegal or unethical act, even if directed to do so.	93	2	8
l) Responsibility not to engage in activities which would cause a conflict-of-interest with the management accountant's employer, without the employer's permission.	88	7	8
m) Obligation to avoid personal profit or gain as a result of confidential information gained through employment.	89	8	6
n) Obligation to maintain confidentiality of information about employer.	94	5	3

Even though each of the preceding topics might be appropriate for a code of ethics for management accountants, none of these responsibilities would really impose any new ethical duties. Each of the preceding topics is either contained in the law or is too general to enforce. However, the following provisions would impose new and significantly increased ethical duties upon management accountants. Do you think these should be contained in a code for management accountants?

	Should Be	Not Sure	Not
o) Responsibility to always present information in the most reasonable manner so as not to deceive the primary user.	94	5	4
p) Responsibility to follow generally accepted accounting principles where applicable.	94	2	7
q) Responsibility to report violation of the code by other management accountants.	43	18	42
r) Responsibility to report any violations of the law within the organization to someone in the organization—either to the owners or to an appropriate level of management; i.e., responsibility to "blow the whistle."	85	3	15

	Should Be	Not Sure	Not
s) Responsibility to make top management of the employing organization aware of the code of ethics for management accountants.	77	13	13
t) Responsibility to cooperate with external auditors by informing them of all items which would materially affect the entity's financial statements.	78	7	18
u) Is there any ethical issue which was not mentioned but which you feel is important?			

Question 3.

The material we sent you contained three sample formats for a code. Forget for a minute the specific provisions in those samples and consider the format. (Hand interviewee a copy of the three if he or she does not have them present.) Do you prefer the: 1) "Obligations to," 2) "Canon," or 3) "Absolute Conduct-Contemporary Ethics" format? Why?

"Obligations to" 51 ; "Canon" 17 ; "Absolute Conduct" 17 ;

"No Preference" 20 .

Question 4.

In the sample codes, the provisions were written differently. For example, the continuing education clause was written in very general terms in one code and quite specific terms in another code. Would you prefer that a code for management accountants be written in general or specific terms? Why?

General 68 ; Specific 34 ; Not Sure 2 .

Question 5.

This question deals with whom a code for management accountants should apply to. The following suggestions have been made by various persons:

1) The code of ethics should apply to all members of NAA. 21
2) The code should apply only to CMAs. 22

3) The code should apply only to NAA members when they are performing management accounting functions. 61

Since NAA membership is so diverse and since the practice of management accounting is so diverse, it will not be easy to specify who must follow a code and when he or she must follow it. Which of the alternatives do you prefer or do you have another suggestion?

Question 6.

If NAA adopted a code of ethics, the Association's tax-exempt status as an educational organization might be lost. Taxes and increased mailing costs could increase operating costs as much as $4 per member per year. Do you think that such increased costs should significantly influence whether or not NAA develops and adopts a code?

Cost is Significant 35 .
Cost is Not Significant 71 .

Question 7.

In your current job situation do you think that a code of ethics for management accountants would either: 1) help you, 2) hinder you, or 3) have little or no effect? Why?

Help 37 ; Hinder 0 ; Little or No Effect 68 .

Question 8.

To be really effective, a code for management accountants would need acceptance and support by the accountants' employers. Do you think that your management would either: 1) strongly support a code, 2) be mostly neutral toward a code, or 3) strongly oppose a code? Why?

Support 81 ; Mostly Neutral 18 ; Oppose 0 ;
Not Sure 4 .

Question 9.

Our intent is to represent your opinion as accurately as possible. Is there any aspect of a code of ethics you feel is important that we have not discussed?

Question 10.

If necessary, request additional demographic information to complete the following checklist.

INTERVIEWEE DEMOGRAPHICS
(Check Appropriate Category)

1. Sex: __93__ Male __14__ Female
2. Age: __17__ 20s __37__ 30s __31__ 40s __22__ 50+
3. CPA: __34__ Yes __73__ No
4. CMA: __11__ Yes __96__ No
5. College: __9__ No Degree __80__ Bachelor's __18__ Master's
6. Supervisory Level: __23__ Top Management __31__ Middle Management
   __26__ Lower Management __27__ Staff Accountant
7. Organization Type: __98__ Profit __9__ Not-for-Profit or Government
8. Organization Ownership:
   __76__ Public Corporation
   __16__ Private Corporation
   __9__ Proprietorship or Partnership
   __6__ Not Applicable (Not-for-Profit or Government)
9. Organization Size: __18__ Small __20__ Medium __69__ Large
10. Level in the Organization:
   __52__ Corporate Office or Single Entity Organization
   __40__ Division or Subsidiary or Group Office
   __15__ Operating Plant

Structured Interview No. ____________

Prepared By __________________

Date ______________________

Appendix E

Mail Survey Documents

BOISE STATE UNIVERSITY • 1910 UNIVERSITY DRIVE • BOISE, IDAHO 83725

DEPARTMENT OF ACCOUNTING AND DATA PROCESSING
SCHOOL OF BUSINESS

Date

Mrs. Mary Smith
XYZ Corporation
5678 Main Street
City, State 00000

Dear Mrs. Smith:

We are writing to seek your help in a research study we are conducting for the National Association of Accountants. The NAA commissioned our study in July 1979 to help determine whether or not management accountants should develop a code of ethics, and if so, what form the code should take.

Our background research and a series of interviews with NAA members already conducted at nine locations in the United States have revealed a number of issues concerning a code of ethics that management accountants apparently feel are important. For example, technical competence was an important issue for some of the people we interviewed. Company management sometimes directed the accountant to undertake a task for which the accountant was not technically prepared and the accountant was not able to either decline performing the task or take the necessary time to become competent. Other management accountants faced ethical dilemmas in trying to decide what and how much to tell outside auditors. In certain cases, a management accountant felt pressure to present data in a manner which conflicted with Generally Accepted Accounting Principles (GAAP).

In order to determine what ethical issues seem important to a broad cross section of management accountants, a mail questionnaire will be sent to a large random sample of NAA members. You were one of the persons randomly selected. In about one week you will receive the questionnaire which requires a short time to complete.

The outcome of this study will assist NAA in deciding if a code of ethics should be developed. Therefore it is important to share your experiences and opinions with us.

Sincerely,

David F. Groebner	C. Mike Merz
Associate Professor	Professor

BOISE STATE UNIVERSITY • 1910 UNIVERSITY DRIVE • BOISE, IDAHO 83725

DEPARTMENT OF ACCOUNTING AND DATA PROCESSING
SCHOOL OF BUSINESS

Date

Mrs. Mary Smith
XYZ Corporation
5678 Main Street
City, State 00000

Dear Mrs. Smith:

Enclosed with this letter is the questionnaire for NAA's ethics study which we wrote to you about last week. Please take the short time required to complete the questionnaire and return it in the enclosed envelope.

You will be participating in the mail questionnaire portion of the study which has the following three principal stages:

1. Background Research—We reviewed ethical theory in general and examined many codes of ethics for other professional persons.
2. Surveys of Management Accountants—In a series of personal interviews, we asked a small sample (135) of management accountants how they felt about ethical issues. Now a large random sample is being asked to respond to a mail questionnaire which will yield statistically valid measures of how NAA members feel about ethical issues.
3. Recommendations—We will analyze results of the surveys of management accountants to enable NAA to judge the importance of various ethical dilemmas and whether to act towards addressing those dilemmas.

The following questionnaire was developed from the positions taken and the issues raised during the personal interviews. There are no "right" or "wrong" answers. We need your opinion. Your name, company, industry and geographic locations will be kept strictly confidential. The number on the upper right corner of the questionnaire is for our internal control purposes only. If you desire, a summary of the responses will be sent to you (see item 8 of the questionnaire). Thank you for your help in this important and exciting study.

Sincerely,

David F. Groebner	C. Mike Merz
Associate Professor	Professor

Enclosure

Control No. 1193

Questionnaire for NAA's Ethics Study*

1. Some of the 135 management accountants who were interviewed had faced ethical dilemmas in their work or had strong ethical concerns in certain areas related to management accounting. Most of the issues which seem important to at least some of the interviewees are listed below. Do *you* believe each of these issues is a real ethical concern to management accountants, and, if so, how important a concern is it to most management accountants? Your answer should reflect your own personal experiences (if you are a management accountant) and experiences which you know have happened to other management accountants.

	Area of Ethical Concern	Is It Important? Very	Somewhat	No
a)	Maintaining your professional competence.	536	54	6
b)	Being directed to undertake work for which you are not technically competent.	201	310	81
c)	Not being given sufficient time to become technically competent for work which you must undertake.	244	275	72
d)	Recognizing that the management accountant's primary responsibility is to the owners of the firm or the trustees of the organization, while refusing to follow orders to perform illegal or unethical acts.	463	103	27

*The frequency of responses for the 600 usable questionnaires which were returned has been entered next to each question; totals don't always sum to 600 because some respondents didn't answer each question.

Area of Ethical Concern	Is It Important? Very	Somewhat	No
e) Treating other management accountants with professional courtesy.	304	229	62
f) Deciding which external activities will cause a significant conflict of interest with your employer.	218	275	99
g) Maintaining the appropriate degree of confidentiality for information about your employer.	464	105	28
h) Following Generally Accepted Accounting Principles even if asked to use other methods.	362	201	32
i) Presenting information in the most reasonable manner so as not to deceive the primary user of the information.	467	121	8
j) Deciding whether to report a significant violation of law to someone within the business organization and then what to do if the report is ignored.	425	136	31
k) Deciding how much to cooperate with external auditors in informing them of items which might materially affect the entity's financial statements.	327	222	38
l) Being asked to "recalculate" certain financial figures to make a division or organization look more profitable this year.	338	202	50
m) Balancing your fiduciary responsibility to control costs and preserve assets with the necessity to treat employees fairly.	264	268	55
n) Deciding to which organizational level to attach your primary loyalty; for example, corporate headquarters or to a division or plant.	147	279	159

2. Do you think a code of ethics personally would help you resolve any of the ethical concerns listed above?

Yes 223 No 209 Not Sure 160

3. Do you think a code of ethics would help other NAA members resolve ethical concerns they might have?

Yes 296 No 86 Not Sure 214

4. During the personal interviews previously conducted in this study, NAA members cited some potential advantages and disadvantages to a code of ethics for management accountants. Please circle the response which most accurately reflects your opinion about each of the following advantages or disadvantages.

a) A code of ethics would enhance the professional image of management accountants and NAA.

Strongly Agree	Agree	Not Sure	Disagree	Strongly Disagree
87	333	110	60	7

b) A code would be meaningless since NAA has no effective method of enforcing it.

Strongly Agree	Agree	Not Sure	Disagree	Strongly Disagree
35	159	130	249	23

c) A code would have important public relations benefits.

Strongly Agree	Agree	Not Sure	Disagree	Strongly Disagree
46	302	168	73	7

d) If NAA adopted a code, this would encourage the inclusion of ethics for management accountants in college curricula.

Strongly Agree	Agree	Not Sure	Disagree	Strongly Disagree
39	284	198	69	6

e) A code of ethics for management accountants would essentially be window dressing; each person acts according to his or her own personal convictions.

Strongly Agree	Agree	Not Sure	Disagree	Strongly Disagree
69	177	98	232	23

f) Many NAA members are not really professional accountants. A code is not appropriate unless NAA limits its membership somehow.

Strongly Agree	Agree	Not Sure	Disagree	Strongly Disagree
41	151	84	272	47

g) If a management accountant accepted a code of ethics at the beginning of his or her career, the code would assist the management accountant to resist any management pressure to perform unethical acts.

Strongly Agree	Agree	Not Sure	Disagree	Strongly Disagree
36	272	146	118	22

h) Management accounting differs from public accounting since the management accountant must follow management's directions. Therefore, a code of ethics is not needed for management accountants.

Strongly Agree	Agree	Not Sure	Disagree	Strongly Disagree
6	39	86	392	70

i) Voluntary adoption of a code by NAA would tend to forestall government regulation of management accountants.

Strongly Agree	Agree	Not Sure	Disagree	Strongly Disagree
17	156	249	145	29

5. Based upon your own professional experience, your contact with NAA and your knowledge of other professional groups, do you believe that NAA should adopt a code of ethics for management accountants?

Definitely Yes	Probably Yes	Not Sure	Probably Not	Definitely Not
109	322	41	111	15

6. If NAA adopts a code of ethics, to whom should the code apply? Those members interviewed suggested the following alternatives. Circle those alternatives with which you generally agree. *You may circle more than one.*

a) The broad scope and diversity of NAA's membership is one of its major advantages. Any code must be broad enough to cover all members. 204

b) If a code is adopted, the code should apply only to those NAA members who practice as management accountants. 132

c) Only CMAs should have a code of ethics since CMAs are the only group of management accountants who represent themselves as certified professionals. 89

d) NAA should adopt a broad outline of ethical objectives for its members and a more specific code of ethics should be adopted for CMAs. 221

e) NAA is the only organization which represents management accountants. A code of ethics should be written to apply to *all* management accountants, not just NAA members. 317

7. *Demographics.* Please provide the following information about yourself which will aid us in analyzing the results of the survey.

Age: 98 20s 229 30s 121 40s 150 50 and over

Sex: 534 Male 64 Female

Job Title: ____________________

Nature of Your Current Work: (Please check only one)

404 Substantially involved with management accounting

94 Public accounting 9 Teacher

64 General management not closely related to management accounting

21 Other function, i.e., sales or personnel work, not related to management accounting

Type of Employer:

203 Public Corporation for Profit 240 Private Corporation for Profit

99 Proprietorship or Partnership for Profit

30 Not-for-Profit 22 Governmental

Size of Employer: (based upon the appropriate measures for parent organization)

275 Large 166 Medium 146 Small

Years of Membership in NAA:

102 0-2 Years 185 2-5 Years 137 6-10 Years

172 Over 10 years

Have you ever been on the Board of Directors in an NAA chapter?

179 Yes   419 No

Certification: Please check if you:

201 are a licensed CPA*   13 hold a CMA*

*includes 5 with both CPA and CMA

8. If you want to receive a summary of the responses to this survey, provide your mailing address:

Name: ______________________________

Address: ______________________________

____

____

(This information will be kept strictly confidential!)

9. Please add any additional comments that you desire in the space below.

____

____

____

____

____

____

THANKS FOR YOUR HELP

Appendix F

Sample Computer Printouts from the Statistical Analyses

TABLE 8
Chi Square Contingency Table Analysis of Question 1h Versus Question 2

```
SPSS BATCH SYSTEM                                                                    09/11/81        PAGE    7

FILE    NONAME    (CREATION DATE = 09/11/81)

* * * * * * * * * * * * * * * * * * *  C R O S S T A B U L A T I O N   O F  * * * * * * * * * * * * * * * * * * * *
   Q2       WOULD CODE OF ETHICS HELP YOU                       BY  Q1H       FOLLOWING GAAP
* * * * * * * * * * * * * * * * * * * * * * * * * * * * * * * * * * * * * * * * * * * * * * * * * * PAGE  1 OF  1

                      Q1H
           COUNT   I
           ROW PCT IVERY IMP SOMEWHAT NOT IMPO    ROW
           COL PCT IORTANT    IMPORTA RTANT      TOTAL
           TOT PCT I      1 I      2 I      3 I
Q2         --------I--------I--------I--------I
                 1 I   162  I   55   I    6   I    223
  YES              I  72.6  I  24.7  I   2.7  I   37.9
                   I  45.4  I  27.5  I  18.8  I
                   I  27.5  I   9.3  I   1.0  I
                  -I--------I--------I--------I
                 2 I   105  I   84   I   17   I    206
  NO               I  51.0  I  40.8  I   8.3  I   35.0
                   I  29.4  I  42.0  I  53.1  I
                   I  17.8  I  14.3  I   2.9  I
                  -I--------I--------I--------I
                 3 I    90  I   61   I    9   I    160
  NOT SURE         I  56.3  I  38.1  I   5.6  I   27.2
                   I  25.2  I  30.5  I  28.1  I
                   I  15.3  I  10.4  I   1.5  I
                  -I--------I--------I--------I
           COLUMN      357      200       32       589
            TOTAL     60.6     34.0      5.4     100.0

RAW CHI SQUARE =     24.41322 WITH     4 DEGREES OF FREEDOM.  SIGNIFICANCE =  0.0001
CRAMER'S V =  0.14396
CONTINGENCY COEFFICIENT =  0.19950
LAMBDA (ASYMMETRIC) =  0.10929 WITH Q2        DEPENDENT.          =  0.0      WITH Q1H      DEPENDENT.
LAMBDA (SYMMETRIC) =  0.06689
UNCERTAINTY COEFFICIENT (ASYMMETRIC) =  0.01947 WITH Q2        DEPENDENT.          =  0.02560 WITH Q1H      DEPENDENT.
UNCERTAINTY COEFFICIENT (SYMMETRIC) =  0.02212
KENDALL'S TAU B =  0.14189.    SIGNIFICANCE =  0.0001
KENDALL'S TAU C =  0.12406.    SIGNIFICANCE =  0.0001
GAMMA =  0.23858
SOMERS'S D (ASYMMETRIC) =  0.16079 WITH Q2        DEPENDENT.          =  0.12521 WITH Q1H      DEPENDENT.
SOMERS'S D (SYMMETRIC) =  0.14078
ETA =  0.14802 WITH Q2        DEPENDENT.          =  0.20014 WITH Q1H      DEPENDENT.
PEARSON'S R = 0.14326   SIGNIFICANCE =  0.0002

NUMBER OF MISSING OBSERVATIONS =    11
```

TABLE 9
Chi Square Significance Levels Between Question 1 and Demographics

Question	Age	Sex	Nature of Work	Type of Employer	Size of Employer
1a	.415	.288	.738	.038	.809
1b	.104	.013	.024	.211	.172
1c	.593	.014	.202	.543	.218
1d	.119	.807	.206	.672	.135
1e	.552	.507	.053	.000	.628
1f	.001	.301	.794	.238	.816
1g	.096	.157	.474	.042	.109
1h	.183	.906	.162	.030	.790
1i	.586	.593	.729	.897	.797
1j	.187	.580	.901	.164	.825
1k	.966	.030	.189	.000	.858
1l	.092	.388	.089	.158	.603
1m	.008	.196	.203	.260	.465
1n	.067	.486	.115	.298	.093

Question	Years In NAA	Supr. Level	On NAA Board	Certifi-cation
1a	.521	.446	.018	.352
1b	.665	.261	.706	.044
1c	.519	.204	.986	.938
1d	.030	.096	.411	.865
1e	.059	.011	.129	.000
1f	.009	.140	.533	.828
1g	.035	.101	.591	.079
1h	.909	.688	.972	.227
1i	.307	.633	.169	.217
1j	.481	.491	.781	.161
1k	.992	.494	.663	.008
1l	.343	.762	.069	.867
1m	.396	.022	.828	.000
1n	.702	.002	.553	.014

TABLE 10
Discriminant Analysis Relating Demographics and Question 5

SPSS BATCH SYSTEM 09/14/81 PAGE 10

SUMMARY TABLE

STEP	ACTION ENTERED	ACTION REMOVED	VARS IN	WILKS' LAMBDA	SIG.	LABEL
1	TYPE4		1	0.976762	0.0009	MEMBER WORKS FOR NOT FOR PROFIT
2	CERT		2	0.960309	0.0001	CERTIFICATION LEVEL
3	Q7A		3	0.947886	0.0000	AGE
4	WORK5		4	0.937623	0.0000	MEMBER WORKS IN OTHER AREA
5	TYPE3		5	0.930821	0.0000	MEMBER WORKS FOR PROP OR PART
6	WORK2		6	0.923625	0.0000	MEMBER IS IN PUBLIC ACCTING
7	L		7	0.920432	0.0000	ORGANIZATIONAL LEVEL

CLASSIFICATION FUNCTION COEFFICIENTS
(FISHER'S LINEAR DISCRIMINANT FUNCTIONS)

WANT =	1 YES	2 NOT SURE	3 NO
Q7A	2.513147	2.057905	2.564490
CERT	4.541700	4.443400	4.148804
L	0.6441754	0.7467152	0.6167204
WORK2	5.750286	4.034752	5.463411
WORK5	+2.476580	-0.4442392	-2.269404
TYPE3	0.6102687	2.667082	0.5629910
TYPE4	0.3674017	1.575572	2.082420
(CONSTANT)	-13.39719	-12.68282	-12.26200

CANONICAL DISCRIMINANT FUNCTIONS

FUNCTION	EIGENVALUE	PERCENT OF VARIANCE	CUMULATIVE PERCENT	CANONICAL CORRELATION	:	AFTER FUNCTION	WILKS' LAMBDA	CHI-SQUARED	D.F.	SIGNIFICANCE
					:	0	0.9204323	49.084	14	0.0000
1*	0.04422	52.23	52.23	0.2057773	:	1	0.9611307	23.470	6	0.0007
2*	0.04044	47.77	100.00	0.1971530	:					

* MARKS THE 2 CANONICAL DISCRIMINANT FUNCTION(S) TO BE USED IN THE REMAINING ANALYSIS.

STANDARDIZED CANONICAL DISCRIMINANT FUNCTION COEFFICIENTS

	FUNC 1	FUNC 2
Q7A	-0.04515	-0.63440
CERT	0.71811	0.06372
L	0.08050	0.28863
WORK2	0.27270	+0.73400
WORK5	-0.11666	0.44972
TYPE3	-0.05844	0.96645
TYPE4	-0.73178	0.14808

TABLE 11
Confusion Matrix for Discriminant Analysis

SPSS BATCH SYSTEM

CLASSIFICATION RESULTS -

ACTUAL GROUP		NO. OF CASES	PREDICTED GROUP MEMBERSHIP 1	2	3
GROUP YES	1	431	222 51.5%	106 24.6%	103 23.9%
GROUP NOT SURE	2	41	12 29.3%	20 48.8%	9 22.0%
GROUP NO	3	126	47 37.3%	24 19.0%	55 43.7%
UNGROUPED CASES		2	2 100.0%	0 0.0%	0 0.0%

PERCENT OF "GROUPED" CASES CORRECTLY CLASSIFIED: 49.67%

CLASSIFICATION PROCESSING SUMMARY

600 CASES WERE PROCESSED.
600 CASES WERE USED FOR PRINTED OUTPUT.

National Association of Accountants Committee on Research 1981–82

Calvin A. Vobroucek
Chairman
Caterpillar Tractor Company
Peoria, Illinois

George Bannon
Bethlehem Steel Corporation
Bethlehem, Pennsylvania

Robert U. Boehman
Jasper Rubber Products
Jasper, Indiana

Germain Boer
Vanderbilt University
Nashville, Tennessee

Willard Cox
Oil City Iron Works
Corsicana, Texas

Paul E. Dascher
Drexel University
Philadelphia, Pennsylvania

Dwight H. Davis
A. O. Smith Corporation
Kankakee, Illinois

Paul H. Davis
Solar Turbines International
San Diego, California

Geraldine F. Dominiak
Texas Christian University
Fort Worth, Texas

Patricia P. Douglas
University of Montana
Missoula, Montana

J. Bernard Eck
May Zima & Company
Daytona Beach, Florida

Homer R. Figler
CBN University
Virginia Beach, Virginia

Theodore C. Gearhart
U.S. General Accounting Office
Arlington, Virginia

Charles L. Grant
Becton Dickinson & Company
Rochelle Park, New Jersey

Robert E. Hampel
Keller-Crescent Company
Evansville, Indiana

John L. Hanson
Electro Corporation
Sarasota, Florida

John H. Holzapfel
Coopers & Lybrand
Pittsburgh, Pennsylvania

Henry M. Klein
General Instrument
El Paso, Texas

Thomas J. O'Reilly
Coopers & Lybrand
Cleveland, Ohio

Ronald J. Patten
University of Connecticut
Storrs, Connecticut

W. Peter Salzarulo
Miami University
Oxford, Ohio

Henry A. Schwartz
IBM
Armonk, New York

James W. Truitt
Martin Industries, Inc.
Florence, Alabama

Milton F. Usry
Oklahoma State University
Stillwater, Oklahoma

George W. Van Dam
Vanmark Corporation
Creston, Iowa

Robert N. Williams
First National Bank
Dalton, Georgia

Thomas H. Williams
University of Wisconsin
Madison, Wisconsin

No. 81129-CP-2.5M-12/81

MAD GERRY

Welsh Wartime Medical Officer

A TRUE STORY BY A MAJOR IN THE ROYAL ARMY MEDICAL CORPS 1939-1945

GERALD F PETTY, TD. FRCGP

THE STARLING PRESS LTD.
PRINTERS & PUBLISHERS
RISCA NEWPORT GWENT
GREAT BRITAIN
1982

DEDICATION

This book is dedicated to
GENERAL SIR HUGH STOCKWELL, GCB, KBE, DSO AND BAR

Profile of Dr Gerald F Petty, TD. FRCGP

A number of Welsh doctors recently received the Queen's Jubilee Medal and amongst them was a medical practitioner of many parts —Dr G F Petty of Llandaff. Gerald Fitzmaurice Petty TD is the son of a West Country clergyman and a Welsh mother, the latter accounting for his ardent interest in Welsh affairs. "Gerald", as he is widely known, qualified in 1931 with the Conjoint Diploma and has spent most of his professional life in general practice in Cardiff. In 1970 he became a Fellow of the RCGP, but his interest in routine practice is enriched on the one hand by a lively interest in psychiatry, whilst at the other extreme, he is an ardent exponent of manipulative medicine.

Gerald's name has appeared as either a member or chairman on a long list of committees, including an Enquiry into the Cost of Prescribing, the Mental and Geriatric Commission, the MOH's Liaison committee, the Executive Council, Medical Officer to the Pilotage Authority and Medical Councillor to the Marriage Guidance Council. He is Past President of Cardiff Medical Society (1965) and for many years has been an active member of the Cardiff Division of the BMA.

As an energetic practitioner of medicine, his "vivre" spills over into the political scene where his interests are especially centred on Wales. Dr Petty has recently acquired a working knowledge of Welsh; it is his home that is the address of the "Well Wales Group", the non-political group that is pressing for reforms in the organisation of the Health Service in Wales, with the formation of a Health Commission to replace the direct control of the Welsh Office.

During the 1939-45 war, Gerald Petty served as a Major in the RAMC in France and Germany and was twice mentioned in dispatches. He continued his army medical interests into the Territorials and holds the Territorial Decoration.

In all he does, Gerald Petty, a confirmed bon-vivant, is always an enthusiast.

(reproduced from Welsh Medical Gazette, 1977)

Introduction

"Mad Gerry"! Was I mad or not? I never minded the title, because it was a term of admiration and affection, of companionship without loss of discipline, and was used by my troops about me because I was equal to performing any physical task or effort that I demanded of them, whether it was heaving large lumps of coal from railway wagons into trucks, or racing over any Commando battle course!

My Early Life in Cornwall

It would seem that character springs from one's upbringing primarily and one's environment. I was born on 5th April 1906 in the village of Breage, three miles from Helston in Cornwall, where my father was Vicar of St Breage. My father apart from teaching me how to box, also taught me to shoot. While we were living in Devonport I remember that I was about nine years old at the time, and away from school with a cold. All the family were out leaving me by the coal fire in the dining room, where I had been told by my father to study my Latin Grammar book. Being rather bored I found two small tins and a bag full of pinfire 12 bore cartridges and proceeded to cut open a number of them. I put the shot into one tin and powder into another, and put the felt and pieces of cardboard aside for disposal before the family returned. I then collected more coal, banked down the fire with plenty of coal dust, and put the remnants of the cartridges on top, adding more coal dust to bury them from view.

Later that evening the family were all in the hall giving their opinions on where to hang the head of an ibex that a parishioner had given father, when there was an almighty BANG from the dining room. I was the first to run in, not thinking for a moment that I had anything to do with the explosion. There were bits of blown out grate, large pieces of coal and ash sticking to the silk lampshades, curtains, ceiling and carpet. Father with great indignation said, "I'll be after that coalman in the morning; he must have left a 'shot' in the bag of coal". However, the following day our maid told father what I had been doing and there was a loud bellow from him; "Gerald, come into my study at once". This I did in all innocence assuming that the coalman had got it in the neck and father was to tell me all about it. Father then asked me if I had been cutting up cartridges, and I quite cheerfully replied "Yes". Father then asked if I had any more, and went very pale and did not speak for a moment as I handed them over from my pocket. "My son, if you had fallen over, you would have blown your hip off and probably killed yourself, apart from hurting anyone else". He was so shocked and shaken at the possible prospect he did not tell me off, and when I saw how shocked he was, I burst into tears myself. So much for bravado. Perhaps this little bomb episode was the first indication of "Mad Gerry", when many years later I enjoyed defusing unexploded bombs!

Schooldays in Devonport

Whilst living in Devonport I attended Mount House School which was a Preparatory School for boys destined to go into the Navy. Discipline was very strict with your ears boxed for any minor complaint, or six of the best on the backside. I then attended Berkhamstead School until I became a Medical Student at Bart's Hospital and went to live at Oxford House, Bethnal Green where I paid two guineas a week for my keep, and every evening went as Assistant Manager to a working lads club. There I really learnt to box and became sparring partner to George Kent and Alf Pattenden, both professional bantam weights. In fact I failed my first MB exam because of the hours I should have spent in study.

Medical Student at St Bart's

As a medical student I had numerous Rugby injuries and was knocked out more than once on the field, to quote the *Evening Standard* of 1929 "It is strange how some rugby players have an unhappy knack of getting most of the hard knocks that happen in a match. The game between St Bart's Hospital and the Harlequins at Winchmore Hill was certainly an unlucky one for G F Petty who played at right wing three-quarter for the hospital. He was 'laid-out' four times during the match and kicked in the head twice, and it was only his pluck that enabled him to carry on. But the fourth time Petty's ankle was broken and he had to be carried off. I am afraid he will not be able to play again this season, which is bad luck for the man and the team, in view of the Hospital Cup Competition".

In my final year at Bart's Hospital I was attached to Sir Charles Gordon Watson's surgical firm as Clerk to the Pathology Laboratory. This training was useful later when I went into practice in Cardiff as 'Physician and Surgeon'. This was a true title. We had a complete kit of surgical instruments for operating in the home, in the bedroom or on the kitchen table.

This book deals with the onset of War as a Territorial Army Medical Officer to the 6th Battalion Welch Regiment and many other Units to follow; finally to be appointed as Senior Medical Officer of No 8 Beach Group attached to the 3rd Canadian Division for the assault on D Day in France, and its follow-up in Belgium and Holland—part of my six years of service, which to my surprise, I survived!

Explanation of Abbreviations in Text:

RAMC	— Royal Army Medical Corps
SMO	— Senior Medical Officer
DG	— Director General, eg Army Medical Services
ADMS	— Assistant Director of Medical Services (Full Colonel)
DADMS	— Deputy Assistant Director of Medical Services (Major)
RSM	— Regimental Sergeant Major
CO	— Commanding Officer
DUKW	— Four wheeled amphibious boat commonly called 'DUCK'
MO	— Medical Officer
NCO	— Non commissioned officer up to Staff Sergeant
CCS	— Casualty Clearing Station
GOC	— General Officer Commanding
FDS	— Field Dressing Station, eg 33 FDS
HQ	— Headquarters
DDMS	— Deputy Director of Medical Services (Brigadier rank)
DAQMG	— Deputy Assistant Quarter-Master General
DMS	— Director of Medical Services, eg in overall command of an area or army
GP	— General Practitioner
WO	— War Office
WO1	— Warrant Officer Class 1
BAMM	— British Association of Manipulative Medicine

Publisher's Note

Reproduction of some of these photographs has been impaired due to age. They are included however since it is important to have them as historical records. The reader is requested to make allowances when bearing this in mind, since the Printers have attempted to overcome this difficulty. Blurred images and variations in tone are due to faulty photographs and are not the product of printing inadequacies.

1 General Sir Hugh Stockwell, GCB, KBE, DSO and Bar

2 Staff of Commando Training School 1942
(Numbers from reader's left to right) Names I recall are: 1 ?, 2 Captain Douglas Fairbairn, 3 Major Todhunter, 4 ?, 5 ?, 6 Captain Bobby Holmes, 7 Major Brown, 8 ?, 9 The CO Colonel Stockwell, 10 Tommy Clepton, 11 O'Brien Twohigg, 12 Mackworth Praed, 13 ?, 14 Bill Sykes, 15 The Author Gerald Petty, 16 ?, 17 ?, 18 ?, 19 ?

3 Training Brigade—Dragging casualty under visible tracer bullets; one in five, heads down and heels down

4 Training Brigade—Casualties evacuated from beach at Herne Bay under fire and explosive blasts from the beach

5 Stretcher Bearer looped into "chair knot" for walking up the cliff face

6 Stretcher Bearer being hauled up cliff with casualty

Acknowledgements

I dedicate this book to General Sir Hugh Stockwell, GCB, KBE, DSO and Bar.

I served under him when he was in command of five Independent Companies. These were Guerilla troops. They were the product of General Ironside who visualised self contained groups of specialists in all arms of the service.

Colonel Stockwell led the successful assault into North Norway through Bodo (pronounced Booder) after Auchinlech had completed the capture of Narvik.

The right flank guard, the Bodo Force was withdrawn from Harstad to Scotland after the fall of France when all troops— ours, and our allies —were evacuated.

His next appointment was Commandant to the Commando Training School in the Western Highlands of Scotland.

He sent for me, via the War Office, to act as his Medical Officer where I learned the Art of War.

His staff were specialists in their own field—a Himalayan Mountain Climber, two from the Shanghai Police, experts in Karate, and sharp shooters, a Sapper officer to instruct in all types of demolition and Surgeon Commander Murray Levick, expert in snow warfare (ex polar explorer). His commandos became famous for their exploits.

Later on he became Deputy Allied Commander, Europe, during the War with Egypt, triggered off by their closure of the Suez Canal. He was ordered to cease fire by Anthony Eden the Prime Minister, three hours before he anticipated their final rout.

I first considered writing this book following a suggestion at a Welch Regiment Dinner when I discussed with Bryn Owen, the Curator of the Welch Regiment Museum, the possibility of recording my wartime experiences as a Welch Regiment Medical Officer, notwithstanding that I had been transferred from one unit to another during my six years in the Royal Army Medical Corps.

My sincere thanks to all and each of the following—

. . . to Colonel M de Lacey, RAMC and Sergeant Major Tom Meyrick . . . to those who came to my rescue with names, photographs, dates and newspaper extracts covering this era . . . to my secretary Avril Calford for her patience and persistence in seeing it through . . . to the unknown American pressmen for the photographs which illustrate many aspects of the new methods of RAMC training . . . to Professor Bernard Knight, author of so many books, for his constructive criticism of my first efforts at writing this narrative which encouraged me to write with enthusiasm . . . to Professor Levy and Professor Halkin for their considerable correspondence concerning Breendonk Fort in Belgium . . . and finally to F E Alan Yates, my publisher, for his advice and personal help during the editing of my manuscript.

Contents

Index of Photographs

1. General Sir Hugh Stockwell, GCB, KBE, DSO and Bar.
2. Staff of Commando Training School, 1942.
3. Training Brigade—dragging casualty under visible tracer bullets, one in five, heads down and heels down.
4. Training Brigade—casualties evacuated from beach at Herne Bay under fire and explosive blasts on the beach.
5. Stretcher bearer looped into "chair knot" for walking up the cliff face.
6. Stretcher bearer being hauled up cliff face with casualty.
7. Lowering casualty from height.
8. "Fireman's lift"—Training Brigade.
9. One closed stretcher above lower stretcher attached, to be hauled across the water.
10. Raft made from 4 open stretchers, canopy of 3 ton lorry. Carrying two stretcher cases, four men with spades for paddles.
11. Evacuation of stretcher cases between two bicycles—on fairly good roads was very successful. Started in Commando Training School following observation by Major Brown, Second-in-Command (CO of Bicycle Battalion, World War One).
12. Lochailort—the day we netted the salmon (Author in uniform behind the boy).
13. A pleasant break from training in Scotland, with Colonel Stockwell (far left of photo) and Captain Petty (author) alongside, with three other crew members on a sailing trip.
14. No 33 Field Dressing Station 1943-44 (Centre front row, left to right, 7th, 8th, 9th, Major Richardson, Psychiatrist. Major Petty, and Captain Nuttal-Smith, MC).
15. May 1944—Message from General Montgomery.
16. The Right Reverend Dr Timothy Rees, Lord Bishop of Llandaff, who understood more than anyone the failure of humanity, as he was for four years Senior Chaplain to the Venereal Disease Hospital at Rouen in World War One. The Bishop was a dying man when I had my "call up". He had been all his life a parish priest and disliked the isolation of a Bishop. Easy of approach, with a gentle humour, he was loved by all and had cared for the worst possible afflictions. Surrounded by doctors, Lord Horder, and Cardiff consultants, he said to us "I am sorry to be such an unconscionable time dying gentlemen", and smiling all the time. I had to leave at once for my regiment and said goodbye.
17. British and Canadian Troops going ashore at zero hour, 6th June 1944, Bernieres-sur-mer.
18. Bernieres-sur-mer—the third house up was where the Canadians caught two women who were snipers after having lived with the German soldiers for four years. They hanged them.
19. This was the church which housed the German Paratroopers, sniping for three days down the roads.

Index to Photographs (continued)

20. Le Fief Pelloquin, Chateau of Colonel and Madame Bois Lambert.
21. Breendonk—the half underground headquarters of King Leopold of Belgium during the 1914-1918 War were used by the Germans to imprison the Belgians.
22. Sentries with machine guns and searchlights shot any escapees from Breendonk.
23. Breendonk torture chamber otherwise called the interrogation room. The prisoners were stripped naked, their hands manacled behind their backs and hoisted high on the pulley. If answers were slow two electric wires applied to any part of the anatomy helped the screaming. The photograph does not show the runnels to wash away the blood in the concrete floor from lashings, cuts, and eventual dropping of victims bare footed on the sharp edges of the triangular pieces of wood. I saw the dried blood on the floor, not all was washed away.
24. 48 Belgians slept here where the floors and walls were always damp, as Breendonk was half underground.
25. Breendonk—hanging area Breendonk.
26. Breendonk—two "lucky" prisoners slept here, one on the boards the other underneath.
27. Breendonk—after being starved and tortured, prisoners were dragged to the ten black posts and shot.
28. Notes on the National Memorial of Fort Breendonk. Reproduced as text in Chapter Ten.
29. The author, Gerald F Petty, TD, FRCGP.
30. Vught, Holland—this was the nearest other incinerator to Breendonk and therefore a likely site for Breendonk bodies, except that with the threat of the progress of the British Forces there would have been no opportunity of getting rid of the bodies. (RSM Meyrick's photograph).
31. Vught, Holland—the prisoner stood on a rocker with a rope around his neck and strangled himself when the rocker moved.
32. (See story on page 23.) At the end of the War I am left with:
    1) Fins of high explosive oil bomb;
    2) Steel helmet with circular white band for easy recognition on the beach, covered with netting for camouflage;
    3) Respirator;
    4) Tin of ten tubes marked on lid "Ointment anti-Gas" No 5. For decontamination swab off free liquid from skin and apply ointment freely to the affected area. AS SOON AS POSSIBLE. Rub in vigorously for at least 30 seconds. If applied to the skin *before* exposure to an atmosphere containing mustard gas *vapour only*, the ointment will prevent, or lessen the severity of a burn. KEEP AWAY FROM EYES. To obtain ointment from tube, see directions on base of box. TO OBTAIN OINTMENT FROM TUBE. Hold tube at folded end between thumb and forefinger. Flatten end of tube by squeezing. Then holding end so flattened between thumb and forefinger of each hand, tear off end of tube close to fold. 6MB/1/431.

1. No 9 Independent Company

I had at last freed myself from the remnants of the 6th Battalion, The Welch Regiment, who, to their sorrow and shame, had been converted to the 67th Searchlight Regiment, guarding the British coast. My application for transfer had been approved and off I went to join a Field Ambulance, as prospective Company Commander, on Chepstow Racecourse.

The stables made comfortable billets, but the officers were a dull lot. Training seemed to consist of walks through the delightful Wye Valley countryside, and very soon I became bored and exasperated. Imagine my delight then, when one day the ADMS turned up and I was interviewed. "Petty, I want you to volunteer for a secret unit; I cannot tell you what it is all about, but it is dangerous. Officially, you can say you are joining a unit in the Caucasus". (This was typical of the Army volunteering method; "Volunteers one pace forward march, you, you and you, now don't rush it.") So the Colonel cracked his swagger stick across his leg and said; "I'll give you twenty-four hours to think it over, Petty".

"I don't want twenty-four hours, sir; I'll go now." Any place was an improvement on that lot!

Major Bill Siddons RWF

Thus I found myself on the train to Ross-on-Wye. I was met by the CO of No 9 Independent Company, Major Bill Siddons RWF, once a "Black and Tan", who had burned down twenty-seven houses at Limerick and Curragh as a reprisal and never dared show his face in Ireland again. In his dilapidated car, he drove me to our camp like a demented racing driver—flat out, screaming wheels, sudden brakes, and cutting corners. Determined not to show any fear, I whistled a rude tune 'Bollocks and the same to you' all the way. After a while he slowed down and said, "You'll do".

No 9 Independent Company was formed from the 38th Welch Division to implement General Ironside's theory of a Company of Specialists to act as guerillas to destroy lines of communication. For us, it was to be the North/South Road in Norway carrying supplies to Narvik.

Trooper Bill Siddons, DCM and Bar

During the First World War, Trooper Bill Siddons, DCM and Bar (which is rarer than a VC) was detailed with another, to disguise themselves as French women peasants, and swim the Marne in order to locate the German gun positions and the reinforcement areas. After this they were to report back to General Lord French at his HQ. These two buxom women, their brassieres stuffed with hand-grenades, tired of wandering the countryside, stopped at a farm. The door was open and drunken German singing was heard from the cellar below, so upstairs they went and found a girl spreadeagled on a bed. She had been tied up and raped by the Huns below. Bill and his companion cut her loose, went downstairs and tossed a couple of grenades into the cellar. This was followed by bangs, and then a groaning silence. Eventually they swam the river again, reported back with their precious information, and the Battle of the Marne began.

Training in Close Combat

Now this same Bill Siddons, with his lead-loaded swagger stick, which he swung to and fro while using the foulest non-repetitive language of any man I've met, started to train his volunteers in close combat, Black and Tan style, and in small arms. Fighting was all he knew.

"Medical Officer, tonight we are having a night operation, it's a bit damp, so look up the page and sanction a rum issue."

I looked up the page in King's Regulations; 'a 1/64 of a gallon per man with a tea issue'. Strangely my arithmetic wasn't too good, and I drew double the amount. Having dished out rough measures with a soup ladle into a cup of tea, I had an enormous stone jar and a half left over, so we finished the rest of the ration in the Officers' Mess tent. We were seventeen officers drinking, less one, Murray Threipland a teetotaller and archaeologist. He was fluent in Arabic—so he was detailed to this Company which was going to Norway! The Army mind is marvellous!

The following morning I was called at 5.30 am for Sick Parade which I held at 6.00 am. Apart from watching the tent pole spin a few times, I felt pretty good. So off I tottered to the Officer's Mess, half a mile away. On the way I came across a young woman delivering milk and stopped to chat. Appropriately, she said "What can I do for you, sir?". I answered, "Nothing, but let me help you deliver your wares". Forthwith I placed the bottles at every other doorway without breaking one. This surprised me! Eventually I reached the Mess and ate a hearty breakfast. I had a word with the CO to ask if I could go to Newport to say goodbye to Charles Nicholl and my friends. He said "OK, take a taxi". Which I did. What was money anyway?

At that time I wore two revolvers, not one, encouraged by Bill Siddons. I happily arrived to meet some of my former officers and friends and was persuaded to have a farewell drink. Just to show how glad I was to get away from a Searchlight Regiment, I demonstrated my ability to do a 'quick draw' with both hands. Fortunately I did not pull the trigger, but I well remember the look of anxiety on their faces. The time came for me to leave them. They had seemed very pleased to see me arrive, and were even more so to see me depart! After an hour's drive in the taxi I suddenly felt ill and realised, for the first time that I had wakened up drunk and had remained so during the morning. I swore to be an abstainer thereafter. I forgot my oath in due course, but never, oh never, could I touch rum again—especially 'proof' Army issue rum.

We finished our brief training and then it was all aboard the train for Glasgow and a camp at Bellahouston Park, opposite the Queen's Park football ground. Captain Peter Hoffman was our Second in Command; he had been a Pentathlon winner in the Olympic Games before the War, and was sober, dependable, and also a gentleman.

The Norway Operation

We embarked at King George V Dock for Norway. The three Independent Companies streamed onto the ship—we were packed pretty tight. Down past Greenock and out to sea we went. But we never reached Norway. While we were at sea France fell and, although our troops had just taken Narvik, the orders came to evacuate Norway. All the troops returned to Glasgow, including a company of the Chasseurs Alpins with their hundred mules. The mules were uncared for, underfed, unbrushed; and the troops the filthiest I had ever come across. Coming from the Haute Savoie, where they squat on tiles over a hole in the ground to evacuate their bowels, they adopted the same practice in our latrines and missed each time. The dung piled up on the seats and stayed there. The officers left their troops and stayed in a hotel in Glasgow, and all that the demoralised French soldiers wanted to do was to get back to France—by rowing boat if necessary.

French Foreign Legion

I never had the opportunity of meeting any of the French officers. I know that our men were jealous of the daily issue their troops had of a litre of wine. Soon after that, there arrived a Company of the French Foreign Legion—a very different type. There was one Glaswegian serving in this Company and, being back among friends, he was dead drunk for days. I doubt if he even remembered coming back to his home town and all his kinsfolk. When the Foreign Legion left Glasgow in column, the Legionnaire from Glasgow was carried by four of his comrades, two holding his hands and two his feet, completely unconscious!

The Poles v The French

The Glasgow civilians were generosity itself. No soldier was allowed to buy a drink in a pub. There was always someone on hand to say, "Have one on me". A few days later a Company of Polish soldiers arrived and, because of the shortage of space they had to be squeezed in on top of a small hill between the English and the Chasseurs Alpins. Their tents on the slope looked a bit askew but they did not seem to mind. One afternoon a Polish Officer chatting to me, said quite out of the blue, "We are going to attack the French tonight".

"What the hell for?" I asked.

"They are taking their arms into Glasgow and selling them to the Communists."

My CO was absent as usual, so I went to Staff HQ in Sauchiehall Street where the Staff Captain said, "Right, you are in charge, carry on".

"But I am supposed to be a non-combatant RAMC Officer".

"I don't care a damn; you are still in charge".

I thought, "Well there's a nutcase born every minute, and here we have one". I pondered whether I should set up a dressing station to attend to the French/Polish casualties, but luckily I met Captain Hoffman and was happy to hand the job over to him. That night he had two platoons with fixed bayonets marching around the camp. They disarmed every Frenchman leaving the camp, and there was no more trouble. Dumb argument with bayonets fixed was enough. One Corporal was heard to say, "Le fini est arrivé n'est pas permittee pour aller à Glasgow". The Poles were satisfied with our action so there was no battle after all. I wondered what happened to the French after they were very suddenly formed up, and moved off?

Royal Indian Army Service Corps

They were succeeded by a Royal Indian Army Service Corps. The Sikhs, handsome men in turbans and smart uniforms, were well disciplined troops. They were the complete opposite of the French Company. Spotlessly clean themselves, they soon cleaned up the mess that camp was in. The following day there was not a piece of paper, cigarette-end or bit of rubbish to be seen anywhere. The RIASC was the smartest unit at Bellahouston Park.

Royal Army Veterinary Corps

I had a section of eight men from the Royal Army Veterinary Corps posted to me. They had to wait impatiently until the French had gone, and they then took over the wretched mules. They were properly fed at once, scrubbed down and brushed daily. I had never heard of the Veterinary Corps before. Presumably during the first World War they must have been available in considerable numbers for the Cavalry and the RA Gunners before they became mechanised.

Bill Siddons enjoys Glasgow

One night Bill Siddons got very drunk, by himself, as usual. He went to the North British Hotel and, when the barmaid refused to serve him, he poured a jug of water down her blouse and walked down the bar with his hand outstretched, sweeping all the glasses off. By chance, Peter Hoffman and I arrived at the critical moment. We grabbed him, bundled him into the car, and took him back to his tent, where I tied him up with rope and secured the tent flap. I then sent for his batman and said, "The CO is not to be disturbed; he is not well, call me at 0.600 hours and I will attend to him myself".

I visited him the following morning to untie him and told him,

"To hell with King's Regulations, if you ever do that again I'll knock your face through the back of your * * * * neck".

All he said was "Thank you for looking after me".

Following his drunken, almost lunatic escapades in Glasgow, he was returned to his Battalion in the Royal Welch Fusiliers. He owed money to every Subaltern in our Unit and they were thankful to see him go. After I left the Unit, I heard he had been court martialled and dismissed the service for shooting up a cookhouse, and shooting holes in the clothes of the Sgt Cook. (He had an obsession about hygiene for cooks and could not bear to see jackets hung among the pots and pans in the cookhouse.)

A Grateful Legionnaire

Before the French Foreign Legion left Glasgow, I treated a Legionnaire for some minor complaint. He spoke perfect English and his thanks were profuse.

"What can I do for you?" he said.

"Well, you could give me your dagger" I said.

"I cannot, I would rather give you my life".

The Commandos had an issue of daggers, but being a Medical Officer and non combatant, I had to comply with the Geneva Convention, although this allowed the use of small arms for medical personnel in savage warfare. I therefore carried a 0.38 revolver in my holster as an Army issue. The French Foreign Legion had been the assault troops to take Narvik; the key point in the far north for the relief of Norway and our former destination.

"Did you take any prisoners?" I asked my patient.

"No, we killed them all, except a boy of sixteen and we kept him as a mascot. We crawled on our bellies to take Narvik and had no time for prisoners. Every man had one job to do—go forward".

"How did you kill them?"

"We used 'le coupé cabache a la maroccain' ". (Cutting the gourd, Morrocan style.)

"And what was that?"

"We lined them up and walked past them, and with the left hand we slapped the tip of the helmet down on the nose. Then as each soldier instinctively tipped up his head to see, we gave him a back-hand knife slash across his throat with the right hand. We could not afford to waste a bullet on a German. Now you can understand why you cannot have my dagger, but take this button as a memento." He cut off a button from his jacket and I still have this. It is like our own brass button but is inscribed "La Legion Etrangère".

I am quite sure that if we had landed and fought in Norway, Bill Siddons, our CO, would have behaved exactly like the Foreign Legion and taken no prisoners. But I often wondered what my reaction or that of Peter Hoffman would have been; one of us might have shot him!

To The Scilly Isles

No 9 Independent Company, now under the command of Major Glendenning, a regular soldier with a smart up-curl to his moustache and a polished manner, went to the Scilly Isles to protect them against becoming a possible stepping stone for the Germans. These four inhabited islands were then under the Governor, Sir Dorrien Smith. Tresco Island, sometimes called Paradise Island and luxuriant with sub-tropical plants, was his own home. His grandfather had been made first Governor of the Scilly Islands by Queen Victoria. Before then the islanders were very poor; their only occupation was fishing and acting as pilots to shipping. He introduced the flower trade, taking advantage of the highest sunshine rate in the British Isles. Following successful exporting of early spring flowers, their development as holiday resorts soon brought a better life and more money to the Islanders.

Colonel Hugh Stockwell, his Naval Commander, the CO and myself, visited the Governor. Sir Dorrien Smith had reported the Naval Commander about the "unwarrantable interference with the liberty of the subject". I cannot remember now what the brush was all about, except that the Naval Officer wanted to lay down the law about restraining the inhabitants in their fishing. He was duly posted elsewhere by the Royal Navy.

Dorrien Smith asked us if we would like to go fishing off the Bishop's Light in his steam pinnace. He showed us his book of records of catches of conger eels amounting to the total of 3,000 lbs and more. The Bishop's Light was still flashing merrily and provided an excellent guide point for Germans flying from France, where they turned right-handed up the Bristol Channel for their night raids. After a time, when the light was put out, the Germans dropped fire bombs on the uninhabited islands to give themselves the necessary guidelines at night.

HQ on St Mary's Isle

We had our Headquarters on the biggest island—St Mary's Isle—and one platoon each on St Martin's, St Agnes and Tresco; each of which had fifty civilians, some of whom had never left the islands even to go to the mainland of Cornwall. The priest of this parish took me aside and said; "I think I should warn you doctor, that the morals on this island are very low and leave much to be desired".

"Don't worry padre, our troops will appreciate what you say, they are volunteers from criminals of the 38th Division".

I, and my party of eight nursing orderlies had a 32ft motorboat and a crew of two to visit all the islands in the wonderful summer of 1940. My 'uniform' was my cap, shorts, and canvas shoes. The people were very friendly. I tried to shoot some seals. The island fishermen were very keen on this because of the damage the seals did to fish in the local waters. I used a short French Carbine, a parting gift from the Chasseur Alpins when they left Scotland. It is extremely difficult to fire from a rocking boat, but I was not sorry that I missed so often, looking down the sights at the rather pathetic face—so much like a man with a swimming cap on!

We had six weeks of wonderful friendship and co-operation with the islanders, who had not seen soldiers since Cromwell's time, when the last survivors of the Royalist Army had blown themselves up in their small fort, rather than surrender.

The Atlantic Hotel

In the Atlantic Hotel was a pleasant bar, and from this room one could see the seagulls swooping down within a few feet looking for scraps. We were drinking there one day with Quartermaster Crookes, a burly, balding man who had been a planter somewhere in the Pacific. He had had a bitter quarrel with his partner over some 'fiddle' and decided to walk out on him. In his anger he shot his partner's two dogs. I did not take kindly to this tale, nor did the bloke on his other side at dinner who offered him a bowl of chilli peppers. Even a small piece was too hot for me. 'Crookey' took a mouthful and chewed them up without the slightest grimace, while his audience waited for him to choke! He was tough, and didn't he like to show it! He remained completely expressionless, and then washed them down with a pint of beer. Then he threw a handful to the seagulls who swallowed them greedily, but immediately hopped off with open beaks and shaking heads and tried to wash them out with seawater. He thought this extremely funny! Like most Quartermasters, he led a profitable life, and much later when he joined me in the 33 Field Dressing Station, I kept a weather eye on him.

I met a very attractive young woman in the bar of the Atlantic Hotel. Dolly was slim with a tinge of grey in her hair and sparkling eyes; a wonderful conversationalist, but also a good listener. She had worked in London and was waiting to join the WAAF. She was a good swimmer and, when not on duty, I took my boat to some of the islands with her. I thought she was the love of my life for six weeks in this sunny haven. One afternoon I took off and landed with Dolly on the sandy beach of a tiny island called Samson Island, where we swam and lay in the sun. I got very sunburnt on my back and after returning to my billet in the Atlantic Hotel she put me to bed and gently rubbed on soothing oil until I went to sleep.

I had to get up at 5.30 am to report for practice landing where silence in the attack was the important feature. I woke with a start, and pushed Dolly aside; I was twenty minutes late on parade. I ran all the way down to the starting point to find my boat and crew waiting for me. The other boats were well away. Approaching the shore I told my crew to shut down the engine so that I could drift in unobserved and unheard.

I expected to get the most almighty rocket from Stockwell, and he and his Naval Officer Commander Murray Levick, with their backs to me, were standing on the beach watching the troops creeping silently towards the target. I did the same and approached quietly behind them. I got very close and heard Stockwell say: "Where is the MO?".

From a couple of yards behind them, I said, "Here, sir". So I got away with that one!

Officers of No 9 Independent Company

The Officers of No 9 Independent Company were a fine bunch of young men. I remember some of them well.

Tim Evill, with his series of naive funny stories was an asset in any party; and Graeme Metcalfe, who later became a paratrooper, and after that transferred to the RAF. Once Graeme was due to play football for his Unit. He missed the train, so he changed into his football togs, got into a plane, and was parachuted into the field of play, on time. (He is now a well known accountant, living in Cardiff, who rescues companies in difficulties.)

Ronnie Swain, tall and strong, frequently tried wrestling with me in the Mess. I generally managed to floor him but on one occasion I took a 'purler' when I went flat on my back. Grinning all over his face, he exclaimed "I knew I could beat you in time". He was always cheerful and a good leader. He was taken prisoner at St Nazaire with his CO, Lt Colonel Newman and nine commandos. St Nazaire was a harbour for German U-boats on the French coast. The Commandos went in by torpedo boat and after disembarking, had left delayed mines aboard them. They anchored in the harbour entrance and, after getting ashore, attacked the Germans in the town. The Germans went to capture the torpedo boat and were blown up by the massive amount of explosives. The ships had been sent to blockade the U-boats inside. This was successful but the Commandos suffiered many casualties and most were taken prisoner including Ronnie Swain. The attack succeeded in its objective and Col Newman got his VC. (His shooting must have improved since I had last seen him, when he missed a stag when we were poaching together at Lochailort in the Western Highlands.)

Another Gerald of Scilly Isles

Whilst on St Mary's Isle, I got to know Dr Owen the local doctor very well, and was happy to give him a hand when required. One night I went to help him deliver a child with forceps; because the infant had a large head and the mother a small pelvis. Now somewhere in the Scilly Isles there must be a man born in 1940 whose Christian name is Gerald—my reward for services rendered!

Almost daily we had German bombers droping 250 kg bombs of high explosive at 1600 hours sharp; the RAF turned up fifteen minutes later—too late. The RAF, had they studied the German mind, should have arrived twenty minutes earlier. These high explosive bombs had three trembler springs forming an electronic detonator, screwed into the side. It was charged on leaving the 'plane and, as the trembler springs were in three dimensions, each should have flicked over at any angle on contact with the ground and thus detonated. But many of them did not do so and there were numerous unexploded bombs. Lieut Bobby Holmes, the Sapper Officer, by trial and no error, managed to unscrew these aluminium detonators of 3 ins diameter. He always wanted me to go with him "to give him confidence".

I said "A fat lot of use either of us would be if you made a mistake".

He didn't—not then—and I always used to stand by and help.

Off to Penzance

After the radio mast on St Mary's Isle was finally blown up during the Battle of Britain, the Unit moved to Penzance where I stationed myself and my four RAMC corporals and four privates at the West Cornwall General Hospital. One morning early a 'tip and run' raider, flying very low, dropped a 500 kg bomb. This passed straight through the back of a house, above the double bed, just missing a sleeping couple, and out through the bay window, when it broke without exploding on the road. Bobby Holmes and I arrived in our small trucks with two orderlies. We had not heard or seen this type of bomb which was lying right in the centre of the road.

In the middle of the bomb was a round cannister tube 3 ins wide, containing high explosive; the whole outer container being full of oil. The street was evacuated by the Police; I tipped up the bomb and Bobby unscrewed the cap at the bottom. This tube was full of packets of TNT. Putting his hand in with great care, he removed these one by one. He then said; "That's the lot, old boy, put this in your truck and drop it in the garden of my office". My RAMC Corporal, Lieberman, an ex-medical student, and I picked up the bomb and slung it in the back of a truck, drove back and duly delivered it to Sgt Guy, Bobby's Sapper Sergeant.

At 1400 hours, while I was in the hospital there was a loud bang, I guessed what had happened and drove straight to the Sappers' office. Sgt Guy had taken another look at the bomb, rolled it over, and undiscovered TNT blew him as high as the first storey, then he dropped back to the ground. We picked him up and took him straight to the Operating Theatre where I amputated his left arm, and the House Surgeon amputated his leg. He was blind from eye injuries. The Matron, a Cornishwoman born and bred, assisted us. I sent for one of the surgeons to help. He came in, looked at our patient and said to Corporal Lieberman who was giving the chloroform and ether "You are killing him with chloroform".

I turned and shouted at him; "If that is all the help you can give, you can get out; my Corporal is working under my instructions".

Matron said afterwards "Now you know what I have to put up with here".

Sgt Guy, a fine upstanding man, died two hours later. That evening Bobby saw me and said "This had to happen to me".

I sweetly retorted, "It did not, Sgt Guy is dead—not you".

I defuse a few Bristol bombs

After leaving the Unit I went to a Field Ambulance and from there I went on to an Unexploded Bomb Course at Bristol, just after the city was bombed. There was plenty of material there for one to practise on, and with this experience, given the opportunity, I defused a few bombs. (I still have the fins of the oil bomb which I am giving to the Welch Regiment Museum in Cardiff Castle.)

In addition to the various specialities of troops, twenty men from the Welch Regiment were posted to us as anti-tank riflemen. This rifle was 18 ins longer than the .303 rifle with a bore twice the size. The bullets were about 8 ins long. The intention was to cripple the tank by aiming at the tracks. Whilst on the Scilly Isles they used them enthusiastically on the low-flying Hun aircraft, which must have been holed, but none came down.

Bomb Disposal

Howard Jackson of Cardiff, one of Bobby Holmes's Sappers was detailed to remove an unexploded bomb from some motor showrooms in Camborne, and then deliver it to Marazion Beach, a long sandy stretch opposite the small island of St Michael's Mount. This, with one other bomb was due for explosion on the empty beach. It was the biggest bomb they had to deal with, and it was duly blown up with a colossal explosion, which blew the roof off a church half a mile away! Fortunately no-one was injured, but they were more circumspect with the second. One way and another Bobby Holmes and Co were not too popular with the local inhabitants after that incident!

Graeme Metcalfe's amazing escape

Graeme Metcalfe, a self contained quiet chap whom I have mentioned previously, was commissioned into the Royal Welch Fusiliers and then transferred to No 9 Independent Company, responded to an Army Council Instruction for volunteers wishing to join the newly formed Paratroop Brigade. I also applied but was told by the CO; "You're mad enough, but not young enough, and the answer is NO".

Graeme told me years later the most amazing story I have ever heard. He went, and having got used to aircraft as a paratrooper passenger decided to ask for a transfer to the RAF to fly the planes as a pilot. This he did and went into training at once.

The Tiger Moth biplane was used for this with seats for two, the rear seat being occupied by the trainee. Each had a 'joy stick' for controlling the angle of the plane, linked together so that ultimate control could be taken by the trainer. Graeme was anxious to practise a slow roll which meant a downward dip to gather momentum, and a slow roll. He put the nose down to gather speed, levelled out on the horizon, right stick and rudder, and to his amazement came up straight and level.

His instructor shouted to him; "That's excellent when you are upside down next time, keep the nose up on the horizon and try again". So he did it again and lost the horizon twice.

The instructor shouted for him not to be scared and try again. So the third time he dropped the nose of the horizon upside down and the instructor shouted; "Get the * * * * stick forward".

Graeme said; "The stick shot from my hand due to the instructor. It was my * * * * stick, so I pulled it forward, and my instructor in the effort to control had inadvertently unhooked his safety belt and shot out of his seat. I heard a 'bang' as he hit his head on the petrol tank above him, and he fell out of the plane while we were upside down. On recovery to the normal position I put the nose down as he was dropping through the air, and came underneath him at 32 feet per second per second, and he shot back into his seat again, semi conscious from the blow on the head. (32 feet per second per second is the normal increasing speed of gravity when dropped through the air.)"

Can you believe this story? I can. I know the man who told me. Calm, philosophical, and meticulously accurate in everything he did, then, and now!

2. Commando Training School, Lochailort, 1941

My days with the Field Ambulance ended when I was suddenly instructed to report to Inverary for duty as a Medical Officer attached to the Commandos. When I eventually arrived there, no-one was expecting me. The Commandos were occupying themselves with practice landings so I attached myself to a Canadian Officer who seemed to have a roving commission. I met the Old Duke of Argyll, a funny little man who wandered around on his own, his eyebrows raised in vacant astonishment at the ever-moving groups of soldiers. He enjoyed his beer and a pleasant chat. After three days the local Headquarters had a telegram for me; "Where are you? Report to Commando Training Centre, Lochailort at once, Stockwell."

I then knew who had applied for me and why! Colonel Hugh Stockwell, RWF had been CO of the group of Independent Companies in the landing at Narvik. After the withdrawal from Narvik, while the Independent Companies were kicking their heels in Glasgow, Churchill ordered him to send a small group to Guernsey by night to attack the main hotel where forty-two German Officers were staying, capture some of them and bring them back. This was calculated to put a little hope into our country after the retreat from Dunkirk.

No 11 Independent Company

No 11 Independent Company was formed for this purpose. A naval vessel with longboats went out by night, and four boatloads of officers and men were put off the ship and rowed towards the shore with muffled rowlocks, looking for the flashing torchlights of the Resistance Movement on the beach. No lights were seen, but the Commandos pressed on and landed—only to find no large hotel, and no Germans. Eventually, it dawned on them that they had landed on the Isle of Sark, thanks to the ineptitude of the British Navy. Stockwell received 'a Rocket' from Churchill, and doubtless the Naval Commander also incurred "the displeasure of the Lords of the Admiralty". And so Stockwell became Commandant of the Commando Training School at Lochailort in the Western Highlands, on the Road to the Isles.

The Headquarters at Lochailort was a castle belonging to the Laird, Francis Cameron-Head. It was in the shadow of the north side of the steep slopes of a mountain overlooking a grim loch, bare of trees, with crows, rooks, buzzards, and occasional fish eagle, sheep cropping the poor grass, and the odd deer outlined on the hill-tops. It never saw the sun, except for an hour or two past mid-day. Here I reluctantly reported to the very group from whom I had succeeded in escaping. So I went straight to the Commandant's Office, saluted smartly and said; "Sir, the Commandos are a volunteer force; I do not wish to volunteer, I wish to return to my Field Ambulance".

"You are quite right" Col Stockwell replied. "But this is not a Commando Unit, it is a Training Unit with direct orders from the War Office. You will stay." Then he said; "On the other hand, this is a depressing place and friends quarrel, so you can go after three months". In fact Stockwell himself went after three months, I stayed seven.

Commando Training School Staff

O'Brien Twohig took over, a very different type to Stockwell. Stockwell was dynamic, a soldier, and a politician. He had the art of surrounding himself with experts in their own field. To train the Commandos in close combat he employed Douglas Fairbairn, ex-Chief of Police in Shanghai, and a Black Belt in Judo. Fairbairn told me that in Shanghai, he had to deal with a murder every day. He always carried two guns, one was a .38 revolver with a sawn-off barrel and trigger-guard, and this he kept in his belt. By leaving a button undone in the centre of his tunic he could slap his hand on the gun, put his finger straight on the trigger and, in two seconds —fire. It was his proud boast that he had never allowed himself to be bribed—the only present he was ever prepared to accept was flowers. He said that the Japanese were worse than the Chinese. He employed his own Japanese spies to inform on their own countrymen.

He told me that every important Japanese or European coming to live in Shanghai was assessed as to what his weaknesses were, and what he enjoyed doing. Where necessary, a Geisha Girl was detailed to infatuate him, and live with him and report back. Or, if that was not his interest, perhaps he collected jade, bronze, ivory or china. In that case, he was not only invited to dinner and shown his host's collection, but, as a gesture of goodwill, he was also asked to accept a small token of friendship. The idea, apart from direct bribery, was to instil some degree of obligation which could temper an ill-wind in any future difficulties.

When Douglas Fairbairn was demonstrating to the Commandos he would lie on the floor and challenge anyone, however strong (and plenty were) to pick him up from the floor and carry him off. Not one succeeded. He could make every joint of his body completely loose and the efforts of a strong young man to lift him up onto his shoulders then became ludicrously funny.

He taught me how to kill a man in seconds bare-handed, and how to blind a man with forefinger and middle finger outstretched. So that I, having spent my adult life in learning how to preserve life and health, now knew how to kill.

With Fairbairn at Lochailort was Bill Sykes—unlike his namesake—was a gentleman of culture and ability. He was chosen by Stockwell to assist in training the Commandos in small arms. He had been a volunteer in the Shanghai Police Force as a Sharpshooter. His chief joy was big game hunting. He would never shoot a stag unless it was a 'Royal' with a magnificent head. When on safari he hated having to shoot for food. (I could never understand this outlook, because my father taught me to shoot at a very early age, and later on I always enjoyed a rough shoot, bringing back fodder for the family.)

Bill Sykes built a small stone cottage on a hill nearby. It was one with three dividing stone walls and a passage down the centre. One day he told me "Bring your .45 automatic and .38 revolver; I have 200 rounds for you". I was then taught to fire from the hip; elbow in the centre of the tummy and forearm held fixed. "Keep your eyes, head and shoulder firmly fixed and swing to look at the target and then fire two rounds quickly" he instructed.

Man-sized cardboard targets popped from each dividing wall on both sides, and at the end a life-sized target went fast across the back wall. The whole exercise was repeated in semi-darkness. I had to shoot on sound more than sight. After 200 rounds, I could put two shots within two inches of each other.

Ministry of Economic Warfare

In addition to my work at Lochailort I had to take care of a number of large shooting lodges off the Road to the Isles, which were under the control of the Ministry of Economic Warfare (MEW). However, the Colonel and Officers in over-all charge were seconded from the Army and responsible to the MEW and to no-one else.

The Director of Medical Services for Scotland was not even aware of their existence until I went to Edinburgh to ask him for an additional MO to cover these Units. He tore me off a strip for not completing returns of all Units in my area. I pointed out that these men were seconded to the Ministry and no returns of any kind were made to Scottish Command. They were top secret.

Sabotage Training

Based at these lodges were Units of French, Spaniards (in case Spain became involved in the War), Italians, Belgians and Poles. Each of the Units was trained in map reading, explosives, and all forms of sabotage, small arms, close combat, and how to kill sentries quietly. After this training, the men were sent in pairs to Liverpool where they practised parachuting. Each pair was then given a task overseas, a bridge to be blown up, a train derailed etc. When the mission was accomplished (which could take up to six weeks), they had to find their way back to a spot on the coast where a submarine would pick them up.

My job was to examine each pair physically and to try and test the aptitude of each man for the type of job. The Italians were the worst—how they found them I shall never know! The French, the Belgians and the Poles had all suffered at German hands and were itching to go, the Italians did not have this incentive and did the job only for money. I considered they were traitors to their own country.

When a party of seventeen Polish Navy Officers and men arrived by train in their uniforms, I was asked to join their train and accompany them to the fishing port of Mallaig. We then embarked on a large ketch and, while out to sea, the Poles changed from their uniforms into British battledress. They were told to throw their naval uniforms into the sea. During this changeover time I was told to examine them. I found that four had scabies and said that

I would make arrangements to admit this lot into my Reception Station under the personal care of my Sergeant, who would be given orders not to divulge to anyone who or what they were. Having sailed out to sea, we then turned round to land the Poles eight miles up the coast. Now dressed as soldiers they marched back to their Unit near Lochailort. But this great effort at secrecy came to nothing. Colonel Jenkins of the Training Staff of the Ministry of Economic Warfare refused to let them come to my Reception Station for treatment in case it leaked out who they were. Instead he asked one of the local country doctors to treat them in their billets. Full of enthusiasm the GP did his job, and then related the whole story in his local pub the following night!

The Colonel had no authority over me, and was not in the Army officially, so I told him angrily and loudly; "You have failed to keep this mission a secret, and turned it into a pub story. You've wasted a whole day for me, and my working day is twenty-four hours. I shall not respond to any future appeal for medical help from you, and this shall be recorded". But naturally I did not keep my word and responded to urgent appeals that occurred.

One day I had an urgent message to come at once to see one of the Polish Officers who had been wounded. I went immediately, expecting a gun-shot wound; but what I found of all things—a sword thrust in the man's right lower chest. He and another officer, to alleviate the boredom of their isolation, had been practising fencing. The button came off the foil, which penetrated his chest just above the diaphragm on the right side, missing his liver. He was evacuated at once in the Red Cross ambulance to Fort William, the nearest hospital, where he recovered completely from his punctured lung.

Most Charming Ambulance Drivers

The two ambulance drivers at Lochailort, Margaret Anderson in charge, and "Toolie" were charming women. "Toolie" the younger, later married Cameron Head, the Laird, after a lot of encouragement and help from my friend Ouilleamina McCrea.

There was a single railway line running between Fort William and the port at Mallaig and, in view of casualties having to travel over thirty miles of very bumpy road surfaces with stones falling from the hillside frequently, I asked for and obtained a railway coach on constant standby at Lochailort. An engine could readily be obtained from Fort William and thus the journey to the hospital was much more comfortable. When the coach first arrived, Miss McCrea collected the Officers' wives as well as local women, and proceeded to decorate it. Pretty curtains filled the windows and with some carpentry, the interior was turned into a spacious ambulance coach, with a small kitchen.

Having waved their magic wand, the Nursing Home on wheels became a great stimulus for this happy band of helpers, and next, my Reception Centre was converted into a Nursing Home with twelve beds for the minor sick. There were bedside tables—each with a lamp with a frilly shade; the Army issue brown blankets were covered with colourful bedspreads, and pillows appeared from nowhere! I felt as though I was back at my old trade of General Practitioner!

Salmon fishing near Mallaig

Going along the road to Mallaig it was wonderful to stop and watch the water with fifteen to twenty salmon at a time jumping the rocks in the falls by the White Sands of Morar, further down the Road to the Isles. Apart from the civilian inhabitants, no-one was allowed to stop off at the railway station from Fort William to Mallaig. All visitors for the salmon fishing (or for any other purpose) were banned unless they were MPs or Members of the Armed Services. The Laird, Francis Cameron Head and Miss Nicholson, owned either side of the river bank and the Loch, shared the fishing rights. In those days it cost £50 a week which allowed fishing from a boat or from the bank on alternate days. A sizeable revenue was being lost, so the owners closed the sluice gates at the mouth of the river when the salmon shoals came up from the sea to spawn. In the shallows hundreds of salmon milled around, searching instinctively for a way to swim upstream against the current.

Cox, the Laird's Agent, was a friend of mine. He ran the whole Estate, from fishing to farming, and stalking the deer, for the enormous salary of £5 per week, plus a cottage. I would watch him walking over a ploughed and rough harrowed field, scattering oats with his hand from a basket slung over his shoulders, a method unchanged in two thousand years.

The day of closing the sluice gates at the mouth of the river was a secret carefully kept from everyone, particularly the locals. But somehow I managed to find it out, and so my car passed shortly after dawn, and lo and behold—there was Cox and his small boat by the entrance of the sluice gates, dropping his net in a wide sweep from one bank to another. Naturally I jumped out of the car and ran down the bank to give him a hand. I had Matty with me, rising eighteen, a fine young Scotsman in his kilt (handed down through four generations—they wove clothes to last in those days!). He was nephew to Ouilleamina McCrea who owned the small hotel in Lochailort and looked after the visiting fishermen with her excellent cuisine. (She was a wonderful woman, the Queen of the Western Highlands who knew little of World War I and II, the Boer War or the Zulu War—in fact knew little of any war except the '15 and '45 when Bonnie Prince Charlie landed at Glenfynnan, eight miles up river.)

Without any hesitation Matty and I waded into the loch in our clothes and dragged the heaving net to the bank. Three hundred and fifty salmon we took that day. Packed in ice most of them were dumped into a lorry and taken to Glasgow for sale at 7s 6d a pound—a lot of money then. Inevitably a few locals 'passing by' offered to help. Later, they were seen walking off with one stiff leg, splinted by a salmon with its nose nestling in the armpit and the tail down the trouser leg!

Matty and I had flung some salmon far into the heather above the bank before helping to load the rest into the lorry. Afterwards, I went to Francis Cameron Head and asked if he would donate two salmon to the sick soldiers in my Reception Centre, to which he agreed, so I picked out a large one and a smaller one, weight 23lbs and 18lbs. I knew the weights because Cameron Head asked Cox to weigh them and make a note in his notebook. I asked Cox why the Laird weighed the salmon he was giving away. The answer I got was; "Miss Nicholson owns the far bank, and any fish given away have to be paid for. I thought; "My God, the meanness of it." But then I suppose it was no worse than the Lairds who chased the crofters off their land for collecting firewood. In this treeless country wood is precious and worth money.

Later that night, by the light of a full moon, armed with a long length of twine from Miss McCrea, Matty and I walked towards our cache not far off the road. When we came to the top of the hill, we saw Cox riding his bicycle up and down the road, hoping to catch those dreadful poachers (some of whom were his kinsfolk) coming back to collect their scaly gains. We scrambled through the heather and down the other side. Twenty-two salmon we laced together through their gills, and then we crawled back over the hill dragging behind our beautiful catch, shining in the moonlight. Back at the Inn we had fried salmon steaks, then I carried away two salmon for the Officers' Mess and two for the Sergeants' Mess.

(The Sergeant Instructors were good voluntary gamekeepers, stopping the Commandos from throwing hand grenades into the river and collecting the stunned fish which floated to the surface. We all disapproved of this because of killing the young salmon and trout.)

Whilst eating our fried salmon, Miss McCrea had asked me if I could go round the following morning and bring my car. Of course I agreed, and called about eleven o'clock to find that she had sixteen salmon all covered and bound, nose to tail with round stemmed reeds. I supposed that this was an old method of keeping them fresh—no refrigerators in those days! So, on the Sunday morning off we all went. "Now we will call on Robert McClean our policeman first" she said. "And after that you will take me round every But and Ben, for every crofter shall have salmon today" (But and Ben being a two-roomed croft). As we arrived at the policeman's cottage, Robert McClean came up to the car and was told by Miss McCrea; "There is something for you in the back of the car, but don't ask where it came from".

He said "I know where it came from, Miss McCrea, the Guid God sent it".

Miss McCrea, who never used her married name of Graham, had married the Chief PT Instructor—Sgt Major Graham, at Lochailort, and he had been posted to the Middle East. He was fifteen years younger than she. (I have known a number of marriages with this age gap and they were all successful.) Sadly, while I was there, news came of his death—'Killed in action'.

Remember 'Whisky Galore'?

At this time we were able to purchase bottles of whisky in the Mess for 12s 6d. They were square bottles with the raised imprint in the glass 'Federal Government of USA'. A ship going to America laden with whisky had been torpedoed off the coast and half sunk. The locals always took full advantage of scavenging in any wreck until the Customs Officer caught up with them. In this case, the Highlands Customs man caught a rowing-boat full. The culprits were sentenced to ten days in prison by the Magistrates to the great indignation of the countryside—local rights had been interfered with! (A film called 'Whisky Galore' was later made about this incident, but I did not see it, I believe it was written by Compton Mackenzie.)

Captain Sandy Wedderburn

I shared a large room in the Castle with Captain Sandy Wedderburn of the Highland Light Infantry. He had been mountaineering before the War and had climbed in the Himalayas, so he had been appointed to train the Commandos in rock climbing. Sharing a room with someone for seven months leads either to dislike or friendship and in our case it was the latter. Sandy suffered from asthma and could not go into the Officers' Mess anteroom because of the Officers' dogs (being allergic to dog hair). Up in the mountains his lungs were always completely clear. He used to take a Section for a week at a time up into the hills fifteen miles away. He gave up trying to persuade me to go, I would always refuse, saying to him; "I'll face up to anything, except that I have no head for heights". He understood and was always patient with the occasional officer who froze after climbing only ten feet. These he sent back without criticism.

We shared our personal problems. He had married a beautiful blonde WRAF woman, fifteen years older than himself and was very much in love with her, and not a little jealous. I had my own disappointments. When not actively engaged in work, it was a lonely life.

I had two young boys, aged seven and six years old, cared for by my wife who also looked after her widower father Colonel Sir Hamish Knox,a retired Inspector of Prisons. I begged her to come to Lochailort and bring the boys for any part of the school holidays, for I longed to give them the opportunity of knowing the Highlands, the fishing and the shooting, but always she said she would not come. I appealed to her snobbery and wrote that Lord

Jellicoe's daughter, married to the Staff Captain had arrived, bringing with her two children, three dogs and twenty-four chickens. Why could she not come? The answer I got was; "You should have married someone like that, not me". Some time later, I did!

Survival Kit

Once Sandy telephoned me from his mountain camp to say he thought his men had scurvy, and enumerated the symptoms. The men were irritable and quarrelsome. They bruised easily, had bleeding gums when brushing their teeth. I told him to stop their 'Iron Rations' and to give them fruit and green vegetables, plus fresh meat. These troops had been given the basic portable ration devised by Surgeon Commander Murray Levick. This was on the same lines as the food that he had carried on his mission to the Pole, consisting of Pemmican which was a compressed strip of dried meat (he used to have reindeer meat), and very hard ship's biscuit (as hard as a dog biscuit), tea and sugar. The main omission from this survival kit was vitamins. Tablets of 50 milligrams of Ascorbic Acid would have given them all the Vitamin C they needed.

Colonel Newman (VC of St Nazaire)

One evening on the way back from Arisaig, I saw the Northern Lights. For a brief moment I thought "Those are searchlights over the hills", and then moments later realised that searchlights do not bend. They waved to and fro, slowly, like a long reed twisting in the wind. As I watched, there, thirty yards from the road, my eyes fell on the magnificent spectacle of the head and antlers of a Royal stag looking straight at me in the moonlight. I stopped off at the Inn and said to Matty, "There's a stag a mile down the road". Out came Miss McCrea and some officers, and with them was Colonel Newman in command of a Commando training course. I turned my car round, and two other cars made up the party. It was getting darker, the stag however was still there. I had a spot-light on the roof of my car and turned this onto the stag. Matty steadied the rifle on the bonnet and fired, the stag fell on his haunches, and we scrambled down the hillside. I turned to Newman and shouted "Use your .45 and put the bullet between his eyes and ear". He aimed and fired, but the stag did not move. He had missed! His next bullet fortunately went home. I thought, "What sort of a Commando is this, who can miss at a few feet?" Not long afterwards "This man" was to win the VC at St Nazaire, as I previously related.

Matty took his knife and disembowelled the stag on the hillside. We then dragged it up onto the road, all sixteen stone of it, and dumped it in the boot of the car. Back to the Inn at speed, where we had fried venison liver. Matty butchered the stag into joints for the Officers' and Sergeants' Messes and the rest went for distribution to the locals.

Research into Fatigue

Surgeon Commander Murray Levick and myself were the two medical officers at Lochailort commissioned to perform research work as well as routine MO work. Murray Levick who had a white medal ribbon in World War One (this was the Polar Star for the expedition to reach the Pole), his job now was to assist in training troops in cold conditions, and in research.

One of our projects was to find something for the relief of fatigue. We tried large doses of Vitamin C tablets four hourly, and also measured urinary excretion of Vitamin C four hourly. Our findings were not conclusive, but the facts that these experiments were being done at Lochailort were made use of by the Ministry of Economic Warfare.

Raw carrots were served in the Officers' Mess. At an Officers' Mess meeting I protested at being made to eat raw carrots in addition to the Vitamin C and got smartly ticked off by the Colonel. I did not know then that this method was being deliberately leaked to the Germans as being a means of relieving fatigue, and improving the night vision of RAF pilots. Nor did I know at the time that all Beaufighter aircraft were being equipped with Radar for night fighting. This picked up the German aircraft in front of them and shot them down easily. It was a great success and accounted for hundreds of German aircraft being shot down as they crossed the Channel.

The Radar Secret

The Ministry of Economic Warfare arranged for a dead body of an airman to be washed up on the shore of Minorca. This was found and examined by the Italians, and in his pocket was a reference to the Vitamin C tablets regarding massive doses of such for the pilot and observer to take for night time fighting. Therefore the Radar was kept a secret leading to the enemy thinking that the Vitamin C was responsible for the improvement of night vision and great losses of the Luftwaffe.

While I was at Lochailort we heard the sad news of Russian and German Armies closing in on Poland from both side and crushing this fine country. I asked a Polish Officer training at the Commando Centre; "Whom do you hate the most, the Germans or the Russians?" He said; "The Germans; the Russian is a savage beast; the Germans should know better".

Ethyl Chloride

Among numerous visitors from the War Office was a Major Campbell RAMC who was responsible for drug research. He had been before to enquire on the efficiency of quickly and silently knocking out German sentries using "Dollies" of Ethyl Chloride. These were thin glass bulbs normally used for anaesthetic purposes, sprayed onto a gauze covered mouth-and-nose frame, to produce a fast loss of consciousness. The thin bulb was covered with gauze to be smashed into the sentry's face in an attack from behind, and then to be quickly and silently killed with a knife. The War Office raised an objection about this on the grounds of the possibility of this being used within the terms of 'Gas Warfare'. (The Germans were the first to use gas warfare in World War One by releasing in the front line large cylinders of Chlorine—a choking and blinding gas, to be followed later by more deadly gas.

Use of Benzedrine

Now, on this second occasion Major Campbell arrived with a view to our trying out Amphetamine Sulphate (the official name) or Benzedrine, made by the Baer Pharmaceutical Company which had been used by the Germans on their tank crews to keep them awake for long periods of time. I had a report that some of these crews, as a result of taking Benzedrine daily had come out of their tanks with hands shaking, and incapable of accurate thought and controlled movement.

After our useless efforts with Vitamin C to relieve fatigue, we began to research the use of Benzedrine. Two Commando Platoons were detailed to proceed as fast as possible across country to a map reference twenty miles away. One platoon was given (as a control) Bicarbonate of Soda tablets every four hours, and the other platoon had Benzedrine every four hours. They all had to go as fast as possible with normal battle order and equipment. The platoon on Benzedrine came in one-and-a-half hours ahead of the control platoon, alert and cheerful and with no signs of exhaustion. The others were completely exhausted trying to catch up. Both platoons were physically first class and in very good training. The Benzedrine platoon sat down to a large meal, and afterwards sang all evening and night!

The conclusion was, of course, that Benzedrine was a very potent cerebral stimulant. Secondly, that the dose was excessive. Finally, these tablets were ideal for Commandos on a twenty-four or forty-eight hour task, because not only did they get relief from fatigue but that the stimulant was such that it produced elation and fearlessness.

A full report was submitted to the Commandant, who forwarded it to the War Office, and as a result an Army Council Instruction was issued to the effect that all troops on Benzedrine would be confined to barracks for forty-eight hours after the event. It is not possible to *order* a soldier to sleep, and there was also the risk that in contact with the public, particularly in a bar when the sense of responsibility was reduced to a minimum, emotional excitement would involve breaches of discipline.

Sexual Prowess!

The Commandos coming to Lochailort for training were given these tablets in much lesser doses than originally. The men accepted them, but then quite unexpectedly refused to take them. Some idiot had spread the rumour that Benzedrine caused impotence. Most soldiers are proud and sometimes very boastful of their sexual prowess, and this threat was just "not on". I then gave them a short lecture on the exact effect of Benzedrine. In no way did it ever cause impotence, in fact the reverse occurred because the tablets increased their physical strength, gave them confidence, and their unfortunate girl friend would have to put up with more prolonged vigorous love making than she had ever known before! It worked, and a number of them asked for more tablets to take home on leave!

Research with String Vests

I had instructions from the War Office to try out the effect of troops wearing Norwegian string vests to decide whether they should be made Army issue generally for warfare in cold conditions. There were already available to the troops special Army Issue White Suits for use in snow, making recognition at a distance very difficult. The string vests were different and concerned retention of body heat.

I was told to take two Platoons of Commandos to the top of Ben Nevis (4,004 ft) in the evening and stay there all night. A Scientific Officer, a Major from Edinburgh was detailed for the assessment. One Platoon was to wear the vests, and the other, as a control, went without them.

As the body keeps cool by the evaporation of sweat, all liquids evaporating lose heat. There is a heat control centre at the base of the brain which constantly adjusts the body temperature according to conditions. In hot, damp weather—as in tropical swampy areas, the sweat pours off with the body soaking and becoming exhausted. In dry hot climates, the life is pleasant. I asked Murray-Levick who had lived in Polar expeditions as well as Tropical expeditions—which was worse. He said "I would much rather go to the Pole. In cold weather you can always keep warm, in really hot damp weather, you are exhausted and never really comfortable".

Our Scientific Officer had two tabs of electrodes, one to be stuck onto the skin of the chest and the other on the inner side of the battle-dress. The electric wire from the tabs connected to a galvanometer gave an immediate reading of the temperature at starting level and every 1,000 ft further up. He estimated the outside temperature and the humidity at these levels.

Each of us had to wear a scarf around the neck, and all buttons were secure. The principle of this was to stop the convection currents of air around the body surface. Heat is lost if acquired by radiation from the sun or by artificial means eg, radiant heat loss, or secondly, by conduction. All metals have their specific conduction; railway tracks take up heat by the sun and the friction of the wheels. That is why there is a gap between the rails to allow for expansion, otherwise they would bend and derail the train. Wool is a non-conductor of heat, and for that reason woollen vests are warmer.

Loss of Body Heat

Loss of heat by convection takes place in liquids and vapour. This is easily seen with a glass of hot water with a teaspoonful of sawdust dropped into it. Following this there is a constant movement from the bottom upwards, and then down again as the surface water cools and so increases the specific gravity allowing the cold water to sink.

So, the body is protected against loss of heat by radiation, conduction and convection.

We started at the base of the north face of Ben Nevis which required no rock climbing, and went up at a steady pace. Every 1,000 ft, our Major recorded the body skin temperature and the temperature of our battle-dress. The humidity, temperature and atmospheric pressure were also taken. We reached the top without incident, except that those wearing string vests were sweating hard. Our respirations were increased in frequency and depth. There is some loss of heat from evaporation of moist lung air. (Dogs do not sweat, they have no sweat glands and so they lose heat by panting with their tongue hanging out and increased salivation, the evaporation of which is the cooling factor. Horses do sweat, their nostrils dilate and they lose heat via the lungs and skin.)

Cold on Ben Nevis

We stayed at the top of Ben Nevis, but with a piercing wind, it was bitterly cold. With the agreement of our Major, who had gathered enough material now for this particular investigation, we half-trotted down the hill by the light of a full moon. We had one casualty—a sprained ankle! I had no idea what report was sent on from our investigations, but I put in my own report for the Commandant for transfer to the War Office:

> "Having not only arranged the investigation and taken part in this myself, I have come to this conclusion. In continuous cold weather this form of protective heat loss would be justified. During considerable physical exercise recently undergone, the general sweating was excessive. On exertion ceasing, and in conditions of considerable cold and icy wind, this proved a handicap—relieved only by further exertion in descending fast from Ben Nevis. It would appear therefore that, the vest worn with instructions to keep all buttons done up and a scarf around the neck, that there is insufficient convection current to

produce normal cooling of the skin. I would therefore suggest that there string vests are worn by sentries as an issue together with the anti-mosquito cream for the ears and face."

'Cured' by Castor Oil

Sergeant Tipstaff, an ex-chemist, was my medical orderly in charge. He acquired an excellent knowledge and was reliable with a degree of efficiency and loyalty. I could safely leave him in charge for a day or two. On the Road to the Isles from Glen Fynnan to Inverailort Castle, there was a Pioneer Company of ninety men under the command of Major Adams, MP, and were responsible for repairing the road. At Sick Parade one day, twenty-two men reported with vague maladies. "Sergeant, take these men to the Treatment Room and give them a dose of castor oil". The following day, nine reported sick. NAD (nothing abnormal discovered), and so the same treatment was given. On the third day there were only three left on Sick Parade. Treatment given on this occasion was normal. After that Sergeant Tipstaff took over, and only sent for me for anything outside his 'ken'. I seldom had to go.

The Road Builders!

I had many other Units to care for. It was the practice of these men working in groups resurfacing the very narrow potholed road to have a 'ganger'. Groups of men were working with a 'ganger' at both ends of the section of road, standing at a bend. When a car or military lorry approached, up would go his arm—pick in hand, to signal their approach. The men would leap to their feet (from lying down in the comfort of the heather-bordered road) and start digging and shovelling with obvious energy. As the vehicle went by, normal reclining posture was resumed and so the road never was properly finished. (In fact, going back thirty-eight years later, I found a beautiful second-class road which had taken seven years to complete from 1961 with a perfect surface glistening in the rain, along which my wife Ann-Marie, in a fit of enthusiasm driving our new blue Saab, at times went more than 80 mph.)

There were times when sleeping in the heather, which was always wet at the roots, when we had to put up with the occasional uninvited companion, and once, right in the centre of my chest, I noticed a sheep tick. I made no attempt to pull it off. It had six legs curving inwards, buried in the skin. To pull it off with the legs embedded could turn this septic. We put salt on the ticks in the same way as for leeches. They then regurgitate the blood and unhook themselves. This I did, and lost the sheep tick. Sometimes the soldiers would chase them off with a burning cigarette.

Transfer to Field Ambulance

I appealed to Colonel Strachan for a posting back to a Field Ambulance, having served for four months at the Commando Training School after Colonel Stockwell had gone. (He pronounced his name "Shawn".) I noticed that his field uniform was not the regular pattern, he wore a jacket, Sam Browne belt, riding breeches and boots but his jacket was different. The lapels were cut away and he had three brass buttons above and below the belt. It then dawned on me that he had been the Medical Officer to the Royal Household Cavalry. I requested a transfer to the Field Ambulance in order to get some active service, and to regain command of a company as Major. His reply to my request for transfer was; "Of course you shall go, I only wish that I could join an active service unit myself".

3. 202 Field Ambulance

So thanks to Colonel Strachan, in the Autumn of 1941 I at last got my posting to the 202 Field Ambulance as a Company Commander. They were stationed at Dromore, County Down, Northern Ireland. I thought this place was like a gin palace after the Western Highlands—no shortage of food, and comfortable billets. Lt Colonel Stanton was in Command. He was a very smart regular Army Officer who trained all his men in daily drill until they were as near perfect as Guardsmen. The Sergeants were in competition with each other in voluntarily taking squads to try and reach the 'faultless' stage.

Service in Northern Ireland

Colonel Stanton was a Catholic, and every Sunday afternoon he called on the Protestant vicar and his family for tea. Such co-operation was rare in Northern Ireland. The other Company Commander, Major Logan, had his wife staying with him in lodgings. One day he went shopping and brought back a cardboard box of iced cakes. (In England we had little sugar and certainly no icing sugar.) He offered these to his landlady who immediately asked; "Where did you get those from?" He named the shop and she smartly retorted; "You can just take them back; it is a Catholic shop." This rather trivial incident showed me the intensity of religious feeling of which, not having been there before, I was totally unaware, and very surprised.

As an officer of field rank I was shown a large number of official documents basically relating to the strength of the Eire Armed Forces. They were then equivalent to one English Division. There was the complete list of all their armaments; guns, tanks, motorised transport, shells, ammunition—the lot! As we had a turnover of three Divisions in Northern Ireland, in addition to the Royal Irish Constabulary and the 'B Specials' (armed volunteers), any warlike threat was anticipated—but not expected.

The first time I realised the presence of the 'B Specials', was when on an exercise to take my Company to a target area to set up an Advanced Dressing Station. I had gone into an empty farm house and saw on the kitchen table a .303 rifle and a couple of hundred rounds of ammunition. On my return, I duly reported this to the CO who told me of the 'B Specials' and their function.

The Government were never completely certain, when we later left Northern Ireland for operations abroad, whether Dublin would come in on the German side or remain neutral. We already had Irish troops in the Army at home, but the uncertainty remained. It was after all, only twenty five years since the Easter Rebellion. This remained in older memories with some underlying sympathy for the Independence of Ireland. The problem is still unresolved today in 1981.

I duly settled down; training was more interesting than arduous and we were also useful to the local villagers who were short of transport. I was asked if I would help with the unloading of a train of coal wagons which had been stationary for some time in a side-line not far away. I took four three-ton trucks and a party of men, and we manually offloaded the coal into the trucks. It was a hot day and I, with others, stripped to the waist and clambered onto the wagons, heaving the lumps of coal into the trucks. The Colonel arrived, immaculately dressed as usual, looked at me and said; "What is an officer doing like this, when he should be supervising?". I said; "Sir, I have always believed in not only showing my men how to do the job, but also showing them that there is nothing I would order any man to do that I could not do myself".

He made no comment, and I carried on.

Transferred to the Midlands

I walked a lot in the lovely countryside on my own, but then quite suddenly we left Northern Ireland and proceeded to the Midlands to Loxley Hall, near Uttoxeter. Colonel Stanton went off to another command abroad, and by that time my senior Major had also left, so I was acting CO. I had instructions that Lt Colonel Matthew de Lacey would take over. He arrived by car and I saluted smartly and bade him welcome. The surprising retort was: "How far is it to the nearest pub?" I told him that it was not far and that I would take him as soon as his batman had collected the bags! We got on very well! He was easy-going, but very efficient, and well liked.

Uttoxeter Scenery

Loxley Hall was a large mansion on the top of a hill, amid lovely surroundings. The lady of the house was a widow and a charming woman. I apologised for having to take over the estate. She had her own separate rooms and I made a point of calling on her for tea, from courtesy in the first place, secondly to make sure that the troops had not trespassed, and that there would be no barrackroom damage to pay for, after we had left.

Once she asked me if I had ever handled a .45 revolver. I told her that we only had an issue of .38 revolvers. She enquired whether I would like to see her late husband's .45 revolver, and handed me a very long barrelled 'six shooter' with ivory plates on the butt. The outer ivory plate was plain, the inner one had a Mexican Eagle carved on it. She then explained; "My husband inherited this place and miles of countryside from his uncle; the old man having died while his heir was in America. He had gone off whilst a young man and became a cowboy. One day, when drinking in a saloon, he heard the sounds of shots outside. Two cowboys were shooting it out and he shouted at them to stop. One turned and fired at him and the bullet hit the butt of his revolver in its holster. He then promptly drew his gun and shot the both of them, and went back and finished his drinks. He got a gunsmith to put another ivory plate on his gun and it was this plain bit of ivory which was not carved. When his uncle died they took some time finding him, the heir to a fabulous fortune. Eventually he was traced and came back to take over the estate. Not long afterwards, I met and married him. He was a quiet and gentle man".

Mansion at Colton in Rugely—Haunted?

I was not at Loxley Hall for long. When the Colonel took over, I went to Colton in Rugeley to take over a very old mansion to house part of the Company. There was a plaque of the sun on the wall over the front door. This dated from the time when the Insurance Companies put their signs up to show that the house was insured against fire. There were two windows which had been bricked up. This followed the Window Tax—the more windows the owner had, the more he had to pay. We are a nation of tax dodgers, and this was one more method of beating the government of that particular time.

When accommodating men, there had to be so many square feet per person, so, with my Staff Sergeant, we went around measuring to find out how many men we could put into any one room. There was a big room in the front with a large chimney breast and two large unstained mahogany cupboards on each side. I noticed that there were two holes in the back of one of the cupboards and put my stick through one of these. I was surprised to find that the stick went in three foot deep and still had not touched the back of it. I got one of my clerks who had previously had training in an architect's office to draw me a plan of the ground floor. The drawing showed an empty space big enough for a small room, with no door or opening to it. I was very tempted to remove the back of the cupboard but refrained because of 'barrack-room damage' which would have followed. I thought that this might very well conceal a 'priest's hole' where such men were hidden at the time of Cromwell and his anti-papist persecution.

I had my bedroom on the first floor. This was quite a large room and right at the back of it was a long passage leading to a spiral staircase which went down and led out into the garden by a side entrance. Staff Sergeant Wall told me that just before dawn he had got up to relieve himself and, as he stepped into the passage, he saw a woman disappearing towards the end. The woman had a narrow waist, long skirts ,balloon sleeves, and hair which was in a bun at the back. Because no women were allowed in the men's quarters, he called out to her, but she disappeared down the spiral staircase. He leaned out of the window to see which direction she took, but there was no sign whatsoever of her. I pulled his leg and told him to stick to beer, and cut out the hard stuff!

Later I had a chat with Mr Reilly who was a wealthy shoemaker, married to a chatty, friendly young woman, who cheered up a lot when the young officers came to call. He told me that at the beginning of the century, a young woman had gone out by the same door to the garden and drowned herself in the pond. Her ghost had been seen on a great number of occasions since. I then told him of the possibility of the 'priest's hole', with which he agreed, and told me of the history of the underground passage from the house to the Priory which was the escape route for the persecuted Catholics. I was intrigued but disbelieving in the ghost story.

The 'Ghost' visits me

One night, however, alseep on my camp bed in my room, I awoke to see a nun-like figure standing at the foot of my bed. I promptly said "Can I do anything to help you?". The figure went, or faded away. Was I dreaming? Anyway, unmoved, I turned over and went to sleep. I prefer ghosts to armed, unfriendly men!

While I was at Colton I was asked if I would examine a farmer not far away who had had an accident. With no-one else about, I went to find this fat and very dull man who had cut his forearm open with a billhook. I looked at this astonishing wound, only to see no tendons from the muscles. I asked him again what happened and he said; "Them strings were hanging down, so I cut them off with scissors." Astounded I said "Well, where are they?". He then said, "Oh, the dog had them." This sort of incredible stupidity was almost unbelievable. I packed him off without comment to the nearest General Hospital and heard no more of what happened to him, but undoubtedly he had paralysed his arm for life!

South of England

From Colton we went to Canterbury, where the Headquarters were at St Edmund's School on a hill on the north side of Canterbury. I was sent with my Company to St Leonards-on-Sea to a large convalescent home, which I then took over. It was in pleasant surroundings about a halfmile to the cliffs and down to the beach.

One sunny afternoon in the countryside I heard a bang high above, and saw a Spitfire with a damaged wing eddying like a falling leaf. The pilot baled out. I watched through my binoculars and saw two large holes in his parachute—he was dropping too fast. I took a bearing with my compass and drove quickly across country to his landing spot. When I got there, he had fallen into a tree and from there down onto the ground. A few other people came running at the same time I got there myself. He had smashed his leg as well as having other injuries and was dead when I examined him. A young RAF Lance Corporal shouted at me; "Why don't you send for a doctor?". I answered "Just because I am in uniform does not mean that I am not a doctor! This man is dead." It was the first time he had seen anyone killed, and he burst into tears.

Conscientious Objectors

On 6 May 1941, while Colonel de Lacey was on leave, I took over command and received an Army Council Instruction issued to all Commanding Officers RAMC, amending the rules of Conscientious Objectors, to have this fact entered in red ink on their Field Conduct Sheet. We had five in our Unit. As acting CO I interviewed them individually and informally, telling each to sit on a chair in front of me instead of standing to attention. I pointed out that up to now all records of Conscientious Objectors were kept in a secret file under the control of the Senior Office Clerk and their Commanding Officer, but now it could be known to anyone in the Unit under these new circumstances. I told them that they were entitled to withdraw their conscientious objections and that their names would be removed immediately from the register. It was interesting to hear their reasons for declaring that they were Conscientious Objectors *before* their enlistment.

One young man said; "Sir, I am the eldest of five children and my father was injured in his job and could not work, so I declared my conscientious objections to be called up, as somebody had to feed the family. I never was a true conscientious objector, but felt that this was a way out of my difficulty. Now I would like my name removed as I love my life in the Army and the friends I have made."

Another told me "I was scared stiff of going into the Army. I have always been a studious type and afraid of violence. My life has been completely changed and I am not a true conscientious objector." And so it was with all of them. It was a very happy occasion, but it could not be celebrated in any way because secrecy was still maintained. The Colonel was most surprised on his return from leave when I told him we no longer had any conscientious objectors in the Unit. He said, "How the hell? What have you been doing now?". I told him; we had a quiet celebration ourselves that night in the Mess.

Air Raids on Canterbury

On 1 June 1942, we were awakened at 1 am by anti-aircraft fire. Hitler had started his Baedeker Raids. This raid lasted about one hour. Previously, the RAF had dropped one bomb which hit the Cathedral in Cologne. This was not deliberate, but now new targets for the Germans were the Cathedral cities. The whole city appeared to be in flames as we watched from the hill at St Edmunds. Headquarters was then available as a Casualty Clearing Centre. We opened up immediately and my ambulances were sent to Canterbury to evacuate the casualties. We had seventy-five wounded soldiers and civilians in by 3 am.

During the next two nights Canterbury Cathedral was ringed with fires. The Medical Officer of Health went into the city centre and was killed. By God's Grace, not one bomb hit the Cathedral itself. Nearly all the telephones were cut off and communication was by Despatch Riders. My girl friend Diana was visiting me at Herne Bay when Canterbury was bombed, and we had the occasional bomb drop nearby. I can remember her sitting behind a table, which served as my desk, in the large Orderly Room when a bomb fell and every soldier in the room ducked. But not Diana. She superciliously lit a cigarette and did not move, looking too blasé for words, with a contemptuous shake of her head. I asked her why she didn't lie down or at least kneel? She said, "Don't be silly. If I did that, who would give me a new pair of silk stockings?"

At the first air raid warning, the whole of St Edmunds School in Canterbury was evacuated in eight minutes when the patients and personnel went into the shelters. The Colonel at Headquarters sent two Medical Officers with thirty bottles of plasma for transfusion to the Kent and Canterbury Hospital. He also sent men and trucks to help extricate casualties from wrecked or burning buildings. Later, the RASC personnel with picks and shovels helped to clear the streets.

Every house around the Cathedral was in flames and hundreds of fire bombs showered around it. The Air Raid Precautions men on the roof of the Cathedral threw these bombs off by the dozen. Some were tubular bombs incorporating high explosives as well as the intense white heat of the mercury compound, and had a red letter "A" on the bottom. It was these brave ARP men who saved the Cathedral from burning. (The Black Prince—still there—survived a very different war. His black effigy covered the gold of his armour, hitherto unseen for centuries, which a careless tool revealed.)

Tommy Ryan RAMC

Just afterwards Colonel de Lacey's War Diary recorded the

following; "Major Petty returned to the Unit after relief as CO of the Military Hospital, Sheerness." It was the first and only time that I had complete charge of a hospital, and I can't remember much about it! I recall one incident only; that was meeting there, an old Bart's friend—Tommy Ryan, RAMC, the CO. He had been a full back in the Rugby Inter Hospital Match Final when we won the Cup in 1931 playing against Guy's. This had been my fifth year playing for the hospital and Tommy Ryan's third. I asked him how he managed to get into the Army. He told me, "I managed it by being accepted as Category C, which excludes the Tropics". I understood—he only had one kidney!

Tommy Ryan had been a good full back, but he was temperamental and if he had an off day, he would limp across the field. Towards the end of this particular match, he certainly was limping. His play had not been bad; in fact we had won the Cup. In the bath afterwards he said to me, "Give me a hand, I have a pain in my side and I want to pee". So I did, and we both saw he was passing blood. Within a short time he was escorted into Bart's where, on operating it was found he had split his kidney into two. This was then removed, while the rest of us were drinking and dining in celebration, toasting his absence—not knowing how serious it was.

Beach Under Fire

On 21 July 1942 I was told by Colonel de Lacey to lay on a demonstration of stretcher bearers evacuating casualties from the beach under fire. With exposure to noise from blasts of TNT on eighteen inch sticks, electronically detonated, the stretcher bearers dragged their loaded stretchers through barbed wires and under the protective beach scaffolding. For good measure, '69' bombs made of bakelite exploding on contact, were also thrown with care in their direction to add to the noise and blast, and to encourage all bearers to crawl with head, tail and heels down. (A World War One common wound was being shot in the heel.)

The fire power was provided from Bren guns by the Sergeant Major and Senior RASC NCO's using visible one-in-five tracer bullets coming overhead. It was unfortunate that a few of these hit the side of the ship, and then ricochetted off into the sea. The Captain also broke his rudder in the too shallow water when approaching the beach. He had always been most co-operative on previous exercises, but this time the demonstration was a bit too real for his liking. From then on, when requested for his help, he unfortunately had other work to do! I appreciated what he did, and also sympathised with his viewpoint.

This demonstration was seen by the Deputy Director of Medical Services 12th Corps, and the ADMS 43rd Division, plus all officers and NCO's of 230 and 130 Field Ambulance.

I remembered how on one such demonstration in Scotland, one of the Instructors hurled a '36' grenade over the heads of the advancing soldiers, and that it failed to explode and lay in the heather. He waited for the appropriate two minutes, timing this with his watch, then approached and picked it up. At that very moment it exploded, blowing his hand off and embedding shrapnel in his chest. We got him to hospital in Fort William for operation, where he survived. A year later after this incident, I had a letter from Captain Tasker, RAMC who had left our Company to become MO to a Commando Unit, which read, "Thanks for the training you gave me, active service in the desert is chickenfeed compared with your lot." I liked that!

This sort of training should have been harmless, and it got the stretcher bearers and men accustomed to heat and blast so that, when they came to have a go at the real thing, they regarded blast and noise on active service, as Captain Tasker did—'chickenfeed'! Even those training exercises took their toll in the battle school.

Commando Training

I once put myself down for an Infantry Training Course at the Commando Training School at Lochailort (this being whilst I was still in Canterbury and Colonel de Lacey was away and I had taken over as CO). The Brigade Major rang me and asked why I wanted to go as I was not an Infantry Officer. I replied; "As I was posted there as Medical Officer and spent seven months going through the Infantry training, I would like the opportunity of seeing my old friends again, particularly as I am now training your Field Ambulance crews that 'where a Commando goes, stretcher bearers must follow' to bring them back over the same obstacles which requires strength and know-how when handling stretchers up cliffs and over rivers and ditches".

He agreed and so I went and did my course with the rest of them. On the sixth day, running through the scrub I hit my leg below the knee on a concealed tree trunk, and got myself a very nice wound with swelling of the shin. All I could do was hobble about with a stick, following at a distance.

Came the final day of the course and Colonel Hugh Stockwell addressed us all; "You will embark in the boats which will cross the lock, scramble ashore and climb the hill above. During this time when crawling up the hill, keep your heels and bottoms down, because flying over your heads will be Bren gun bullets with one-in-five tracer bullets. You will experience blast from explosives simulating beach mines, and '69' grenades which produce blast on hitting the ground. If any casualty occurs a red Verey-light will go up. All firing will cease, and every man will be completely still. When a green Verey-light is seen, firing will recommence and you will continue to advance."

Due to my injured leg I could not take active part, but I joined a boat to see it through. The beach was very rocky, so I decided not to go ashore and risk further damage to my leg. Bobby Holmes, the Engineer Officer responsible for the explosives, was ashore checking his bombs and shouting to everyone to keep their heads and heels down. A red Verey-light went up; all firing ceased. In fact it was the last bang from one of the '69' bombs which scored a direct hit on Major Lefevre when he was scrambling ashore. I struggled over the rocks with a couple of stretcher bearers, cut off his boot and put on a Field Dressing. We got him back to the boat and turned around as the green Verey-light went up for the recommencement of the attack.

I found in the boat that he had had his heel blown off. On our way back over the loch, about half way across, another red Verey-light went up. I told the skipper not to turn around but I would send an MO by road to the other side. I learnt on reaching the shore that one of the officers had been shot dead. Every battle school had its deaths. Tragic though these were, nevertheless the survivors of this type of training were attuned to noise and blast on landing on D Day. Some American troops, not having our experience 'froze' on the beaches instead of continuing to crawl forward steadily, or running a short distance with covering fire. Their casualties were much higher than ours.

4. The Training Brigade

In 1942 there was a shortage of officers in all Corps Troops and Infantrymen. So a Brigade was detailed to train other ranks selected to become officers in the Royal Engineers, The Royal Corps of Signals, REME and RAMC, as well as the Infantry.

At Lullingstone Castle

I had a posting direct from the War Office to report to the 221 Field Ambulance at Lullingstone Castle in Kent as Chief Instructor in RAMC training. The owner of the castle, Lady Zoe Hart Dyke, I knew well. She was a remarkably dynamic lady, married to the Baronet whose title went back to Elizabeth the First. She owned the only silk-worm farm in Britain at that time.

In an enormous hall, huge wire-netting trays, one layer on top of another, housed a million silk-worms, feeding on mulberry leaves collected daily by gypsies from the orchard of mulberry bushes on the estate. There was a curious, constant, loud rustling sound as the silk-worms crunched their way through their special diet. Lady Zoe spun and wove the silk, and among her achievements she numbered the Royal velvet cloaks for the marriage of Princess Elizabeth, and later for her Coronation. (She was god-mother to my daughter and her christening present was a piece of this velvet —my daughter now being a GP -married to another GP in Bournemouth.—Time marches on!)

I reported to Lieutenant Colonel Lowe and handed him my instructions. I was to have a free hand in training the stretcher bearers' officers, and my reports would be sent by me directly to the Brigadier in charge of RAMC training at the War Office. Colonel Lowe did not like this at all and told me to follow his own programme of routine training on regular Army lines, but I insisted that I was responsible for a new type of training altogether, and this—and this alone—would be taught to the new stretcher bearer officers receiving the King's Commission. Previously in the RAMC the only medically unqualified officers were the lieutenants and quartermasters.

Training Stretcher Bearers

The new stretcher bearer officers were brought in to relieve the RAMC officers of administrative duties, and to command sections. Men chosen for this task were to be taught First Aid and treatment of minor surgery for wounds. I was ordered to train them on Commando lines, for where a Commando goes—the stretcher bearer must follow.

Twenty men were posted to me for training, many of whom were qualified chemists, or had some scientific qualification. In the first intake was a very fashionable young man, an osteopath from Harley Street. He was the best dressed of us all, and had his battle dress tailor-made in Savile Row. All he wanted to do was to get back to his profitable practice as soon as possible!

Steep Rock Faces

Early on in training, while demonstrating how to slide down a crumbling steep rock face, I did it so spectacularly, that I developed abscesses on my backside. I used to ask one of the MO's to freeze the abscess with Ethyl Chloride and stick a knife in it, but eventually I had to be admitted to Joyce Green Hospital not far away where I was operated on. Healing was a slow business in those days, taking two weeks. I stuck it out in hospital for four weeks and then discharged myself to resume training, still using a stick. I did this because while in hospital I heard that one of the young men in our first intake had dropped dead in the course of a training run. At the post mortem, the only feature that could be found was a very full distended stomach. To have sent a group off on a run immediately after a large meal was just sheer stupidity. It was this that made me get out of bed and discharge myself back to duty.

The Assault Course for Stretcher Bearers

Within the confines of the extensive castle grounds I built an assault course through the rough woodland. It included a river crossing of the same type as was used in the Commando Training School at Lochailort. Ditches were dug and walls were put up. Ropes hung from trees to be grabbed and swung from. First, every man went over the assault course as fast as possible, and after this they had to overcome the same obstacles with four stretcher bearers carrying a man on the stretcher. To cross the river they were taught to hang a stretcher with webbing onto a tight rope and haul it across the water. Any man to beat my own time across the assault course, got a chit for a pint of beer at the local pub—not very fair, because the more times you go over the obstacles the quicker you know the most effective way of tackling them. Also for crossing the river, a tarpaulin with four stretchers tied together at right angles produced an efficient improvised raft for casualties or equipment.

Skills in Cliff Climbing

When ascending a cliff, wounded men could be carried from the beach to the top in safety and comfort, using only Army equipment and 120 ft of 2½ ins rope. Twenty seven feet of this is used on the stretcher. It is put through the four runnels and at one end, tied in a chair knot. This consisted of two large loops for the stretcher bearers to sit in, while four men at the top of the cliff would pull the pair up. The wounded man was completely encased in canvas, and the stretcher bearer walked up the cliff at right angles, guiding the stretcher to avoid any jutting rocks or overhanging spurs, and the journey was comfortable and speedy.

After training, the first intake of stretcher bearer officers were put on parade for inspection by the Director General of the Army Medical Services, Sir Arthur Hood, accompanied by the General of Medical Services for Eastern Command, and the Brigadier in Charge of RAMC training. My CO Colonel Lowe told me that the Sergeant Major would issue all orders for the men of the sections on parade, and that the men would respond with "IAMA". This was "I am a Section Leader my duties are, etc, etc". I answered him, "No, he will not, as Chief Instructor of this new training, I am in charge of demonstrating their duties and I will issue the orders myself, not the Sergeant Major". He went red in the face, swallowed hard, but said nothing from then on, and the demonstration went ahead.

The Use of Small Arms

I also trained all stretcher bearer officer intakes in the use of handling small arms. The RASC Sergeant Major in charge of all vehicles, handled their instruction in .303 rifles, sten and bren guns, plus hand grenades. I was criticised by the Director of Medical

Services for South Eastern Command on why I taught the use of small arms for non combatant soldiers.

He said, "It is against the Geneva Convention".

I responded with, "My father, a country parson taught me to shoot at the age of eight and said it was always the unloaded gun that killed! RAMC personnel pick up casualties and generally put their weapons on the stretcher. If they had not handled firearms then accidents can, and will occur. Here they are taught where the safety catch is to unload the gun, whether sten, bren or rifle".

Sir Arthur Hood said "What have you got to say to that?". The other General remained silent, but I did appreciate listening to a General being ticked off!

Mock up of Field Dressing Station

Our Lt Quartermaster White, with model soldiers, made a replica of the Field Dressing Station with its officers and men, plus equipment. Giving instructions in this way to the stretcher bearers about the possible units they would be posted to, gave them an easy appreciation of the size and breakdown of the duties of all sections, together with the types and number of vehicles with their casualty carrying capacity.

In the evenings we resorted to the local inn where, occasionally, wives or girl friends would stay. Wives were officially barred from living in the immediate vicinity but they could not stop girl friends as it was not a closed area.

Survival Course

Sleeping in the open, in constant training, we were physically very fit. Among other things, I taught each intake self sufficiency. This is termed today a 'survival course'. They learnt how to shoot squirrels. These beautiful rodents always climb the bark of a tree on the opposite side to the observer, so it takes two men on both sides to shoot them with a firearm or improvised bow and arrow. The squirrel is then skinned and roasted, and tastes very like turkey. Hedgehogs also were killed and roasted in clay on a hot bonfire. The clay on cooling is peeled off, taking the spikey skin with it. Small birds, also fish, can give you enough on which to survive.

7 Lowering casualty from height

8 "Fireman's Lift"—Training Brigade

9 One closed stretcher above lower stretcher attached, to be hauled across the water

10 Raft made from 4 opened stretchers, canopy of 3 ton lorry. Carrying two stretcher cases., four men, with spades for paddles

11 Evacuation of stretcher cases between two bicycles—on fairly good roads was very successful. Started in Commando Training School following observation by Major Brown, Second-in-Command (CO of Bicycle Battalion, World War One)

Motorcycle Training for me

It was here that I learned to ride a motorcycle. I asked the RASC Officer, Lieutenant Gorden Orr to give me a lesson. His idea of a lesson was to say, "Follow me" and off he went, careering away on his motorcycle, with me duly following. After a short time he suddenly went off the road towards a sandy quarry, drove straight down it and up the other side. I followed, declutched and braked, and shot straight over the handlebars, doubling myself up in the air as I fell, watching the motorbike somersaulting through the air. Knowing how to fall and roll, I did not injure myself. I straightened the handlebars and tried again—twice—with the same result. I then rode back, saw the RASC Sergeant Major and told him what had happened. He said, "You should have left it in a lower gear and, leaning back or standing, let the engine control the bike". Without more ado he came with me, and taking his good advice I managed quite well. Thereafter over any rough ground, with further practice, I could ride standing on the saddle. Indeed afterwards with any inspecting officer, I went ahead on the motor-bike rather than use a car.

5. 33 Field Dressing Station

After leaving Lullingstone I was posted as CO of No 33 Field Dressing Station, where I had to form and mobilise this new Unit. This time I was sent to Westbury in Wiltshire to a school. In the background was a huge white horse cut into the side of the hill, revealing the chalk underlying the -grass. This had remained unchanged for many centuries and no-one knew the date of origin. I arrived to find two Officers and twenty other ranks, with no vehicles and no equipment. Slowly, over what seemed an interminable time, more men and officers trickled in. Then three lorries turned up, and a few RASC drivers took over.

Very slowly the Unit gradually increased. I was given the temporary attachment of an officer invalided back from North Africa, who had developed asthma over there. (He was Ernie Hanson, Radiologist at Cardiff Royal Infirmary after the War. Eventually he was invalided back to Cardiff where I met him after demob, and he was the first to use the adrenalin inhaler for relief of asthma.)

I Teach Unarmed Combat

While we were waiting for the equipment to arrive, I taught the troops unarmed combat. Our RASC Corporal Ryan was a professional boxer. So I put on the gloves and after a few rounds he stopped, looked at me in amazement and grinned, saying "What a CO!" Later on, when a part of the Unit was embarked on a craft in Southampton Water, I decided to give them a brief demonstration of unarmed combat. The deck was partly steel and so I could only demonstrate how to throw a man, without performing the movement fully.

A voice from the back shouted "There's a bloke here who reckons he could throw you in ten seconds flat".

I said "I doubt it, but I am not going to try. I don't want to have a death on my hands when he hits his head on the steel deck". I told them how I had seen one young man killed in the ring, when I was boxing at the Stadium Club, London, due to a skull fractured as he hit the canvas. I could not afford to lose one of them before he went on active service. I explained that before this training, I had been with a party of Americans and was watching this kind of situation with two US Army experts in PT. The same challenge had come from an onlooker. There are no Queensberry Rules in war. The instructor was roughly handled and responded stupidly with a quick prod in the eyes with his extended thumb and index finger. That was the finish. The American MO sent the man off to the hospital at once; whether he lost his sight completely, I never knew.

Tommy Richards and SBO Lt Hogarth, both from Glasgow, came together. They were two very good down-to-earth types and did their job well. They were followed by Hand-Bowman, the dental officer, and Captain Reid, who became my second-in-command. Nearly all who were posted to the Unit were stable, and enthusiastic. A few were not, so I enabled them to leave for other Units, safer and more comfortable.

Eventually, without equipment and vehicle nearing completion, I covered the country north and south, training the RASC drivers in column, and in observing camouflage. We went as far North as Yorkshire and later, South to our ultimate objective which was Bournemouth, to become part of the No 8 Beach Group attached to the 3rd Canadian Division for the assault on D Day. On reporting to the HQ in Bournemouth, I met Lt Colonel Taffs of the 6th Battalion Royal Berkshire Regiment, and his second-in-command Major Board, both first class officers, efficient but relaxed.

The Beach Group consisted of many units. Colonel Taffs and his Battalion manhandled thousands of tons of all types of cargo and trucks, ambulance cars, tanks, food, petrol, shells, ammunition etc. All vehicles were treated for landing in water, driving through the sea, and up the beach. Engineers, sappers, gunners, signallers, tank drivers—all took part.

Camouflage Importance

Before arriving at Bournemouth however, whenever near an RAF station, I would apply to the Station Commander for a plane to fly over my Unit. I had to sign his authority that in the event of any accident, I—not the RAF—would assume full responsibility. I did this for the sake of camouflage efficiency, every lorry camouflaged with the netting spread out to avoid the lines of a hard shadow on the ground. Then I gave the Observer of the plane the map reference to look for my Unit. We learnt by our mistakes. Anybody moving could be observed more easily, particularly from a low height when there was an area of small white blobs—which were the faces of the men looking up at the aircraft. They quickly learnt not to move or look up at a plane flying overhead.

On our final exercise before arriving outside Bournemouth near the scrubland of the New Forest, the Unit set up under camouflage. The observer was given an accurate map reference but failed to spot the vehicles as they blended into the background of ferns and small trees. I was then satisfied they knew their camouflage. On that last occasion, I went up with the RAF in an Albermarle—a twin-engined aircraft. All six personnel were kitted out with parachutes and we climbed into the aircraft through an opening in the nose of the plane between the two propellors. When in flight, I asked the pilot why we were wearing parachutes but the crew were not. He replied "They aren't any use to us because in flight we cannot get out of this aircraft anyway". Regulations were obeyed, however pointless!

At Bournemouth with No 8 Beach Group

So, with our brief training completed, we left in column. I reported to the Camp Commander of No 8 Beach Group and I was allocated to the Branksome Dene Hotel in Bournemouth. There was a long sandy valley, flanked with fir trees leading to the sea—the Branksome Dene. We were made welcome by the Canadians who were very bored. They were a fine lot of men having waited for years for the chance to get to grips with the Germans. They were all volunteers. "No Zombies with us" they told me.

I got on with them very well, particularly the Maclean cousins, both with the Corps of Military Police and ultimately responsible for discipline and control of traffic on the Beach. We had quite a few rough Mess nights. They were hard drinkers as were the Welch Regiment, where I learned to hold my liquor. I was very strong in those days, and there was sheer joy in matching myself against tougher, bigger men as we crashed around the Mess, breaking tables and stools—but never our bones—and always finishing up laughing. Our first night like this was followed by a hangover, and a meeting in the Mess tent at 11 am for the 'hair of the dog'.

MacLean stared at me with astonishment when I entered, and said "I thought you were seven feet tall last night—how you have shrunk".

"Not to worry son, I brought you down to size. When you hit me over the head with that stool to no effect. I could not stop laughing! It is not shrunk I am—it was drunk I was!" So we leaned over the bar for another!

The Marshall Murder

Whilst in Bournemouth, I called in at the Norfolk Hotel bar one evening where I met Mr and Mrs Phillips from Llandaff, Cardiff who were on holiday. As I came in, I saw an RAF Squadron Leader escorting an attractive young woman out of the bar. Phillips told me that the girl had asked him to get her a taxi; she did not particularly want to go with that man, but Phillips failed to obtain one in the blackout, and had offered to accompany her himself. The RAF Officer gently took her by the arm and said "Goodnight, it is not far and we can easily walk". That was the last time she was seen alive. The body of this beautiful young woman, who had been battered to death, was found further down Branksome Dene Chine the following day.

I met Phillips after the War on my return home to Llandaff, and he told me he never got over his feeling of guilt in that he had not insisted on helping the girl. It eventually transpired that the officer was not in the RAF. The man was arrested and found insane, to be detained during His Majesty's pleasure; it was not the first time he had murdered.

Casualties of Poison Gas

An old friend of mine, Lt Colonel Fawcett RAMC called on my Unit. He was appointed as Adviser in the treatment of casualties of poison gas. The Germans had introduced Chlorine Gas in the First World War of 1914-18. We had no protection, and deaths from chlorine, temporary blindness and choking, were numerous. I remember meeting my mother's cousin Major Stanley Trick five years after the First World War in 1923, when I was a student in Bart's. He survived the gas attacks, but emphysema and chronic bronchitis followed. He had been a great batsman in his day and had played for Surrey, but now became short of breath on the slightest exertion.

However, we now had an advantage over the Hun. The Royal Engineers were detailed to receive all types of poison gas and use them, when ordered. They were to experiment with them, and with medical assistance, produce adequate preventative respirators. These Sappers were waiting and waiting to take action, which never came. We had sent a Company from the 6th Battalion The Welch Regiment to the Porton Gas School to protect it against possible invasion, as long ago as 1938.

Lt Colonel Fawcett had taught all the different types of gas now available, together with the necessary precautions and First Aid measures, if any. He had harmless test tubes available, simulating the smell of each gas. The 'nerve gas' was much to be feared, producing complete incapacity due to total paralysis of muscles and possibly, without the aid of artificial respiration—death.

Gas Masks

This country had two great advantages over the German Army and Nation. Every man, woman and child was issued with a gas mask, inhaling air through gauze and charcoal. Babies had a special cover for their cot or pram. The Germans, had not supplied their own civilians with this protection. The second advantage, was because of the prevailing wind in France, which is westerly. (The Huns found out when Chlorine was first discharged by them from cylinders towards the Allied trenches during the World War One 1914-18, and the wind turned and blew it back.) In addition, we had ships loaded with gas which were to be sent to Bremerhaven and Hamburg. On approaching the German coast, they were to be abandoned and, by remote control down the coast, blown up. The Royal Engineers had a Company responsible for the care and final use of this gas. They continued to remain unused for all these years —but there they were—ready for action! They were a strategic unit, highly trained—and bored to distraction!

The enemy were not aware of our satisfactory advantage, and therefore they were in no way in a position to risk starting gas warfare themselves. Gas warfare became a strategic weapon and was, therefore, never used. (The nuclear bomb today, is a similar strategic weapon. The threat of its use and consequence of destruction of any capital city or nation, effectively—we hope—will prevent any nation from using it. Within seconds of America or Russia 'pressing the button' the opposite number will retaliate! Smaller nations will be wiped out and the larger continents suffer huge areas of devastation with fallout liable to drop anywhere in the world. Only a megalomaniac would start this—but who knows?)

Security had to be Stressed

Every effort at security was continually stressed. Commanding Officers of the various sections had direct instructions for these to be passed on to the rest of the Officers under my command. Security had to be taught to individuals, and enforced with extreme penalties for those who consciously or unconsciously betrayed plans of defence and offensives. Self discipline is essential to guard the wagging tongue. The Officers and men of the 3rd Canadian Division of No 8 Beach Group kept their mouths shut after the debacle of the Canadian Second Division, who landed at Dieppe in 1942. After having been for such a long time, training and drilling, and bored and homesick, the relief with excitement of the preparations for landing in France at long last, were too much. After drinks in the local pub—careless talk got around. So the Germans were waiting for them at Dieppe! The caterpillar tracks of the tanks were unsatisfactory for the stoney beach, so many of them got stuck. They learnt a lot, at great cost! Their objective was achieved but with grave losses of men, and equipment.

The Government was well aware of the need for security. Propaganda posters were displayed in public places, proclaiming 'Careless Talk Costs Lives'. At one pub I stopped at, I was given a visiting card printed as follows:

U. R. Requested.
2 Refrain From,
Careless Talk.

At the 3rd Canadian Division briefing, we were given a rough cyclostyled map of the contour of the beach on which we were to land, and immediate surroundings. The name of each village or town was fictitious—such as Cairo, Bombay etc. Fortunately none of these maps got into enemy hands. However, a serious error had been made. The magnetic variation of the points of the compass on the corner of the map was noted by the anaesthetist of our Field Ambulance Unit. He showed this to me and we applied them to a real map, which indicated our target area for landing! Immediate withdrawal of all these maps was ordered. The compass on the new maps was now false and the magnetic variation indicated further East. The Germans had been led to believe that the attack would occur East of the Seine, and so their divisions were concentrated in that area. They had 3,300 miles of coastline to protect, from Narvik at the crest of Norway to Denmark, Holland, Belgium, France and Germany. Their concentration of troops were placed near the most likely target.

In fact, they regarded a target at Bernière sur Mère and Arromanches as unlikely, because of the sunken ridge of rocks offshore only barely covered at high tide. The fact was that our landing craft were all flat bottomed and allowed enough time near high tide to land the main assault troops, followed up by the thousands of tons of supplies, petrol, food, equipment etc. This part of the coast appeared to them to be an unlikely landing place, so the German Staff put in a very mixed and weak Division from East Germany, Czechoslovakia and Russia.

D Day Minus 14

Two weeks before D Day, 6 June 1944, all our officers and men were confined to their Unit area behind wire. To any man who broke out and went to the 'local' or met a girl friend, I gave twenty eight days' field punishment. This was the maximum punishment that a Commanding Officer could give under war conditions. (In World War One this punishment consisted of being tied for twenty four hours spreadeagled on the wheel of a gun-carriage. In Wellington's day, the man would have had one hundred lashes.)

Escape Methods

I disliked being cooped up; most of us did. I thought of what it

12 Lochailort—the day we netted the salmon (Author in uniform behind the boy)

13 A pleasant break from training in Scotland, with Colonel Stockwell (far left of photo) and Captain Petty (author) alongside, with three other crew members on a sailing trip.

14 No 33 Field Dressing Station 1943-44
Centre front row, left to right, 7th, 8th, 9th, Major Richardson (Psychiatrist), Major Gerald Petty, Captain Nuttall Smith MC

21 ARMY GROUP

PERSONAL MESSAGE FROM THE C-in-C

To be read out to all Troops

1. The time has come to deal the enemy a terrific blow in Western Europe.

The blow will be struck by the combined sea, land, and air forces of the Allies—together constituting one great Allied team, under the supreme command of General Eisenhower.

2. On the eve of this great adventure I send my best wishes to every soldier in the Allied team.

To us is given the honour of striking a blow for freedom which will live in history; and in the better days that lie ahead men will speak with pride of our doings. We have a great and a righteous cause.

Let us pray that " The Lord Mighty in Battle " will go forth with our armies, and that His special providence will aid us in the struggle.

3. I want every soldier to know that I have complete confidence in the successful outcome of the operations that we are now about to begin.

With stout hearts, and with enthusiasm for the contest, let us go forward to victory.

4. And, as we enter the battle, let us recall the words of a famous soldier spoken many years ago :—

" *He either fears his fate too much,*
Or his deserts are small,
Who dare not put it to the touch,
To win or lose it all."

5. Good luck to each one of you. And good hunting on the mainland of Europe.

B. L. Montgomery
General
C-in-C 21 Army Group.

1944.

15 May 1944—Message from General Montgomery

16 The Right Reverend Dr Timothy Rees, Lord Bishop of Llandaff, who understood more than anyone the failure of humanity, as he was for four years Senior Chaplain to the Venereal Disease Hospital at Rouen in World War One. The Bishop was a dying man when I had my "call up". He had been all his life a parish priest and disliked the isolation of a Bishop. Easy of approach, with a gentle humour, he was loved by all and had cared for the worst posible afflictions. Surrounded by doctors, Lord Horder, and Cardiff consultants, he said to us "I am sorry to be such an unconscionable time dying, gentlemen", and smiling all the time. I had to leave at once for my regiment and said goodbye.

must be like in a German POW camp. We knew that planned escape efforts had been made already, and men and officers had got out, handed on from one resistance group to another through Belgium and France to Spain, and back to this country. To improve the escape methods, one officer and a senior officer, a WO or senior NCO, from each Unit were detailed to attend a course on escaping. I selected myself and Staff Sgt Mace. Our instructor was a young officer who already had successfully escaped from a German POW camp through France, then Spain and Portugal.

We were given a code which varied for each individual. In writing our coded letters home, we had to put this in. I had to put the date in full for the month eg 12/September/1944—this meant that on opening (as all letters from POW's were opened) my coded letter would be taken to the decoder where the last letter of every second word was converted to a number, and then the number allocated to a letter of the alphabet. With the date being spotted and the message recorded, the letter was then sent on to the addressee without delay. Messages relating to the conditions, attitude of guards (good, bad or casual), location of the camp, instructions from the British Command—could be forwarded in a series of letters. It was the duty of any one of us on being taken, to report to the British Commandant of the prisoners at once.

Escape Aids

At these lectures were given practice in letter-writing, also a small hacksaw which was to be sewn into the lining of the outer seam of the trouser leg for cutting through bars. Metal fly buttons were used in the normal issue of battle dress. Two of these however, were substituted for special buttons and were to be cut off when in the POW camp. On the open side of one, there was a small white spot on the outer perimeter; on the second was a minute metal spike in the centre. When the first button was balanced on the spike it moved, with the white spot pointing to the North Pole, ie, it became a very small, but accurate compass. Fortunately, I never needed it!

At the end of the course we had an exam to test our proficiency in the code, which had to be memorised and practised. We then returned to our Units, locked up like prisoners behind the wire, waiting for D Day.

6. Before D Day 6th June 1944

Field Marshall Montomery—'Monty'—lectured all Officers of field rank and above in the 3rd Canadian Division, and No 8 Beach Group consisting of all arms of the Service. For the first time in history, a General passed on to *all* troops the exact mode of the attack, together with the names of the battle ships to give the covering fire with their heavy guns offshore onto the German batteries. We were told the number of bombers, and their load of bombs; the number of fighter planes to give us protection with their air supremacy over the Germans. The Navy had cleared the route across the Channel of mines, and marked the boundaries with buoys. There was also to a balloon barrage for each beach site. He gave us the total number of troops and all equipment we asked for, we got! My own Medical Officers had been allowed to have any special drug they were accustomed to using. This was unheard of before, when the normal issue had been restricted in type and amounts—all applied for in triplicate!

The uplift in morale was terrific. We had up until then pictured ourselves—those who survived—climbing over the bodies of the Assault Sappers and Infantrymen, to get through to the village, shelled, bombed and machine gunned!

Attack Rehearsals

All troops in each Unit were then lectured by their own Commanding Officer in Nissen Huts where there was an exact model replica of the beach, village, the church which was three foot high and the streets with houses all exactly in proportion. I took my own Unit in small parties to show them this model, so that if they landed in the wrong place, they could visualise the outstanding landmarks and follow the route to the beach cleared of mines and then proceed to the Chateau. They were NOT to stray into the field beside it, because I had been shown in April and May air photographs of the mined area in this field by the Staff Captain at Canadian Headquarters.

Services of Supply

The Americans called our Beach Groups—SOS (Services of

Supply). They were similarly responsible for guns, ammunition, petrol, food, care of vehicles etc. dragged to the DVP area. The DVP was the Drowned Vehicle Park, and all vehicles were made waterproof to drive in sea water. The exhaust pipes were taken up to the top of the lorry, and the air inlet pipes accompanied these, allowing the air to go downwards through water level to the carburettor. The plugs and all the wiring were sealed off with plastic putty. All these trucks and lorries were unloaded day and night, with a neverending collection of supplies and equipment.

'The Mixed Bag' said HM King George VI

Although very acceptable in one way, any break in the day I found irksome. We had frequent inspections, on full parade for the two Field Dressing Stations, and these meant half a day off work. First we were inspected by Canadian, General Dempsey—that was one day gone. Later, by HM The King with Colonel Taffs of the 6th Royal Berkshire Regiment, Officer Commanding all personnel in the Beach Group, accompanying the King along our ranks, and explaining the different types of troops of the group. As he passed he turned to Colonel Taffs and in a pleasant but rather blasé tone, said "You have quite a mixed bag with this lot, Colonel". From then on we were nicknamed "The Mixed Bag".

Inspection by Monty

Two days of peace came, followed by another inspection, this time by Monty. He had different ideas from the others; not unusual for him. We were formed into a large square with two ranks facing inwards, opposite each other. Monty stood on the bonnet of his Jeep and said "I don't know you and you don't know me, so I am going to walk between the ranks facing inwards, you will stand easy, and I shall have a good look at you, and you can have a good look at me". This he did and the curious thing was, that the troops regarded his attitude as extremely funny. The two lines facing inwards had their officers standing behind them, and the soldiers in front of me were laughing, and one actually lit a cigarette, which provoked a loud growl from me, and telling him to report to his Sergeant afterwards.

Monty always said "Be damned to spit and polish. In battle wear what you find most comfortable!" Monty played to the gallery, but in the process he improved the morale by his frank, revealing plan of the assault and all the support we should receive. Brigadier de Guingand was the Senior Officer in charge of Administration in Monty's army. He had a brilliant brain and fact there was nothing we, or any other unit could not have which he failed to obtain. He was also a sick man, and was examined by Major Strang one of our surgeons, who clinically diagnosed a severe inflammation of the gall bladder with, or without gall stones. He promptly admitted him to hospital for speedy investigation. The Brigadier brought all his papers with him to the ward, and he was operated on at once successfully. Monty however was furious, he sent for Major Strang and told him to discharge the Brigadier back to duty immediately. Not at all intimidated, the surgeon told Monty that this was impossible, it was too grave a risk, and that he flatly refused to obey his order, for at least a further forty eight hours. The Brigadier could have his desk next to his bed, along with his immediate staff, and so this transpired.

Eisenhower Inspection

We were then inspected by General Ike Eisenhower, the Overall Commander of the Allied troops. Before starting his speech he said to us "All take a look at my driver; she's a beauty". Listening to the conversations of the drivers while waiting in their cars, one of them said to Ike's driver, "I wouldn't like to be General Eisenhower". She said "Why ever not?" Came the reply, "Well, there is no promotion for him ever, is there?" General Eisenhower had a frequent grin, and freely cracked jokes as he talked to us. I thought how all the leaders were just that bit different from each other.

It was to Eisenhower that the decision for naming the 'D Day' fell. All depended on the weather forecast, which was unfavourable on the 3rd, 4th and 5th of June. Sitting around waiting, we wrote letters to our loved ones. Many of us wrote, "If I don't come back, remember always that I loved you"!

We made last minute efforts at checking all drugs and equipment. Every MO was allowed to ask for the specific drug he might require. A number asked for Seconal Capsules which were quicker in action than Phenobarbitone as a sedative. Seconal was to prove very effective later on in dealing with the psychological casualties at our Advanced Exhaustion Centres.

We were told that we would find on landing, white painted notices with a black skull and crossbones and the word "Minen". They were on both sides of the beach wall, and had been put there not only to prevent the German troops, but the civilians from straying onto the dangerous areas. This information was relayed to the men, section by section. Nothing was left out, no greater foresight and detailed care has ever been known, to make sure of the success of an assault.

To Avoid Sea Sickness

Before D Day in Southampton, I was given the job of taking four parties of men in small landing craft around the Needles, off the Isle of Wight. Approaching the Needles the weather was a bit rough but not stormy. The craft rode the waves with only a slight pitching and tossing and the twelve men in each were standing, and tending to sway together. There was no particular observation to be made by any craft. I was issued with four types of tablets, A, B, C and D, and was unaware of the names of any of them but assumed that one contained Hyoscine. I had to report on the effectiveness of them, for selection by the Army Medical Services. The number feeling sick were reported in each craft, as were the number who actually vomited, the degree of severity, and which numbered tablet they had taken. I felt that the exercise would have been more effective if they had been landed and made to shoot at targets, to see if their vision was affected, as it might well have been on Hyoscine. Eventually, all ships' captains received anti-seasickness pills for the issue to troops whether on troop ships, landing craft or DUKWs etc. There was one exception where no anti-seasickness pills were issued and that was on my ship!

7. D Day and Afterwards

Exercise OVERLORD was about to begin. No troops were better trained, equipped, or cared for than ours. They had been put in the picture completely as to what to expect, but many of us in our minds had written ourselves off. I felt sorry for the youngsters, very much in love with the girl of their hearts back home, longing to have the job over and done with. My own marriage, like those of some of my friends had broken up, after being so long away from home.

The best high tides were on the 4th, 5th and 6th June 1944. So the weather and the tides were the first essential factors of success. We were standing by and embarked, waiting for the word GO. The reason for these dates was because of the extensive rocky reef 200-300 yards offshore which showed itself as the tide fell. We had flat bottomed craft which held twenty men under the command of a Sub Lieutenant RN. The craft however could easily clear the reef when the tide was high.

First Assault Wave

These were the first line of the assault. The first troops ashore were the Assault Engineers whose job was to cut lanes through the beach defences of wire and scaffolding poles, and remove the beach mines. In Southampton Water we could not see the horizon for ships—three thousand of them, all shapes and sizes. Everything however depended on 'the weathermen'. It was rough and stormy on 3rd June, the 4th and 5th came and went with high tides and choppy seas. If the 6th of June had not been clear then the assault would have had to be postponed for a further month to get the tides right. The thought of disembarking, re-forming and four weeks of hanging around waiting bored, was formidable and depressing.

D Day Landing Organisation

In order to avoid the loss of whole key units, the D Day landing organisation consisted of mixing very small groups of every section of the Army for the assault. If one assault craft blew up, the remainder, landing safely could carry on with their job. To do this we left our camp as a whole unit and passed through assembly areas, breaking up again and again into smaller groups. Because of this system, during the actual landing, I lost only twelve soldiers out of a Company of two hundred and fifty, this company being commanded by Captain Reynolds.

I was in a Tanklanding Ship. Within half a mile of the French coastline we were stuck on the falling tide, so the CO of a Canadian Field Ambulance, Lt Colonel Caverhill and myself, with three other officers, hailed a DUKW to drive us ashore. Thus, having done practice landings for a year in water up to our necks—we landed in comfort—bone dry!

All Those Wounded

We had to deal with 1100 stretcher cases, apart from any walking wounded who had had their wounds dressed, given food and drink and shepherded to the beach and across the Channel. My instructions were to clear the beach of the wounded as quickly as possible. There was plenty of room on the returning ships. Abdominal wounds had priority of operation and transfusion by our surgical teams, so they were kept forty eight hours before embarking. The teams worked tirelessly day and night, with only very short breaks for sleep.

There was a never ending stream of men and lorries of all types which continued non stop day and night. The tanks had come in earlier. At night, a few thousand pocket torches were laid at 1 ft intervals on the beach to mark out the traffic lanes. At high tide the beach was covered right up to the beach wall, so torch collectors constantly followed the tide level, picking up the torches and then replacing them. At night the winding tracks looked like Christmas decorations.

Dealing with the Casualties

It seemed ridiculously simple to have landed on the beach, walk along the marked lanes through the mined areas, up the main street and right to the Chateau which was our base. Apart from the staccato rattle of a Bren gun and big double bangs overhead from HMS Rodney concentrating on shelling the German gun emplacements, we could hear the German light artillery firing on open sights from a small rise of fields above us. They had picked off three tanks in the field beyond us; they were still burning. I had a section of specially trained RAMC personnel who dealt with the survivors of these tanks, and also with the removal of the dead. Some bodies which were badly charred had hot pitch poured on them. After a time when the pitch hard hardened, the bodies were removed piecemeal. The presence and training of these sections were top secret. It would not have improved morale to permit tank personnel to have any inkling of their possible plight.

We were promised before D Day, air and sea supremacy, and we had both! The Navy shelled Caen and the German bases, producing a comfortable 'bang' as their shells went overhead. In the air, it was not supremacy—it was complete mastery. Only a few low flying German fighters got through periodically by day machine gunning at random. I was told not to expose the 24 ft Red Cross flag on the ground, because the Unit was situated between the oil dump and the ammunition dump, and therefore not protectable by the Geneva Convention.

Chateau Le Fief Pelloquin

There were two small Barrage Balloons over my tentage alongside the Chateau, anchored to the ground by a steel hawser. One of these during the first night completely disappeared—much to my annoyance. Just below each balloon, attached to the hawser was an explosive device so that if the wing of an enemy plane struck the wire, this would pull the balloon down coming into contact with the plane and exploding. It was probably just a bit of 'bull' to increase our confidence.

I had my shooting stick which accompanied me on many a 'Point to Point' before the war. The French inhabitants looked in amazement, pointing to the British Officer with a stick walking across the beach, as I demonstrated appropriately with the pointed end, shouting "Pour les Boches"!

The Chateau we inhabited was Le Fief Pelloquin, nestling in a small wood on the side of the town of Benières Sur Mèr, the home of Colonel and Madame Bois Lambert. The Chateau was already filling up with walking wounded, lying around anywhere where there was a space. These soldiers were treated, and collected into groups, ready to be taken to the beach for embarkation home. I suggested to the Colonel that I give him some men to remove his

17 British and Canadian Troops going ashore at zero hour on 6th June 1944 at Bernieres-sur-Mer

18 Bernieres-sur-Mer. The third house up was where the Canadians caught two women who were snipers after having lived with the German soldiers for 4 years. They hanged them

19 This was the church which housed the German Paratroopers sniping

20 Le Fief Pelloquin, Chateau of Colonel and Madame Bois Lambert

antiques and treasures and lock them up, but he declined. I told him that ours were good soldiers but they could also be 'light fingered'. We set part of his grounds aside for a cemetery. Madame Bois Lambert had crosses erected, and took personal care of this task.

Treatment for the Wounded

As soon as the operating tents were erected, without ceasing day and night they were put to use. The Blood Transfusion Officer was responsible for giving blood to the selected wounded. The intention was to operate as soon as possible on the abdominal wounds, rather than have the delay caused by a Channel crossing.

Our Penicillin Powder with a sterilized spoon was poured into the wound after it had been swabbed out, cleaning it of any debris. Meanwhile my two MO's on the beach carried on with the First Aid under fire, and with their diagnosis cards, they would send the injured up to us at the Chateau. In addition, there were eighteen civilian wounded from the town. They were put in Madame Bois Lambert's large drawing room where she supervised their care. I saw them regularly and apologised for not being able to operate on them at once because of our heavy commitment to our own soldiers. We dressed wounds and only one man with severe abdominal injuries died. Every time I went into the room I was greeted with shouts of "Picure" (injection), so they had their morphia and remained comfortable. It was our own shelling by the Navy that was responsible for their wounds, but they were never resentful. They were only too glad to see us at any cost to save "La Belle France".

After a couple of days Colonel Bois Lambert came to me and said; "Promise me that you will take my wife and me back with you when you leave for England". He thought that this was another Dieppe landing. I told him that we were here to fight and win! We had everything—men, determination, control of the seas and skies, and were here to free Europe!

Women Hanged in Bernières Sur Mer

After four years of German occupation, a number of the women had taken to their beds the German soldiers. These Normandy women were not glad to see us arrive. They had had comfortable lives with their German lovers. A few of these women were snipers, picking off our men one by one. Some hid in the haystacks just outside the town. The Canadian Deputy Assistant Quatermaster General had two Bren guns mounted on his Jeep and careered through the countryside, often into German held territory. One night he bivouaced in a field, and found on waking that his immediate neighbours were six German soldiers whom he promptly shot. Also sleeping in a haystack with their guns, were two French women whom he took into Bernières Sur Mèr and handed over to the Canadian troops: they hanged them in the back garden of their house. Eventually his dramatic adventures came to an end when a German shell blew his Jeep to pieces.

One other clear memory of those fraught and fearful days stands out in my mind. I was inspecting wounded on stretchers and found a man with his head and face bandaged, and deeply unconscious. The MO in charge explained 'He has had his face blown off and I have given him two grains of Morphine intravenously". I made no adverse comment except to say that the next time he had a case like that he was to consult with the commanding officer, as I was immediately responsible for the care of all wounded as well as for the action of any Medical Officer. To myself, I said, that I did not think I would have done that—but then I had not seen the man's face, nor how much of it was left! My mind drifted back to former times when I was well aware of the possibility of facial repairs because in World War 1, Sir Harold Gillies had started with plastic surgery operations. In particular there had been a seaman in the Royal Navy at the Battle of Jutland, who had had the total of forty-two operations over two years, during which time his face had been built up and he was presentable again. He had transplants taken from his arms, abdomen and thighs. I knew Sir Harold Gillies' work well; he had been the plastic surgeon at Bart's Hospital. I remembered one case particularly well that he lectured about; "A young woman had a disfiguring injury to her lips and mouth. I repaired these adequately with skin and subcutaneous tissue grafted from the cheek of her mother's buttock. The result was perfect in every way, but I often wonder whether when her husband is embracing her if he thinks for one moment he is kissing his mother-in-law's bottom".

Caring for German Wounded

On D Day + 2 we received twentythree German wounded and

their Medical Officer. The wounded when we checked them had been well cared for by their MO and were evacuated forthwith to a prisoner-of-war camp in England. I kept the MO, who was no Nazi, but was in fact a Hungarian gynaecologist who had served two years in Russia. Also I kept his four medical orderlies. Their MO spoke no English and I no German, but we both spoke French, and as he was wearing the Iron Cross, I asked him where and when he got this. He answered briefly "Pour la merite". Naively, he asked that when he left for England could he visit two professors he had known in Cambridge? I told him that he would eventually be going to a prisoner-of-war camp in Canada. He was to remain with me for the time being in case there was the possibility of further German casualties to be cared for. I kept him and his orderlies under guard, sleeping under the tarpaulin covered framework of a three ton lorry.

D Day + 3 and War Weary

By D Day + 3 I had not sat down for three days and two nights, and my hands were beginning to shake. My Batman's duty at this time was to supply me with pints of hot sweet tea at frequent intervals. The surgeons were also tired out. I offered to take over surgery for Major Bennett if he would sit down and give me advice, but he carried on. That night I went to my tent and lay down, but not for long. The bombs fell all around the Chateau, and after the bombs came the long dreary cry of "Stretcher-bearer". I staggered up and tried to kick my NCOs awake but failed. With fear dragging feet, I moved with great effort towards the heavy dead silence that follows a nearby explosion.

Direct Hit on the Truck

I went to what was left of the tarpaulin framed truck and saw six bodies without heads, and scattered everywhere like a mad dentist's surgery there were bits of jaw with teeth attached, curved bits of skull bone, bits of brain, with blood and hair attached to bits of scalp. Our bodies were khaki clad, theirs were grey, lying together, close, with heads and helmets gone, silent and inhuman, with no face, unable to stare even blankly at the night. The four German prisoners had been standing up, and my two sentries of necessity had to stand to guard them. Their officer, an old campaigner, had lain flat on the ground, and escaped without a scratch. He came with me to assist in treating our own wounded. I appreciated his skill acquired after two years of war against the Russians. In no way could I feel anger towards him; he was a gentleman in the German Army. His soldiers and mine—all were buried in the little cemetery, thanks to the devotion of Madame Bois Lambert.

We had eight others killed and wounded that night. I attended to my own cases kneeling down where I could for safety. A young Canadian MO from 16 CCS had just arrived and was giving the transfusion when a soldier just outside the tent, stumbled and fell against the tent wall. Instinctively I ducked, but thought "I must stand and set an example". On the other side of me the gynaecologist from Prague worked, dressing the wounds of our injured, and I watched him from the corner of my eye noting his efficient medical skill. He knew more about war wounds than I was ever to know.

My MOs were not hit, but Major Board the Second in Command to Colonel Taffs, was shot through the head—thanks to his distinctive white helmet which they both wore to make them available to all to see. He was a charming, efficient, brave man, and his death was a great loss.

Captain Johnny Nuttal-Smith

I decided that I had to sleep. I took a Seconal and slept in one of the slit trenches for about three hours. I awoke feeling less shaky, but still mortally tired and slow. I decided to go to my MO on the beach to see how he was, as I had not seen him since arrival; Captain Johnny Nuttal-Smith. I knew he was all right from scribbled 'wounded cards' he sent to us with his wounded. I walked down the road to a large stone wall which separated the beach from the road, and stood on the top of the wall at the entrance to the beach, but could see no sand. It was high tide and the whole beach was under water. Looking along, I saw Johnny's Red Cross mark displayed fifty yards away. Dully I asked myself, "How do I get there?" I saw a gap in the wire and walked through it. I looked down and saw that the smooth sand on top of the wide wall was untrodden. A voice outside the wire shouted; "Sir, you are in the middle of a mine field". I wondered what to do, whether to try and run so fast that only my heel would be blown off, or whether to turn round slowly and put my feet into my own footprints. I did the latter and came out unharmed. There is nothing like acute fear to make one become wide awake. With really severe fatigue—reason goes. Then I did the obvious thing that I should have done in the first place, walk along the road by the beach where I found Johnny in his dug-out, exhausted and shaky like myself. I told him to lie down and take a Seconal. He said; "No, I'll carry on, I've still got work to do". I told him; "This is an order, swallow it, lie down and I will too". He was asleep in two minutes flat. He had done a good job alone, and I recommended him for the Military Cross, which I am glad to say, he got.

8. July - August 1944

The Germans were retreating. We moved out towards Caen which was well defended, where we were sited by Brigadier Wallace well in advance of our forward guns. Caen was the key point of the attack. The British on the left wing swept through to the north of the city and the Americans commanded by General Patton (a dynamic, colourful, two-gun cowboy of a man, twin holsters for his pearl-handled six-shooters) driving a wide arc southwards through France, pivoting on Caen.

Close to Corps HQ a few miles behind us, an automatic tank minelayer accidentally dropped a mine like a chicken laying an egg. The following tank ran over it, and blew up with two killed and eight wounded. So even at a safe distance we had our casualties.

One afternoon, low flying aircraft attacked the 33 Field Dental Surgery machine gunning at random, ignoring our large Red Cross mark. We had three tents holed to pieces with no casualties. The Dental Officer, Hand Bowman, whilst filling a soldier's tooth at the time had his tent machine gunned to pieces, with no casualties, dental or otherwise! His patient said that this was the only time he had not been frightened of the dentist! The attack was so sudden that all anyone could do was to duck, and fall flat! What astonished us, was that no one was hit.

We watched hundreds of our heavy bombers pass overhead, not in formation but at all levels through the clouds of 'flak'. The exploding anti-aircraft shells of black puffs of smoke, looked like a huge patterned curtain hanging from the sky. Two bombers were hit and went down in flames. It was like a game of chance, with more winners than losers fortunately.

Attack on Caen

On the ground in the attack on Caen the casualties were heavy; the 3rd Canadian and British Divisions advanced on both flanks, with the 59th Division making a slow advance in the centre. Following this the 210 Field Ambulance admitted four hundred and ten casualties on the first day of the action, where we were still sited in advance of the Light Regiment of Field Artillery shelling Caen.

Seventeen regiments of field artillery make a lot of noise! We were less than 100 yards away from some of them! In the dusk I made a courtesy call on them, approaching from the enemy direction which astonished their CO. "Lucky you called in," he said. "We would have advanced straight through your tentage during the night". I replied "I'll have a large drink on that, thank you", and so we finished the last half of his whisky bottle!

The fall of Caen was essential. The Germans were well aware of this, and had their maximum field power stationed here. We expected a counter attack, which did not come and we all felt a general relief. The Germans defending Caen fought with sterling courage. They remained in their foxholes and came up for air to fight again and again, during the short lulls in our shelling.

On a 'recce' forward in my jeep through the cratered area, I came across prisoners walking back to our lines. I told Driver Keeley as another lot came into view around the corner "You can smell them before you see them". They had had little food and no water, and they made a pretty powerful stench. When they were taken over to the Hygiene Section, they were dusted down the arms and trousers with DDT powder to kill off the lice.

Montgomery put in three Divisions to hold the perimeter of the bridgehead. Each was relieved after four days so that gradually all experienced the effect of shelling and small arms fire, and got used to it. When the 51st Highland Division on the follow-up in the perimeter of the bridgehead took a pasteing from the Hun shell fire, a number of 'exhaustion' casualties came back in groups and passed through to Major Tommy Richardson, the Psychiatric Adviser to the 3rd Canadian Division. He was a Scotsman; a very good practical type.

Deserters: Shoot Them!

Amongst the all too many soldiers coming back from the line without permission were two young men from the Gorbals in Glasgow. "What is your civilian occupation" asked Tommy Richardson. "Thieving, Sir" they replied. "Right" said Tommy, "Don't you realise the golden chances you are missing? In a few days the advance will take you through France with easy pickings from the German prisoners—their watches, pockets full of francs they did not have time to spend, and no-one to say "NO". They looked at each other for a moment, saluted and said; "Can we go back to the line now, Sir". They did! Tommy told me; "My job is to give them incentive to stick it out". Tommy put in a written report saying that the only way to stop soldiers walking out of the lines was to make an example by shooting some as deserters. The Chaplain supported him in this, saying that these men were leaving gaps in the line and betraying their comrades. The report was duly sent to the Brigadier, who decided not to pass it on to the General.

3rd Canadian Division Praise Us

I was happy to receive a letter from the Assistant Director of Medical Services of the 3rd Canadian Division, as follows:

1. The medical unit of 102 sub-beach area and surgical teams 32 Casualty Clearing Station have done most excellent work in the assault.
2. Many British and Canadian lives have been saved by the rapid evacuation and high standard of surgical operative ability provided by these units.
3. The cases which did not require operation received first class medical care during the evacuation.
4. As ADMS for the 3rd Canadian Division it is a great privilege for me to have such a well trained group of officers and men under my command for the task which has been accomplished.
5. The GOC has expressed his deep appreciation for the splendid care of his troops and now wishes to pass his grateful thanks with my own officers and men of the units concerned.

This message was most encouraging for all concerned. It was good to have the occasional pat on the back both for officers and men alike. Especially with the number of orders and counter-orders we were receiving involving constant movement usually without the assistance of the Military Police. However, we learnt from our mistakes, faced our problems and solved them.

6th Canadian CCS

On the 12th July, the 6th Canadian CCS moved in next door, fresh from England under the 1st British Corps. I was ordered to go forward to recce the 6th Airbourne Division HQ for a possible FDS on the east flank of the River Orne, six hundred yards from the enemy. This I did and found that there were four quarries in a line, with the steep sides towards the Germans. I was then told to move half my Unit with Field Surgery and the Blood Transfusion Unit over the canal and the River Orne to reach the 6th Airborne Division who were holding the east flank. I asked for a Movement Order, as this was essential for all units joining columns of trucks, tanks etc. The Military Police had to hold up a column at specific times to allow other vehicles to join the column. The roads were narrow, and traffic blocks caused absolute chaos. Our problem was getting the ambulance cars through. So I asked again for a Movement Order but did not get it, the Brigadier merely replying, "Petty will get through all right". I did, by sneaking a truck in here and there when the Military Police were not looking.

Surgical Unit in a Quarry

Brigadier Wallace decided on the 15th July, that he should have the most advanced surgical unit in military history! The site selected for this was in a quarry, but this was just fifty yards away from a junction where five roads met. This was the most shocking technical error that any officer could make. I had learnt in my early training as a sixteen-year-old Corporal in the Officers Training Corps at Berkhamstead School, *never* to put a site on cross roads for enemy automatically to pinpoint.

That night the enemy dropped a bomb straight down the face of the quarry producing a direct hit where Major Jordan was operating on a wounded man. The Major had a piece of shrapnel in the back of his head, the anaesthetist escaped, unscathed, the two nursing orderlies were wounded. Then a few days later Major Jordan died. We had terrific thunderstorms for a few days with extremely heavy rain, and both the Field Surgical and Field Transfusions Units were flooded out to a depth of over one foot. The Airborne Sappers were very good at pumping us out time and time again.

Our rations were tinned meat and hard biscuit, which we thought were harder than dog biscuits (they certainly looked similar), and even those with sound teeth complained of the soreness of gums. I suggested to our Cook that he crush them up with a hammer, and mix them with tinned meat and local vegetables, producing a passable, sustaining meal of stew. After a week we had 'ten day' bread flown in for all casualty units, which was exceptionally white and soft, like cotton-wool. Apparently this was bleached to prevent it from going stale. Eventually the Army Catering Corps arrived to bake fresh bread, and I noticed a couple of our German wounded breaking their ration of bread and feeling it with amazement; they had not seen or eaten anything like it for years.

Appeal for Gumboots !

The weather had dried slightly by 23rd July and we moved our Field Surgical Unit out of the wettest part of the quarry. I had made a verbal appeal to the Quartermaster General at Corps HQ for six pairs of gumboots for use by those operating all day (and sometimes all night) in 12 ins of water. I was very much afraid that they would develop 'trench feet' and become incapacitated. He told me "There is not one pair of gumboots in the whole of France, but I can put in a 'whitehot indent' as the cable across the Channel has just been linked up". Twenty four hours later, the gumboots were delivered to me in the quarry. The officers and men were very impressed by this postal service. The fact that we could have anything necessary that we asked for, was a big morale booster.

On the morning of the 26th July I visited the Corps Headquarters, and found the St Aubin road was unusually empty as the enemy had been shelling us.

Heavy Shelling

A column had stopped on the road ahead, so we pressed on to overtake them. Shells fell into the field nearby, and we watched as two hit the village on the crest of the hill. One shell hit the road thirty yards in front of us, and we moved forward with another jeep and a 15cwt truck. We went through St Aubin village very fast swinging from side to side, and felt the blast of one shell in the middle of the village which rocked our jeep. Driver Keeley, an excellent youngster, drove well. When a shell burst in the road ahead of us, the 15cwt truck in front of us stopped short. I cursed him and told him to keep moving; he did, and I felt better. Unpleasant, but also exciting for a few moments, and curiously I felt no fear, which afterwards surprised me. We were very lucky, because at this point the Germans had been firing on open sights.

On 29th July about thirty bombs dropped on Ecarde village, with heavy shelling of the Ecarde/York Bridge road. I found that I could sleep between the bangs but the high-pitched hum of the mosquitoes around the head was worse. The mosquitoes got so bad that I made curtains of surgical gauze for the entrance of my slit trench (one advantage of being in a medical unit). I often wondered when lying in my trench when they were straffing, should I keep my tin helmet on my head and face ,or over my balls? I decided that if I got shot through the head, I would have no further use for the other appendages anyway, so I opted for the DSO. In the First World War, the DSO stood for "Doodles Shot Off", not uncommon when the Germans advanced in line firing from the hip.

Major Hugh Smith

I heard on 31st July that my friend Major Hugh Smith had been killed by sniper fire when on his way from base to see me. We had had similar marital troubles, and a lot in common. He was a very fine officer, with a great sense of humour. That day I interviewed the Quartermaster over a deficiency in our blankets, and instead of the massive amount of 151 blankets deficient, I found nil. I was a bit fed up of doing his job for him, and was getting physically overtired, and finding it increasingly difficult to settle down to anything.

The Brigadier Visits Us

We were then visited on 1st August by Brigadier Wallace, who suggested a few 'bull' improvements for the Director General Army Medical Services inspection, which was to take place on 3rd August. On the night of the 2nd/3rd August at about 01.00 hours, ten 105 shells landed in our FDS field. The Germans had done the obvious by shelling the five crossroads. Corporal Jevons had a shrapnel wound through his head, with herniation of the brain. A shell landed between Sergeant Mace and Sergeant Page lying in their trench. Sergeant Page lost most of the fingers of his left hand, with also an open fracture of the patella, plus calf wounds. I attended to Jevons, Page was sent straight for operation. Jevons was unconscious, but I tried blood transfusions anyway, but he died in about half an hour. Father Costello of the Commandos was with him before he died. It was amazing how the Padres sprang from nowhere, just at the right time. Jevons was a very good fellow and had been attending a casualty at the time he was hit—but no medals for him! Sergeant

Page cracked jokes with his stretcher bearers on his way to his operation saying "In-ah, out-Ah" all the way. The best sergeant that I had had—it would be! Staff Sergeant Mace was unscathed but all his belongings were blown to bits, including some of the clothes he had on! Major Strang operated on Page, as he had particularly asked me to let him stay. I'd hoped to get the Unit out of that damned quarry without any deaths, but it was asking too much; we expected to get casualties here—and we got them!

Lt General Sir Arthur Alexander Hood Inspects Us

On the 4th August, we had this inspection by Lt General Sir Arthur Alexander Hood, the Director General of Medical Services accompanied by Major General Tomlinson, Director of Medical Services 21 Army Group, plus a few Brigadiers thrown in for good measure. The men were paraded for General Hood and listened to him congratulating them on behalf of the people of England as they were staffing the most advanced Surgical Centre in military history! Which wasn't a lot of comfort to us. I had asked the CO of the 6th Paratroop Gunners the previous evening if he would put up a barrage at 1305 hours, i.e. five minutes after the General and Brigadier had arrived. "Why?" he said. "Because General Hood is coming with all the Medical Brass in Europe for a front line inspection, and I want to see them duck". The Gunners CO grinned and said that if his operations allowed it he would, but they were rationed and if they had an emergency it would take up their supplies. Alas, due to the German shelling, their total ration was exhausted and the following morning Brigadier Porritt(who had thought this plan very funny) told the Director General, who, I am glad to say, laughed too, and I got let off.

When he referred to our casualties Brigadier Wallace said; "We must take the pluses with the minuses ! !"

Some of the officers were moaning and 'bellyaching' about the unnecessary waste of life when the FDS was not fully employed. Couldn't I send the FDS back? Couldn't I get them out? I told them that the Brigadier and General Hood knew the position, and that the Medical Officers must remain with me, and that I was staying until told otherwise. It was difficult enough, God knows, to stick it out, but a damn sight worse when one had to put up with 'bellyaching' officers who should invariably know better, and who then put the responsibility of further casualties on my shoulders. I decided that I needed to get drunk to escape them, but there wasn't enough gin or whisky to do that. So that evening I walked around to Colonel McEwan, ADMS to the 6th Airborne and asked him what he did with his officers who 'bellyached'. He offered to come back with me, and as we had a few drinks he told us stories of what his own people had been through, how twelve Medical Officers from his Division were lost, some in Glider flights when they landed behind enemy lines before the main assault on the beach. He finished up by telling us of the necessity of having the FDS this side of the river, because the line was thinly held, and if the bridges were blown they would have no surgery or medical attention. He said that we were all there to do a job 'Army Style'. After this talk I felt a good deal better and went to bed worn out.

Danger of Malaria

In the early part of August, the new Assistant Director of Hygiene 1st Corps, Lt Colonel Marco came to see me. I had found, in the pools of water in the marshy ground, mosquito larvae lying on the surface of the water. This was the larvae of the Anophiles Mosquito capable of carrying in its salivary glands the parasite of Malaria. We had some troops with us who had served in the Mediterranean and North Africa, who might have been carrying the Anophiles Mosquito parasite in their blood, and accordingly I had notified the previous Deputy Assistant Director of Hygiene, a bombastic young man, who had landed on D Day on his head, so that he was seen careering round on his commandeered motorcycle with an ostentatious bandage on his forehead chasing the Goddess Hygea! He was a self-opinionated, bumptious little man, seldom seen far from base HQ. However, Colonel Marco confirmed my orders locally that all sections of troops would pour oil on the surface of the pools and marshy ground, which would asphyxiate the larvae breathing below the surface. Prevention being better than cure—we had no malaria.

Canadian Nurses Join Us

We had a very welcome message from DDMS; "We are taking on eight Canadian Nursing Sisters, 12 Pioneers, and 10 RAMC". They were to work with us and they turned out to be a fine, practical lot with a great sense of humour, and quite capable of looking after themselves. Their attitude to Senior Officers was very different from our own Queen Alexandra's Imperial Military Nursing Service and we had more frequent casual visits from senior officers. I remember one day, Brigadier Fenwick walked in when a Sister was on her knees picking up bits of glass, and said "Praying, Sister". With a waggle of her bottom she looked up and retorted; "This place is lousy with brasshats". He smiled at this observation and stopped to chat.

We had a whole series of orders to move, and then cancellations in twelve days. There was little sleep and exhausted troops, who constantly had to erect tentage and equipment. I don't think we had a single tent ,vehicle or stretcher that was not bullet holed. It was quite amazing how we did not have a single casualty of our own men at this time; God was certainly with us. However from 13th August we were working up to twenty hours per session, with up to 1500 casualties a day.

Mobile Surgical Unit—Very Mobile

Hardly a day or night went by when we were on the move again, packing, down with the tents, and off. We always went forward, never retreated. Then the column would halt at a planned stop. I would alight with a couple of officers to have a careful look at the chosen field, and stroll across it, staring at the cows. There was a Standing Order that no Unit would enter any open space to put up tentage until it had been swept by the Sappers with their mine detectors. Not always did I wait for them to arrive. I would walk in through the gate, look around for cattle, and if there were none wait until the Sappers arrived. When I did not wait for the Sappers but walked into the field to allot spaces, my men would remark; "Mad Gerry is just asking to be blown up". Once the Sapper NCO in charge of mine detection came up to me and said; "Sir, it is against orders to open up your Dressing Station until cleared by us". I replied; "You have your tasks to do, so carry on, but your work here has already been done by the cattle who are happily munching the grass over the whole area we need". A smart salute was followed by a sly grin and so my troops followed my orders and set up the tentage.

Meeting Monty

I met Monty several times while I was in France. He had two magnificent caravans, one he used as an office, the other his living quarters. On one occasion he was given a German 'baby tank', which was complete in every detail but only measured 4 ft x 3 ft. Attached to the tank was a long electric cable which was controlled from its starting point, and on reaching its target visibly, the button was pressed and the explosive content blew up.

Sloppy Soldiers

Monty had a hearty dislike of fat majors, and fortunately for me I was in the peak of condition after several months training with the Commando's, so I was lean and very fit. He had great qualities and made frequent contact with the other ranks. He also made a point of all his troops wearing what was most comfortable during the action, but this led to slovenliness when the men lost pride in their battle dress. I know that I have mentioned this before, but I found it difficult to lead men and officers under stress without firm, but just discipline in their manner, bearing and dress.

My Kent Cottage Destroyed

It was while I was in France that I had news of my cottage in Kent—The Lodge at the entrance to Lullingstone Castle—being bombed by a V1, the roof completely blown off. It had then been ransacked by vandals. I therefore applied for compassionate leave which was promptly granted. I had had all my civilian clothing stolen, which included six suits and numerous shirts, but the most valuable thing of all stolen was a small mahogany travelling doctor's pharmacy of over a hundred years old. There were nine slots in this for the small, square bottles containing pills of Hyoscine, Opium, different forms of purgative, Aloes, Rhubarb, etc. There was a small crystal mortar and pestle, a tiny scale balance with weights from half a gain upwards. This was irreplaceable, and I was more upset over this than anything else.

When I went to see the DAQMG of the 3rd Canadian Division, he already knew that I had a divorce on my plate, so he gave me compassionate leave for the loss of my house, provided that he personally telephoned my lawyer in London and so dealt with the two problems. This was help indeed. When I got into London, the lawyer had made all the arrangement for my marriage to the beautiful Diana and we got married in the Registry Office in Victoria Road. Attending were just a few relatives, who were completely unmoved by the shuddering bangs and loud crack of the anti-aircraft guns. The Registrar also ignored the 'air raid in progress' sirens and continued undisturbed.

There was great difficulty in finding any hotel room in London. This struck me with amazement that in spite of the blitz and V-One's the civilian population seemed immune to fear. Every room seemed to be booked, and so after a telephone call to my mother, she invited us to spend the first few days of our honeymoon with her—and this solved our problem. I felt quite thankful to get into the train at Paddington for Torquay, away from all the bangs, shell fire and bombs.

9. Nervous Exhaustion Centre

When we moved further into Belgium I was responsible for a Nervous Exhaustion Centre, which had to be sited within the sound of the guns. All cases of collapse or doubtful illness would be sent to us by the Regimental Medical Officers, so I called on Madame Etienne de Stas Richel, with a view to taking over her charming chateau. She was a dignified, gracious lady who had maintained her responsibilities with the Resistance Movement, and had buried guns in her garden. When a young German Oberleutnant had walked in to say he was going to search her house, she rounded on him and said; "How dare you give me orders. Go back and send your most senior officer and I will instruct him myself". I said that I thought she was a very brave lady indeed, but she replied; "That was nothing, I responded to the Germans by telling them to mind their manners, and never send me an officer who was not of senior rank again. I got what I expected, profuse apologies, clicking heels and a smart salute. I had no interference after that and continued to supervise the burying of arms in my garden by night".

Venereal Diseases

I had posted to me at the Centre, two Venereal Disease Consultants, Captains Blair and Taffs, together with ten RAMC orderlies trained in the treatment of VD, i.e. with daily injections of Penicillin. We had divided the Centre into two parts—one for Nervous Exhaustion and the other half for VD. We averaged at that time 6-10 cases of VD daily, very little considering the number of troops which was in the region of 100,000. With the advent of Penicillin there was a marked decrease in the ravages of VD. We now knew that gonorrhea could be cleared in 2 to 4 days and syphilis in one month, compared to the previous treatment of two years intravenous injection of Novarsenobillon.

In World War 1 there were 10,000 regularly treated at the Military Hospital in Rouen for VD (I learnt these facts from the bachelor Bishop of Llandaff, Dr Timothy Rees, a friend and patient of mine before the War. He was the very best of parish priests and disliked his administrative work as a bishop. He had been the senior chaplain at the Venereal Disease Hospital in Rouen for four years in the First World War).

A French physician a hundred years ago was observed to remark that; "Any fool can diagnose gonorrhea, but God alone knows when it can be cured!" Sir Girling Ball, Dean of Barts, told us students in our final year, "A man is not a man until he has had gonorrhea three times! After all, I bought my house in Harley Street with my fees from clap".

A Russian General Calls

We had an official visit from General Osipov, who was the equivalent of a DMS when he was in charge of the medical administration of the sick and wounded in Stalingrad. He came to see how our Unit was being run and made detailed notes particularly about the treatment for VD with Penicillin. I was told to answer every question, and tell him all he wanted to know. At the same time, the War Office sent a similar mission of our senior officers to Stalingrad who were entertained for a week, but shown nothing! The War Office then threatened to withdraw their mission and give no facilities to the Russian mission in France and Belgium; this produced the necessary result.

I warned some Polish Officers who were in the psychiatric half of the Unit that General Osipov was coming to inspect us, and that although the Russians had been their enemy, they were now fighting for us against the common enemy; I expected them to exercise control. However, my words went unheeded. Two young officers were lying on the grass when this young, blonde general in his striking green uniform with riding breeches went by. He nodded to them but both heads turned sharply away, and they spat on the grass in contempt. His interpreter, a Major in the Intelligence Corps, told me that the General said that, had that conduct happened in Russia, they would have been shot.

After lunch with us, which was improved by the Sergeant Cooks' efforts on the Black Market in buying icing sugar and a curious bottle of simply dreadful wine (which Osipov politely said he liked), he sent for the cooks and congratulated them on the special cake. They had baked it with the Union Jack and Red Flag with the Hammer and Sickle in icing sugar on the top. I asked the General one question only; that was having regard to the fact that we were

Allies and that I was showing him all the advances in medicine and surgery, would the Russians after the War permit visits from our doctors to them? The interpreter told me that the General did not want to commit himself.

(Considering that we after the War, and during it, discovered more new pharmaceutical preparations than the whole of Europe and the USA, it is surprising, is it not, that nothing new had come out from Russia since Professor Pavlov and the birth of the psychological experiments on dogs' stomachs years before. It seems that Professor Pavlov had been the only name to congratulate them, but he lived in Imperialist Russia not the Communist Russia of today. Undoubtedly, their present knowledge of psychotropic drugs is greater than ours, and their misuse of them for political reasons on their fellow countrymen is an abomination of interference with the mental and physical liberty of the human subject. Instead of relieving depression and mental torture, they reproduce these symptoms to increase the feeling of guilt in the Russian who does not obey the Party lines).

Shell Shock—Battle Fatigue

With the two halves of the Unit divided in the spacious grounds of the Chateau, the cases of nervous exhaustion were sent back by the Regimental Medical Officers. (These were known as 'shell shock' in the first World War, and once they were in the line of evacuation from the danger and noise of the guns in the Military Hospital, they were a 'write off' as far as recovery and further service.) The Symptoms were tremors of the hands and gross anxiety, all of which invited sympathy from friends and relatives, and the public in general. Dr Coué introduced a new mass treatment which involved large groups respectively singing; "I am getting better, better, better, all the time, every day".

In World War Two, nervous exhaustion was the only diagnosis permitted for the troops evacuation to the Exhaustion Centre at the Chateau. The words 'Shell Shock' were expressly forbidden to all Medical Officers. The Americans used the words "Battle Fatigue", and in their bomber crews, pilots and crew members after thirty sorties were temporarily withdrawn for a rest period of a month This was routine and very sensible.

Each man was interviewed by our Psychiatrist Tommy

Richardson, and the Medical Officers he had taught in history taking. Every man then was given a Seconal Capsule every four hours, and put to sleep on stretchers. They were woken up for meals and the urine bottle, but spent most of the twentyfour hours asleep. After this complete rest 60% recovered and could return to the Battalion the following day. The other 40% were kept for a further period at the Centre, but still within the sound of the guns, and finally 10% were sent back to the Base Hospital. Once in safety and away from the sound of the gunfire, their recovery was not always complete, in as much as some of them had private emotional anxieties, and the effect of these difficulties produced functional disorders which were physically incapacitating.

I remember one case of Tommy Richardson's particularly, as I sat in with him at the time that the soldier was carried in on the stretcher. His Medical Officer had written; "Suffering from shell blast a few feet away, he is without detectable physical injury, but apparent paralysis of both legs yet has not lost consciousness"; this was a good report from a good MO. So Tommy Richardson gave the soldier an 'abreaction'; this was a small amount of intravenous injection of Pentathol to induce drowsiness but not unconsciousness. This was given while he was still on his stretcher supported by trestles off the ground. Tommy then blew up a paper bag and said to the man; "Did it happen like this?" He clapped his hands bursting the bag, just by the man's ear with the normal loud 'bang'. The man jerked upwards, flung himself on the grass and then staggered to his feet. Pointing a finger, Tommy shouted; "Look, you can walk". The man sat down and burst into tears, and then his analysis began. Tommy found out that apart from being extremely short of sleep, he had letters in his pockets from 'friends' in his home village, telling him about his wife going around with another man. Consciously, all he wanted to do was to go back and deal with the home situation, but he knew that this could not be done in reality. He was a good soldier with a good record of service. Why did he have these symptoms? He did not conjure them up. Subconsciously he had imitated the symptoms of a severe condition that he had been aware of as a child, when he had seen an old uncle who was paralysed from the waist down, sat in the best chair by the fire in the family home. His mother had looked after the uncle devotedly, and he came first in the family for attention. This illness produced sympathy, love, affection, and attention—all of which this man craved for himself. Who doesn't? He was referred back to Base Hospital with a recommendation that he be given sick or compassionate leave to deal with his home problem. This was a very unusual request and we hoped that it was granted (so long as it was not known to his companions), as subconscious imitation of these symptoms could occur.

10. The Horror of Breendonk Prison

After the breakthrough on 31st August, I was sent forward by Brigadier Wallace to find a suitable site for a Minor Accident and Sickness Hospital in the Brussels area. Driver Keeley loaded us up with petrol and rations. Fighting was at a standstill. This was primarily because the Army had done a Blitzkreig, but the supplies of petrol, ammunition and food, had failed to keep pace with the advance. I went to the local policeman in a village north of Brussels who had himself walked out of jail the day before, where he had been awaiting trial for burying guns in his garden. When the Germans had slipped off quietly and hurriedly, he found all the doors in the jail suddenly unlocked.

He took me to a charming Chateau owned by M. Marcel Lamot who had the decorators in already and his gardeners back on the grounds immediately. I roughly measured the area required and found it too small for my purposes. He was looking very forlorn and depressed at having his home taken away by his liberators, the very day it had been restored to him. I said; "Monsieur Lamot, I am sorry but your home is too small". He could hardly express his relief, and out came the champagne and the cigars! He owned breweries in Malines and Brussels and had been allowed by the invading Hun to continue brewing on condition that half his product was reserved for the German Army. They had put in their own Commissar accountants to check the amounts. Marcel told me; "We Belgians are used to being invaded, and we kept two sets of books, one for the invader and the Income Tax man, the other for ourselves".

Marcel became our frequent companion and was very helpful. He wanted to be seen with a British Officer, as he was still unsure whether his enforced deliveries of beer to the German Army would be held against him as a collaborator. His English was fluent; he had spent part of his life in England before the War, and the Lamot Brewery Company was formed and registered in England. He asked me that if I had any wounded officer coming through my hands who would be returning to England would I let him know? I asked why and he said; "I want him to buy for me as many of my shares in Britain as he can, as I have an accumulation of four years interest for all shareholders". I told him that he was a pleasant rogue but that I had no such casualties at present. Typically Marcel found his officer and whether the deal took place or not I do not know but I expect it did!

Collaborators Imprisoned

From his Chateau, Marcel Lamot took me to see Breendonk Fort, some sixteen miles from Brussels. This was a ghastly horror of a prison, in charge of the Gestapo who from 1942 to 1944 had starved, tortured and murdered Belgians accused of resistance. These prisoners wore Khaki uniform, the Jews had pale blue with round caps, and they were housed in the second half of the prison. The surviving Belgian prisoners had been freed the previous day; now I found that the Fort was filled with two hundred prisoners, men and women who had been collaborators. The women's heads were all shaved. This distinction indicated that they had been the mistresses of the German Army and Gestapo.

The Camp Commandant was of the Resistance Movement, wearing an armband denoting this fact and had a rifle over his shoulder. He showed us around. I asked him if my Unit could be of any medical help, but he declined my offer saying; "The present prisoners won't need much medical help". I then watched the long queue of men and women lining up with their tins to collect their ration of soup and bread, getting the same rations as their own countrymen had had earlier from the Gestapo.

Belgian Gestapo

The average large room was for fortyeight people in the Fort; three tiered bunks with shelves for toilet articles, tables, stools, bowls and a stove. The perpetual dampness in the half-underground Fort meant that clothes and towels were never dry. One large room had been converted into numerous very narrow cells, three foot wide and deep. The prisoners could not lie down, and barely sit. The Commandant took us to see two young men chained by ankles and wrists to the wall. They looked about nineteen years old and so I asked why they were there. He told me; 'These are Belgian Gestapo, who were more brutal than the German Gestapo. They volunteered for their job and were sent to Poland for six months training. They came back de-humanised! They tortured and murdered their fellow countrymen. They will be shot tomorrow". Their protests of innocence were unavailing. This must have been the last time that the black posts outside were used. Seeing these two young men, wide eyed wth fear, awaiting death, I felt nothing but anger.

The SS had boasted that they had the most terrible place in Western Europe in Breendonk. There was only one humane man on the staff who was the Catholic Priest of the German Army and gave succour to the dying, according to his calling. He also secretly took messages to relatives of the prisoners and brought answers back. Monseigneur Gromann had to wear the swastika on his uniform, but he was no Nazi. He had to obey official orders. However, his chief weapons were reticence and prayer.

In the empty cell next to the two Belgian Gestapo prisoners, the previous inmate had been there for three months, and had scratched a cross to mark days of the week in a monthly calendar on the bricks in the wall of his cell. This in his solitude was the record of the passing of time. In a lower brick he had scratched; "La vengeance des morts sera terrible en 1945"; (The vengeance of the dead will be terrible in 1945). We got there in 1944 when I noted this.

5,000 Belgians went through the gates of Breendonk, and were of all types—professors, ministers, writers, labourers, bankers etc. Professor Leon E Halkin has written the book; "A L'Ombre de la mort" (The shadow of death). In this he describes his own tortures as well as others. During interrogation he had two handcuffs attached to each ankle and wrist. He remained in this squatting position, starved and beaten for fortyeight hours. The sweat ran off his forehead to form a pool around his feet. He said; "It is easy to make a person scream, but few of us talked".

It was difficult to organise a resistance plan in the barrack room which resembled a morgue, more than a meeting place. He remembers calling out the names of his fellow inmates.
"L'Abbe Boufflette" . . . "He is in hospital".
"M. Ferrion . . . "Il est mort". (dead)
"M. Storey" . . . "Il est mort". (dead)

Professor Halkin said; "While we were making every effort to live, death was striking us down on all sides".

The Gallows

I saw one of the execution areas; the gallows inside a corner of

21 Breendonk—the half underground headquarters of King Leopold of Belgium, during the 1914-18 War, were used by the Germans to imprison Belgians

22 Breendonk fences and watchtower—sentries with machine guns shot escapees from the concentration camp

23 Breendonk torture chamber otherwise called the interrogation room. The prisoners were stripped naked, their hands manacled behind their backs and hoisted high on the pulley. If answers were slow two electric wires applied to any part of the anatomy helped the screaming. The photograph does not show the runnels to wash away the blood in the concrete floor from lashings, cuts, and eventual dropping of victims bare footed on the sharp edges of the triangular pieces of wood. I saw the dried blood in the floor, not all was washed away.

24 Breendonk Fort National Memorial: Chamber. Here slept 48 Belgians where the floors and walls were always damp, as Breendonk was half underground

had not been investigated, as the Commandant of the Resistance told me the two young Belgian SS were to be shot immediately after our arrival at the Fort! Were they? I hope so!

Note when reading the correspondence between myself and Professors Levy and Halkin, there is expressed disbelief about various aspects of Breendonk. I can only repeat what I SAW on August 31st, 1944; that there were empty, paper thin coffins on the ground, and iron hoops that they pushed the coffins through, and the whole of this area covered in white ash.

In order to prove what I saw in Breendonk—that the white ashes were human—I visited the Crematoria just outside Cardiff in November 1980. I went there for the specific purpose of studying the appearance of human ash during the process of cremation. Here, they have a row of gas fired burners producing a temperature of 600 degrees centigrade. The whole coffin with the body in it is taken from the Chapel and put straight into the burner. Many people query whether the body is removed from the often magnificently decorated coffin, inferring sometimes that the Funeral Director uses the coffin again for the next burial or cremation. This is not so. There is a Code of Ethics, and members of The Society of The Federation of British Cremation Authorities lay down very strict rules governing this.

In Cardiff I watched the whole process through a sliding thick steel panel periodically during two hours. The wood of the coffin burns furiously and helps burn the soft fatty tissue which become ignited, with the roaring two foot high flames. Gradually the body disintegrates, the skull falls off and the pelvis with the spinal vertebrae and limbs break up. Many metal articles drop through the grid on which the coffin lies, such as rings, artificial hip joints of nickel which were used many year ago.

I reported back my observation to Mr M Summers, the head of the large family concern of Undertakers here in Cardiff, who had kindly arranged for me to go to the Crematoria. I then collected typewritten foolscap files, newspapers, glossy magazines and papers, and put them on a 2 ins iron mesh grid over the flames of my barbecue I had used in my garden. After the paper burnt, the residue was black. In the breeze a few dark grey flakes floated off, but I emphasise that the ash was *black* not grey, not white! !

REPRODUCED FROM LEAFLET

By law, on the 19th August 1947, and voted unamimously by Parliament, was established the

NATIONAL MEMORIAL OF FORT BREENDONK

The Memorial, which is an independent public undertaking and the only institution of its kind in Western Europe, has as its aims:

a) to ensure the conservation in perpetuity of the Fort and the objects therein;

b) to take all necessary steps to keep alive the memory of the events which took place at Breendonk,to encourage the civic spirit, and to promote the education of young people in the love of their country.

In the name of the governing board, entrusted by HM the King of the Belgians with this imposing charge, we welcome you here and wish you an instructive visit.

*

Men have fought at Breendonk.

For other men it has meant downfall and disgrace: they lost all dignity and were finally vanquished for having believed that forces could win and that democratic Belgium could be crushed.

The nazi regime found its own end through its contempt of humanity.

Those who refused to despair secured victory for the democratic powers.

They suffered, many died.

That is why today Breendonk is a place for meditation.

*

Breendonk is a truly historic building. The rooms where the nazis penned their prisoners have been carefully reconstructed. Only those places which present no historic interest have been re-arranged. Everyone is free to inspect the fort as he wishes. The route indicated on the map is an example of a quick (1 -1½ hour) complete four.

In order to ensure historical accuracy, the recorded evidence of former prisoners is put at the disposal of visitors. This can be listened to by pressing the buttons at the places marked with a cross on the map.

In the notes that follow, the numbers correspond to those marked on the map:

1. **Entrance-gate**—In 1914, the flooring at the entrance was removable, thus creating a drawbridge which prevented access to the Fort. Left of the gate a tablet commemorating the siege of 1914; on the right side the one concerning 1940-44.

2. **SS Canteen**—The Fort was used as an SS concentration camp from 20th September 1940 until 31st August 1944. The front part served as quarters for the guards and for certain SS troops. Here was the SS canteen. The Tribunal which was set up there on the rare occasions when legal procedure was respected has been reconstructed: 15 persons were tried here, and executed afterwards. Nearly all the 3,000 other prisoners at Breendonk were never brought before a trial, the SS concentration camps being usually reserved either for suspects who could not be tried by the military authorities or convicts having served their sentence but still under close observation by the Secret State Police (Gestapo).

2a. **Jacques Ochs memorial room**—Drawings, paintings and literary works inspired during captivity. The main part of this unique set consists of drawings which Jacques Ochs, the great Belgian drawer and painter, was allowed to make when a prisoner in Breendonk in 1940, 1941 and 1942. He succeeded in getting them out of the camp against the will of the nazi wardens who intended keeping them as a private collection about their victims.

3. **Cells**—The "barracks" of the fort consist of 14 casemates, two of which were converted into cells by the erection of brick partitions They were used either for prisoners punished for the so-called "discipline" or for isolating those awaiting interrogation. The walls bear numerous inscriptions, some of which form real testaments.

4. **Second series of cells.**

5. **Reconstruction of an average room**—Three-tiered bunks with straw mattresses (48), shelves for toilet articles, tables, stools, bowls, a stove etc. The dampness was such in these rooms that the towels never dried. All the room are alike. This is the only one open to visitors.

6. **Mortuary**—The bodies of those who succumbed to maltreatment or exhaustion were brought into this former powder-room. It was here that the bodies were put into coffins.

7. **Torture Chamber**—In the autumn of 1942 this former ammunition store was completely walled in except on the side which today still forms

the entrance. The room was converted so as to permit "re-inforced" interrogation—in other words, the torture of prisoners.

8. **Hutments**—From September to the end of November 1940, no "racial" discrimination was made among prisoners. Subsequently, however, "Jews" were lodged in the left wing of the barracks and "Aryans" in the right wing. Finally, the "Jews" were denied the benefit of concrete rooms and relegated to huts like these.

9. **Museum**—Here the museum has been installed in an infirmary constructed in 1941 and 1942 but not much used.

GROUND FLOOR

Room a - -History of Breendonk—Origin; construction of the fort (1906-14); the siege of 1914; GHQ of 1940.

Room b—Occupied Belgium—Various documents about the life in the country under nazi-yoke.

Room c - Breendonk, SS Camp—Illustrating the prisoners' life at Breendonk—uniforms, tools, objects which belonged to prisoners and to their guards, documents concerning captivity. Models showing the work done by prisoners: the Fort was covered by a mountain of earth measuring about 250,000 cubic metres; the prisoners removed this, using the earth to raise the outside edge of the moat.

Room d - The trials—For 4 years, Breendonk was a prison for patriots who had never been sentenced by law. It was ruled by lawlessness and brutality. Between 1946 and 1949 some of those responsible for Breendonk were caught and tried by the Belgian military Courts. Posters proclaiming the death sentence of some of these men are to be found here, as well as photographs and documents relating to the trial of the Breendonk war criminals. German SS man: Sturbannführer (major) Schmitt, former commander of the camp, eight Belgian SS men, three Belgian civilian workers and three former inmates who, unable to endure the rigours of Breendonk, had eventually cooperated in the torture of their colleagues (a Belgian nationalist and two German Jews) were also sentenced to death. The remaining criminals could not be traced or have been sentenced to imprisonment.

FIRST FLOOR

Room a - History of nazisme—How dictatorship grew in Germany. Autographs and documents about the SS organization.

Room b-c - The concentration camps—Over all Europe an intricated network of prison camps, where 10 Million people were jailed, more than 9 Million died before and during the war, and hardly 600,000 survived.

10. **Workshop**—The mound reconstructed here gives some idea of the vast amount of earth removed with primitive tools such as spades, pick-axes, wheelbarrows and tipcarts.

11. **Site of executions**—The gallows and firing-squad posts. Few condemned prisoners were executed at Breendonk but betwen 1942 and 1944 the shooting of hostages (groups of ten men chosen at random among the prisoners) was frequent.

12. **Shrine**—This is not a museum. You will find here no documents, no historical reconstructions, no reproductions—only authentic objects which cannot fail to command respect: urns containing the ashes of prisoners of the SS from Auschwitz, Dachau, Neuengamme, Gross Rosen, Flossenbürg, Natzviller and Mauthausen; bullets recovered from the Breendonk execution posts; the chaplain's chalice; a fragment of a Jewish Book of Law found among human ashes at Birkenau, ribbons from the wreaths laid at the foot of the execution posts and gallows. On the altar is the cross which the Austrian chaplain showed to those about to be shot between 1942 and 1943, whom he was sometimes allowed to succour.

13. **Dungeons**—Here, in 1940 and at the beginning of 1941, were the dungeons. They fell out of use when the barrack cells were built and subsequently converted into dark cells.

*

The National Memorial of Fort Breendonk has a heavy task: that of keeping alive the memory of events, some grievous and some glorious; of paying a lasting tribute to men amongst whom were the flower of Belgium; and of using their example to spur young people to serve their country unfalteringly.

From the day on which Breendonk was turned into an SS concentration camp, it became the scene of the most frightening bestiality. The guards fell ever lower. Some of their victims broke down, but most of them, regardless of nationality, had the will to resist the degrading treatment to which they were subjected. Their example shows that brutality will not prevail against a resolute spirit and brotherly unity. The message of Breendonk is not one of hatred but of mutual understanding and of humanity.

(END OF REPRODUCED COPY FROM LEAFLET).

11. Those Breendonk Letters

MEMORIAL NATIONAL
DU FORT DE
BREENDONK
Etabl. public d'Etat.
(Loi 19-8-1947)
Tél 031/866209

30 June 1980

Dr. G. F. PETTY
CARDIFF

Sir,

I am awfully sorry to have delated such a long time my answer to your most friendly and interesting letter of March 27.

It is our mission to write the exact story of Breendonk and to present to the visitors an accurate picture of what happened there under the nazi occupation. I happened myself to be an inmate of the Fort from Nov. 29 1940 until Nov. 20 1941. I escaped to Britain and came back as a War Correspondent. I am now professor at the Catholic University of Louvain and President of the Board of Directors of the National Memorial created at Fort Breendonk by the Belgian parliament. (This to introduce myself . . .)

Your letter is of great importance to us. What happened in the Fort immediately after the liberation are facts with which quite a few of us disagree: we didn't fight the nazis in order to follow their methods but well in order to suppress them . . . for ever(?). I didn't reach Breendonk in 1944 before the 9th of September, visited the place, addressed the detainees and, going back to Brussels, protested with Belgian authorities against the treatment they "enjoyed" there.

But at the time when you visited Breendonk there were no execution places anymore (the nazis suppressed them before going) and there was never anything like an "incineratour": corpses were not burned in Breendonk.

We would be delighted if you publish some pictures of the Memorial in the book you are about to write. I very sincerely hope to be able to help you. If you wish any other document just tell us, we will not fail to send them promptly and without waiting as long as we did now . . .

I am,

Sir,

your most obedient servant,

Prof. Paul M.G. LEVY

President B.D.

29 Gerald Fitzmaurice Petty, TD, FRCGP

[photo by K T Burrows (Photographer),
11 Pontcanna Place, Cardiff]

30 Vught, Holland—this was the nearest other incinerator to Breendonk and therefore a likely site for Breendonk bodies except that with the threat of the progress of the British Forces there would have been no opportunity of getting rid of the bodies. (RSM Meyrick's photograph)

31 Vught, Holland—the prisoner stood on a rocker with a rope around his neck and strangled himself when the rocker moved.

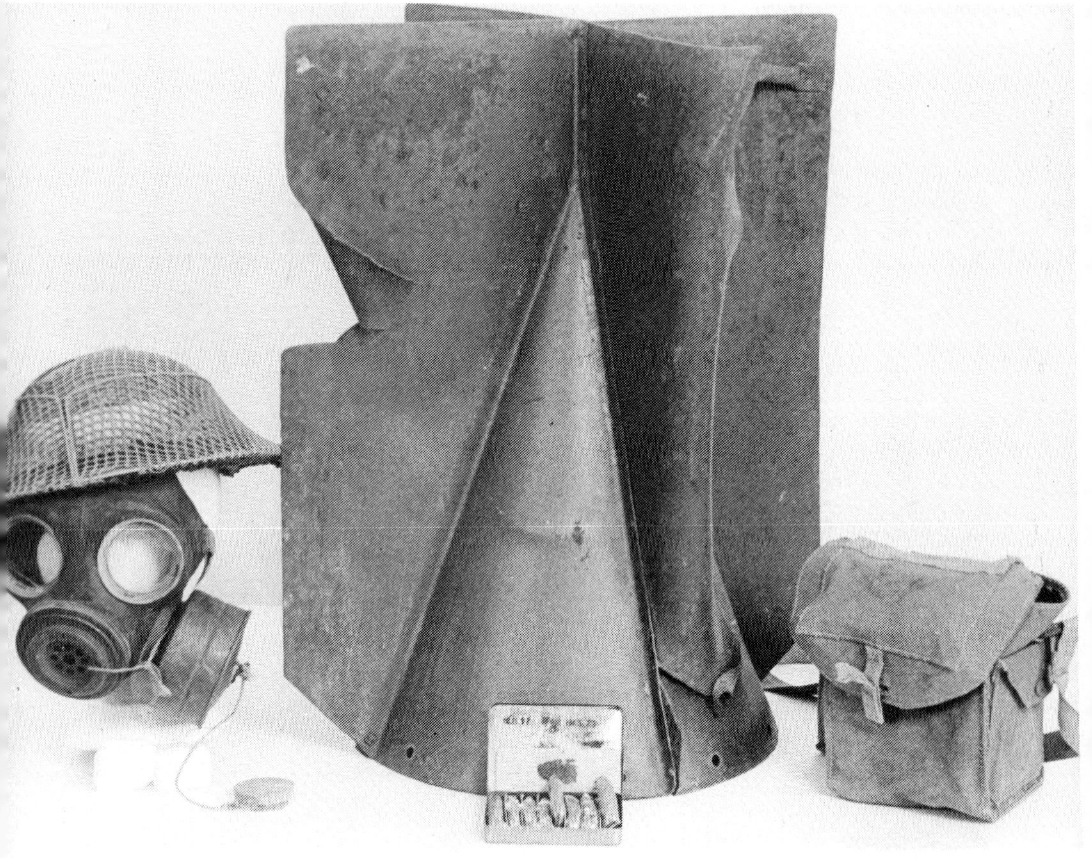

32 (See story on page 23.) At the end of World War Two I am left with :

1) Fins of high explosive oil bomb;
2) Steel helmet with circular white band for easy recognition on the beach, covered with netting for camouflage;
3) Respirator;
4) Tin of ten tubes marked on lid "Ointment anti-Gas" No 5. For decontamination swab off free liquid from skin and apply ointment freely to the affected area. AS SOON AS POSSIBLE. Rub in vigorously for at least 30 seconds. If applied to the skin *before* exposure to an atmosphere containing mustard gas *vapour only*, the ointment will prevent, or lessen the severity of a burn. KEEP AWAY FROM EYES. To obtain ointment from tube, see directions on base of box. TO OBTAIN OINTMENT FROM TUBE. Hold tube at folded end between thumb and forefinger. Flatten end of tube by squeezing. Then holding end so flattened between thumb and forefinger of each hand, tear off end of tube close to fold. 6MB/1/431.

DR. G. F. PETTY

56 PALACE ROAD
LLANDAFF
CARDIFF CF5 2AH
Telephone : Cardiff 561889

11th July 1980

Professor Paul M.G. Levy.
President B.D.
Memorial National Du Fort De
Breendonk.
Belgium.

Dear Professor Levy,

Thank you very much for your letter which I was delighted to receive.

My book which is about the experiences of a Welsh Medical Officer during the War, will, I hope, be published shortly.

I am including with this letter the rough draft of some of my experiences in Belgium when I was in command of No 33 Field Dressing Station, some 250 medical officers and men and I was the Senior Medical Officer attached to the Third Canadian Division landing on the Le Jour (D Day to us) at Bernière sur Mer.

You will see from my record that my observations are my own, and not all drawn from the literature that I later read. I saw the incinerators which had been used up to the time when the Gestapo walked out in a hurry. There were plenty of ashes left and many empty cardboard thin coffins waiting to be used.

I must congratulate you on escaping from Breendonk and returning as a War Correspondent.

When I visited Breendonk last year I took my daughter with me—Dr Geraldine Freeth. I failed to find Marcel Lamot. Madame Stas de Richel, a prominent member of the Resistance movement had also passed away.

I look forward to seeing you. If you are ever in this country be sure to let me know and stay with us, with your wife too.

Yours sincerely,

G.F. Petty.
TD., FRCGP.
Mem BAMM.

15th July 1980

Dear Professor Halkin,

I have been asked to write a book on the experiences of a Welsh Medical Officer during the War, by the Curator of the Welch Regiment Museum.

I landed on Le Jour (D Day to us). Following this after the break-through from the Bridgehead I was sent forward to find a chateau for the care of sick soldiers.

Among other places I was taken to Breendonk after the S.S. had moved out the previous night. I enclose a brief draft of my visit to Breendonk.

I would ask you therefore if you would be kind enough to allow me to publish some observations from A L'Ombre de la Mort.

I have written to Professor Levy to ask for permission of publish photographs of Memorial National du Fort Breendonk. He did not arrive at Breendonk until 9th September and wanted confirmation of what I had seen because of some disagreement as to the conditions.

I have now sent him my personal observations. I felt a deep anger at the appalling senseless savagery of the Huns. I have offered to again return to Breendonk to meet Professor Levy in the future.

Yours sincerely,

G.F. Petty.
TD., FRCGP.
Mem BAMM.

LEON-E. HALKIN

LIEGE, LE
41 RUE DU PERY
10 octobre 1980.

Dr. Gérald-F. Petty,
Palace Road, 56,
Llandaff,
Cardiff CF5 2AH.
South Wales.

Cher Monsieur,

Je suis désolé de répondre si tard à votre aimable lettre du 15 juillet, mal classé en cette période de vacances. Ayez, je vous en prie, l'amabilité d'excuser ce retard.

C'est avec plaisir que je vous autorise à citer des extraits de mon livre *A l'ombre de la mort* qui contient mon témoignage sur Breendonk sous les nazis. Je regrette qu'il n'existe pas de traduction anglaise de cet ouvrage.

Le récit original de votre visite à Breendonk, après la libération, constitue un document passionnant dont l'objectivité sera précieuse aux historiens de la guerre. Je l'ai lu avec intérêt et je le conserve en vous remerciant de me l'avoir envoyé.

Je suis sûr que votre ouvrage sur *Les expériences d'un médecin militair pendant la guerre* intéressera à la fois les spécialistes et le grand public et je me ferai un plaisir de l'acquérir à la Librairie anglaise de Bruxelles, dès sa parution.

Veuillez agréer, Cher Monsieur, l'assurance de mes sentiments les meilleurs.

L.E. Halkin.

(*Readers, please note : letters exactly as written—reprinted with errors made by writers of letters.*)

ENGLISH TRANSLATION

Leon E. Halkin. *Liege, 10 October 1980.*

Dr G.F. Petty,

Dear Sir,

I am most sorry to reply so late to your friendly letter of the 15th July, mislaid at that time of the holidays. Be so kind as to forgive this delay.

With pleasure I authorize you to cite extracts from my book "In the shadow of death' 'which contains my testimony as to Breendonk under the Nazis. I regret there is no English translation of this work.

The original narrative of your visit to Breendonk after the liberation constitutes a fascinating document whose objectivity will be invaluable to historians of the War. I read it with interest and am keeping it with my thanks to you for sending it to me.

I am sure that your work on the Experiences of a Military Doctor in Wartime will interest both specialist historians and the general public. It will be a pleasure for me to get it in the English bookshop in Brussels when it appears.

Assuring you, dear Sir, of my best wishes,

L.E. Halkin.

28th October 1980

Professor Leon E Halkin.
41 Rue de Pery.
Liege.

Dear Professor Halkin,

Thank you for your letter. My apologies for not having answered before.

I enclose copies of my correspondence with Professor Levy. I find his attitude completely in-explicable.

Did he wear the blue striped uniform when he was a prisoner? How did he escape from Breendonk? Was he helped? If so, by whom?

It is nonsense to tell me that "there were no execution places when I arrived there", which was a few hours after the S.S. had left. I saw the ashes still in the incinerator, the pile of carboard thin coffins waiting to be used. The two young Belgians (Gestapo) chained to the wall waiting for their well deserved place in hell.

The people of Belgium have given to the world an example of their sacrifice and having done so those of us who were witness of a part of the appalling slaughter of the Jews in Europe.

On my visit to Belgium I took my daughter Dr Geraldine Freeth who is a doctor in Bournemouth, to visit Breendonk and the value of the personal visit to witness what actually happened must never be forgotten.

My book is waiting to be published and is about the experiences of a Welsh Medical Officer during the War. The chapter about Breendonk is of very great importance. Also I met Tilley Brosens daughter of the Burgomaster of Hoogstraten when I took over the convent for treatment of our soldiers, the memory stands out—never to be forgotten. She saved twelve of our pilots in the R.A.F. She was responsible for the line of evacuation through to France, Spain and then home to England.

She had personal letters expressing the thanks of the Allies from Winston Churchill, Eisenhower and Montgomery under whom I served. She was many times interviewed by the Gestapo as a spy, but on each occasion she talked her way out.

We owe the Belgian people a deep gratitude.

Yours sincerely,

Gerald F Petty

PAUL M.G. LEVY
PROFESSEUR A L'U.C.L.
CHAUSSEE DE TIRLEMONT, 49
5800 GEMBLOUX-SUR-ORNEAU

FERME D'ENEE, LE

Nov. 2nd 1980
Dr.G.F.PETTY
CARDIFF

Dear Dr.Petty,

I am grateful for your kindness and the interesting texts you sent me last July. I would be delighted to see you whenever you come over to Belgium. I was in the U.K. last July when I lectured in Bradford University (Peace Studies) but don't foresee any other crossing of the water in a near future.

I have to stick to my place since I have many things to do here and I wish to lecture up to the"bitter"end . . . I am going to be emeritus at the end of the present academic year.

Breendonk gives also a lot to do:we had trouble these days when former nazis decided to demonstrate in Breendonk on Nov.11th in favour of a general amnesty of the persons condemned for collaboration with the nazis.This is still presented as an actual problem in Belgium and there are some cases(of children and grandchildren of the condemned people) which are not easy to solve.

I say with relief that the Parliament almost unanimously voted to ask the government to forbid the demonstration and that the people who took the initiative capitulated.

And this brings me to your problem. I am sure there was an incinerator in Breendonk but to burn documents and files and not to burn corpses. This is important because it should be said clearly: very often people visiting Breendonk ask for the "crematoria". . . There were none. An other point is that Breendonk was occupied by irregular units after the liberation. And these people arrested a lot of men and women and treated them badly without having any proof that they were culprits. Nobody was ever executed at the time in Breendonk.It was much later that regular tribunals started to work and that people duly tried were condemned.I am personally against death penalty in whatever case.I can tell you that about 2491 death penalties were given by the Belgian tribunals between September 1944 and August 1950.There were 242 executions(including the SS commander and various other criminals who had acted under the occupation in Breendonk). We, the former prisoners, protested against theses ill-treatments immediately after the liberation and we succeeded to have people regularly appointed being put in charge. Therefore,it would be very regrettable nowadays if a book would be published giving people to think that men or women were actually killed in Breendonk after the nazi time. There were no executions there and nobody condemned to death there after 30 Aug.1944.

My remarks, if I may formulate them about your text are the following ones:

first page about Breendonk: Gestapo in charge from 20/9/40 until 31/8/44

—In Breendonk the so-called Jews wore exactly the same uniforms (Belgian army Khaki) as the other prisoners but with a yellow ribbon on the breast. The pale and dark blue striped uniforms were used in Germany, Austria, Poland, Czechoslovakia,Russia and not espeacially for Jews.

—No prisoner was freed on 31/8/44.The remaining prisoners were brought by autobus to Holland(Vught).

page two about Breendonk: nobody had the right at that time to condemn to death or to execute. The black posts were never used for exécution:they symbolise since 1947 the posts which were used by the nazis.

On the other hand all the Gestapo Belgians went with their masters, they didn't stay on the spot and were traced afterwards,sometimes when returning after May 1945,sometimes after being arrested in Germany, sometimes as well disappearing together with the other SS people . . .
page three about Breendonk: what my friend Halkin writes about incinerators and dead bodies is right but *does not* apply to Breendonk. Therefore what you write on this page and on the next one about the ashes does not concern Breendonk.

I remain of course at your disposal.Several books have been written in French,Flemish,German about our Belgian camp.There are references to Breendonk in the Russian and Polish literature.We have regular contacts with the concentration camps musea in Germany(both parts), Poland,Czechoslovakia,Soviet Union, . . . Work(historical work)is being done today in the Belgian Royal Military School and our Universities . . . Certain of your personal eye witnesses should be taken into account.We attach a very great importance to the truth,the whole truth and that nothing but the truth should be said.

Therefore I would be delighted to see you when you happen to cross to

Belgium.My personal telephone number is (081)61.30.20 at the University it is (010)41.81.81,in Breendonk (031)866209

I remain,very faithfully yours,

Paul M.G. Levy

P.S.—Two years ago, invited by the B.B.C.,I participated in the celebration of the 40th anniversary of the French,Italian and German broadcasts in London . . and on the air.

DR. G. F. PETTY

3 COLLOSSEUM TERRACE
ALBANY STREET
REGENTS PARK
LONDON, N.W.1.,
Telephone : EUSton 3356

56 PALACE ROAD
LLANDAFF
CARDIFF CF5 2AH
Telephone : Cardiff 561889

27th November 1980

Professor P.M. Levy.
President B.D.
Breendonk National Memorial.
Belgium.

Dear Professor Levy,

Thank you for your letter. I appreciate your observation.

I would comment on the possibility of incineration of the bodies or papers. I accepted what I saw at the time as I saw it, that is; iron hoops forming a cage for coffins in it to be burnt. There was a considerable amount of greyish white ash on the ground. I did not investigate further, there was no point in doing so.

I noted the bullet holes in the black execution posts further on. I was told that the Belgian hostages were shot here. Some were hanged with their comrades being paraded to see their own future state if they did not give in after being tortured.

I decided to investigate recently the results of incineration of papers compared to those of a body and visited the Crematorium in Cardiff, and then later the effects of burning books and papers on a fire in the barbecue in my garden. The results of the book and papers being burnt were black ash and carbonised sheets.

Obviously I accept what you have written. It is likely that by the time you arrived there after my visiting Breendonk on 31/8/44, a lot of clearing up had been done. I know nothing of what happened after that date. I am frankly very glad to have your figures of the death penalties of the S.S. staff, and those Belgians who had assisted them after being tried by appointed tribunals.

I think that it is very right and necessary to include this record in my book for this reason, and the following reasons. In London there was a request from the right wing British Movement—who uphold Nazism, and wanted to join in the procession of British War Veterans to march past the Cenotaph on November 11th. This was turned down flat by the authorities.

I enclose a cutting of the Western Mail newspaper showing what happened here on 23rd November 1980.

There is a Nazi upsurge in France and England indicated by the bombing of the Synagogue recently in France.

I am pleased to know of your refusal to allow the Belgian Nazi league to hold a parade at Breendonk. Well done! It is essential that every publicity is given to warn all that the ripple which has started on the surface could easily one day become a torrent.

Is it enough in this country to leave it to the Anti Nazi League to suppress this vile and filthy culture of the British Movement before it gets out of hand, and too popular with adolescents who have no proper upbringing and no knowledge of the last war, nor the millions of innocents killed by the followers of Hitler.

Yours sincerely,

G.F. Petty.
TD., FRCGP.

LEON-E. HALKIN

4000 LIEGE, LE
RUE DU PERY, 41

Monsieur le Docteur G. F. Petty,
Palace Road, 56,
Llandaff. Cardiff. CF5 2AH.

Cher Monsieur le Docteur,

Merci de votre lettre du 28 octobre. J'ai lu ce que vous écrit M. Lévy. Son cas est le suivant. Les Anglais avait annoncé son exécution. Pour démentir cette nouvelle et faire la preuve de leur honnêteté (?), les Allemands ont libéré Lévy, qui a rejoint secrétement la Grande-Bretagne.

A ma connaissance, il n'y avait pas de four crématoire à Breendonck et, de mon temps, aucun cimetière. Les corps des exécutés étaient transportés à l'extérieur, je ne sais où. Les cendres que vous avez vues pourraient provenir d'une incinèration de documents (?) par les S.S. avant leur départ ou d'une incinératilon faite par les résistants après la libération du Fort? Les fours crématoires dont je parle dans mon livre sont ceux des camps en Allemagne.

Je serai tou jours heureux d'avoir de vos bonnes nouvelles et je vous prie d'agréer, Cher Monsieur le Docteur, l'expression de mes sentiments les meilleurs.

L.E. Halkin

ENGLISH TRANSLATION

Leon Halkin. *Liege, 10th November 1980*

Dear Dr Petty,

Thank you for your letter of the 28th October. I have read what M. Levy wrote to you. His case is as follows; the English had announced his execution. To refute the news and give proof of their honesty (?) the Germans liberated Levy who went secretly to Great Britain.

To my knowledge there had not been a crematory furnace at Breendonk, and in my time, no cemetery. The bodies of those executed were transported outside, I do not know where. The ashes that you have seen could have come from an incineration of documents(?) by the S.S. before their departure, or from an incineration done by the resistance after the liberation of the Fort? The crematory furnaces about which I speak in my book are those at the camps in Germany.

I shall always be glad to have good news of you, and beg you to accept Dear Dr Petty my good wishes.

L.E. Halkin.

(Reader please note: To maintain accuracy the errors in the spelling in these letters are not printer's errors but as originally written. Remember that these writers are corresponding in a foreign language to them namely English.)

12. Hoogstraten

I had been ordered forward once again to 'recce' a site for a minor casualty hospital, and I came to the village of Hoogstraten not far from Antwerp. It was of importance to the Germans, because of its church tower of 103 metres high, from which there must have been a magnificent view of miles of the complete flat countryside, and in fact it was used as an observation post by the Huns. In spite of this, our artillery and RAF were not allowed to destroy it. The Hun however, whose regard for people or places was non-existent where the exigences of war occurred, put dynamite in the cellars and brought the tower tumbling to the ground, their last act before retreating. There was no warning given to the villagers, and there was hardly a pane of glass left unbroken in the vicinity.

Brave Young Tilley Brosens

I called at the largest building I could see, which was a school and convent, The Kosk E'Cole. I asked Mother Superior for accommodation for my Unit and sick soldiers. "We do not have an empty room in the place" she told me. So then I called at the Mayor's home; he was not in but Tilley Brosens his youngest daughter was. She was a charming young woman with dark hair and a sparkle in her eyes and voice. Her perfect English she had acquired during the War. She was very active in the Resistance Movement and cared for a succession of RAF pilots, whom she hid in their cellars and sent them on their way, through the escape route out of France and home. Had she been caught, she and her father would have been shot. Tilley was questioned repeatedly about spying then eventually arrested. After a couple of days, she demanded to see the Commandant of the SS and told him she had to get back to work. "And what makes it so important that you return to work?" Tilley replied; "Without me there is no-one to teach German to the children". The recall and apology was immediate. She still continued spying and was questioned many times afterwards, but the Germans could never actually prove anything.

Soon I was to find out how much respect her people had for her. When I told her that I had had difficulty at the convent she said;

"What nonsense, they have plenty of room. Come with we!" Off we went to the convent. She went in to see Mother Superior, and returned a few minutes later saying; "It's all right; you can have half the convent". So—in we moved! The nuns cleared out their half, barricading all the doors between the 'brutal and licentious soldiery' and themselves. To their complete surprise the troops took not the slightest notice of them, so after three days their confidence returned. Down came the barricades! In came the nuns to collect the soldiers' washing and mending!!

British Troops Donate Food Allowances

In return, I sent two trucks to Lille where there was a glass factory. I came back with sufficient panes to replace all the broken windows in the convent at first, then gradually enough for the whole village. Autumn was on us and it was getting cold, so I sent trucks to collect coal for the people of the village. I got to know the parish priest and the local doctor well. In early December they held the Feast of St Nicholas, which was more important to the children than Christmas. Therefore it seemed to us that it would be a good thing to give the children a party.

I paraded the Unit and explained the idea. I suggested that the officers and men should give up their chocolate allowance and fruit issue for a month (our rations being very substantial by this time). I asked for volunteers, by the simple Army expedient of Staff Sergeant Mace calling out; "All those not wishing to volunteer, one pace forward, march". The priest calculated that there would be ninety young children whom he could invite. On the appointed day one hundred and twenty came with their mothers as well .However, there was plenty to go around, but what astonished us so much was that many of the children would touch neither the chocolate nor the tinned fruit. They had not seen either for five years of their young lives but their mothers, standing behind them did not mind. They just leaned over the children and happily finished the lot!

After the eating, there was the play acted by Staff Sergeant Mace as Bishop St Nicholas, and the Unit "Funnyman" as Naughty Black Peter, who was duly caught after a chase and put in a bag and carried away.

The Secret Room

After the War, I frequently tried to get in touch with the

numerous members of the Brosen family, but failed. I met three daughters and one son; he must have been about eighteen years old at the time. He was surprisingly gauche and uncommunicative when I first went to their home, and I found out why at once. The Germans never knew that the Brosen's had had this youngest son, because he had been kept in the cellar all day and came up at night. His communication and conversation were limited to the family, and RAF pilots. I have come across this in youths in the village of Lierre when I was stationed with Tommy Richardson. He and I were asked to spend Christmas Day with the local carpenter who had two sons. One morning at 2 am the Gestapo arrived to arrest the eldest boy. This had been in the previous year, and they had not seen or heard of him since. The younger boy had had a similar experience but was returned home after interrogation and imprisonment. He would not tell his parents what had happened, nor where he had been. He was silent, withdrawn and remote. His father told us; "I know I have lost one son, but now I have lost them both". Under the stairs the carpenter had panelled in the space to make room for a bed; there was no door, just a moveable panel. It looked like a wall supporting the stairs. There the boy slept every night, until we came.

The Missing Sons

In the window of a little shop in the town were over two hundred photographs of young men and boys, over a notice; "Will anyone returning to Lierre and recognising anyone of these photographs, please let us have details."

Passive Resistance

The Belgians in general knew how to handle the Germans. They shrugged their shoulders when orders were issued, then got on with daily chores as best they could. They were used to invasion, not just during the First World War by the Germans, but in time past when once they were even a colony of Spain.

The Dutch, although nearer in blood relationship to the Germans, revolted against the invasion of their country and the ruthless smashing of Rotterdam flattened by the Luftwaffe without Declaration of War. The Dutch would not accede to the German demands and orders—and suffered for it!

When we went into Holland before Christmas, I took over

convents near Nijmegen and Turnhout. They had no coal, no windows and no food. They were deprived of everything. They had some bulbs from the previous season, so bulb soup for many was the main diet. Once more I sent trucks off for panes of glass and coal, and we supplied the immediate necessities of food. The coldest Christmas I have ever known, I spent here. We shared our presents of food from our relations at home with the nuns. Everything was frozen—the taps, canals and houses. Many died from privation and we slept in our battle dress, fully clothed except for our boots.

In Belgium, where the shops were well stocked, we had been able to buy glass and china to send home as Christmas presents. In France we had been able to send from Normandy, Camembert cheese and butter which arrived home three weeks later with the postman holding his nose as he handed it over. Some people, I believe, like it that way—but not at my address! However, in Holland there was nothing—absolutely nothing!

13. Reflections

The Germans had been driven back; Brussels was free! I had time to wander and wonder at the cheerful smiling faces, hurrying for no real purpose; shops open with surprising stock. I thought of the years of War, of my home town Cardiff at the beginning of the 1938 crisis, when some of its citizens were uncertain where their loyalty lay. Of how Hitler had almost won the War before it started, by restoring power and pride of being German in the younger generation. I thought of how he had made the non-Aryans suffer—sacrifice their wealth, then freedom—finally their lives in his loathsome concentration camps! From amongst the files found by our Army in the advance, there was a complete dossier of the Jews in Wales. Von Ribbentrop was to have been created Gauleiter for Wales!

Captain Petty Reported : September 1938

My mind wandered back to September 1938—of the constant ringing telephone. Damn it, would it never stop! I lifted the receiver; "Captain Petty, report to Drill Hall in uniform at once". "How the hell can I? I have patients to see here in Cardiff". "Sir, this is an order". I telephoned my partner, Andrew Loudon to say I was being called up and for him to carry on with the practice. None too pleased, he agreed so I dressed quickly and went to Cardiff Drill Hall. Men came in small groups, just walking out from their work—labourers, miners, office clerks etc. Some wore shoes, others daps—no boots because although 1,500 pairs had been ordered, they had not arrived! Major Claude Hurford came over where I was performing a very brief medical on each man and said; "Every man and officer has to have £5 embodiment money, but we have no money except for a small amount of Regimental Funds". I told him that I would contact Lloyds Bank and ask the Manager for a loan on account, but it was after four o'clock so I would have to ring him at home. Mr Richards the Manager thought the situation very funny, but said that as the War Office no doubt would stand surety, he and the Cashier would open up for us and debit my account to pay the British Army.

Stand By—on Chesil Beach by Portland Bill

All went well, apart from having an incomplete uniform, no boots, or steel helmets, only a .303 Lee Enfield rifle, and twenty-five Lewis guns covered in grease from World War One. What a way to start! We were all very cheerfully prepared to defend our country against the Hun. Anti-aircraft guns? (None, but our twenty-five Lewis guns were soon mounted on vertical railway sleepers in front of dug-outs in the cliffs at Chesil Beach—good diggers our colliers.) We also had a Bofors gun on the beach sited to be recognised from the air, but then it had to be seen to do its job—it was made of wood! The troops put up the tents on the boulder-strewn Chesil Beach, which wore out their shoes in two days, then they went about barefoot but happy. "Let them come" said the boys "We will give 'em hell", but God Almighty, what with? Hore Belisha, the Minister of War, was right! We had nothing! (For the previous two years he had been trying to persuade the Government to set up Munitions Factories and failed. Duff Cooper, First Lord of the Admiralty had resigned because he was not allowed to send the Fleet to sea to make straight for the German coast. The Prime Minister then was Chamberlain.)

No Complaints! Nothing Happened!

Three days passed, with nothing happening. I visited each section, no complaints, no-one reported sick. On the beach they still walked barefooted, but not a grumble anywhere. On the fourth day—Emergency over—troops were recalled to barracks. Suddenly sick parade was half a street long. Disembodiment money was paid out—another £5 per man, and troops were given temporary leave. That evening, young subalterns reported with whitefaced alarm. "The boys are mad drunk, and are fighting the sailors, police and civilians". I thought "Serve them right, getting Welsh boys to defend the English, who generously supplied them with peashooters with which to do the job. After all, it was Welsh bowmen who won the battles of Crecy, Poitiers and Agincourt for the English, but at least they had weapons".

That Hitler–Chamberlain Meeting 1938

At the end of September 1938 Neville Chamberlain returned from the Four Power Conference at Munich, attended by Adolf Hitler, Benito Musolini and Daladier. "Peace in our time" he said happily grinning. "Mr Hitler has no warlike intentions". Thus Prime Minister Chamberlain sacrificed the Czechoslovakians to Hitler, together with the munitions factories, the best in Europe. This take-over was completed in just ten days, and Hitler had all the arms he needed for War. Meantime Winston Churchill and Lord Beaverbrook got together and organised the munitions factories which we needed.

Swastika Flag on Cardiff Civic Building

I particularly remembered an article which featured in the Daily Mirror of 1st October 1938, and repeat it here: (with acknowledgements to Daily Mirror)

Risking death to pull down swastika.

*Four members of a Cardiff City Council Committee Meeting, hearing yesterday that a swastika flag was flying from the roof of the Civic Centre, ran out, risked their lives, and pulled the flag down. Cheered by a crowd, two of the Councillors got to the top of the building, despite locked doors*G *and slowly made their way across the roof.*

Faced with a thirty foot drop on either side, they clung desperately as they made a perilous crawl along the footway running the length of the building. "It took them several minutes until they reached the flag" an eyewitness told the Daily Mirror. "Then they grabbed the swastika and pulled it down, leaving three flags fluttering in the breeze."

A storm of indignation broke as soon as the swastika flag was found to be fluttering from the south east corner of the Civic Centre. One councillor attempted to climb a drain pipe to the roof. He failed. So angered was Sir William Williams, senior member of the Council that he rushed to the private room of the Lord Mayor, Alderman C C Purnell and urged him to take down the flag. His request was refused. Ten minutes later the Lord Mayor, leaving his room for a Committee Meeting heard Sir William declare, "It's an insult to the people of Czechoslovakia, it looks as if Germany has won."

Turning to the Lord Mayor, Alderman C H McCales said "You should not have allowed it in the name of the Council. You have no authority from members to fly the flag, and should take it down at once." Several members shouted "We will not tolerate this." Then the four members including Sir William, who tried to reach the roof of the City Hall and found it locked, were unable to find the key at first. Meanwhile, Alderman Charles H McCale went over and had a whispered consultation with Councillor John Heginbottam and together they went inside the building. Alderman McCale is sixty and Councillor Heginbottam sixty-five.

It meant climbing right to the top of the building before they could reach the flag. It was a dangerous task indeed. People cheered them on. The flag was afterwards hidden to prevent its reappearance. "It ought never to have been put up" Councillor Heginbottam told the Daily Mirror afterwards. "Several ex Servicemen who were watching us do the job volunteered, but we preferred to do it ourselves."

Late last night the Lord Mayor said; "We flew the four flags to celebrate the event, four Powers having signed the peace agreement. It is a good job Mr Chamberlain has not the same mentality as these members of Council, or we should have been at war by now. This is an historic occasion and I can see no reasonable objection to my action. It is a gesture of international friendship." It is understood that the matter is to be taken further and that a certain section of Council members are to insist on the flag not being flown.

I thought—God bless those Councillors and their fine example, and damn that Chamberlain!

6th Welch Battalion New Role

In December 1938 conversion of the 6th Battalion to the 67th Searchlight Regiment RA started. There was a new intake of recruits and the officers were given intensive training in the mechanics of searchlights. The change was not popular with anyone; indeed it was bitterly resented. Lt Colonel Charles Nicholl the CO of the 6th Battalion and Major Claude Hurford, his Second in Command ,together with many others did not relish the idea of a completely new aspect of warfare for an infantry batalion, proud of its drill, fighting ability, a wonderful record of battle honours to become permanently on sentry duty, the only challenge to the enemy being a beam of light in the black night sky. At the time I had a Regimental Aid Post in Cathedral Road, Cardiff while the searchlights were being slowly sited. In 1939 just before the real outbreak of War, I remember we went to Newark-on-Trent to man the searchlights on that part of the East Coast. Suddenly orders came to move back to War stations. The Nottingham group of the Searchlight Regiment took over from us and because there was no official transport, our officers used their own cars paid for by the Army! In column we belted for South Wales along roads, which in an incredibly short time had had thousands of miles of white lines painted along them in the centre. (Every local council in the country had turned to for this task of traffic lines.) The dimming of lights on trucks and cars was compulsory but there was a guide light visible on the lorries below the rear axle just, but only just, visible to those behind. We ignored all speed limits. Despatch Riders ahead of the column stopped all traffic at crossroads to let us through. We had a feeling of importance and excitement; even quiet officers became quite cocky. An adolescent emotional reaction perhaps? We passed startled people on the roadside anxiously wondering whether this was the result of the invasion, but surprisingly we had no accident and no breakdowns.

Cardiff and District Searchlights

We took up our stations on the hills around Cardiff, and I acted like a country GP moving from one site to another. Innoculations became routine for all troops on enlisting but at that time were not completed. I recall on the Caerphilly Searchlight site one man with Tetanus (lockjaw). The Rizor Sardonicus—was apparent in his grin, with bared teeth and painful arching back. He was taken to the Fever Hospital near Cardiff and I am glad to say he recovered, many did not.

I was quickly bored with my job of running from one hill to another and applied to ADMS Western Command to go to France; I was posted at once—to Chepstow! While waiting there I met a fellow General Practitioner, Dr "Jumbo" James who said; "Gerald I want to join up; can you get me into the Army?" I asked the ADMS about this and to Jumbo's surprise, he was commissioned and after a few weeks training had an immediate posting. He went to France—happy as a lark. He arrived just in time for the

German Blitzkreig and the retreat from Dunkirk, was taken prisoner after only a few weeks in the Army, and remained a prisoner for the duration. (After returning home he was quiet and morose, walking slowly with bowed head. It took him a long time to recover his old 'joie de vivre', helped by his charming wife.)

14. Anniversary of D Day 1969

In 1969 my wife Ann Marie and I set forth for Normandy with a loaded car on a beautiful day. Twentyfive years previously, it had been wet and stormy. Our ship was full of Americans, all there for the same purpose—the 25th Anniversary of D Day 4th June, 1944.

We went to the Hotel Lion d'Or at Bayeux, an old world coachinghouse of great charm, but we could stay overnight only as it was fully booked after that. We saw the Cathedral at Bayeux with its famous tapestry depicting the Norman Conquest of Britain. They had successfully hidden this tapestry from the Germans during their occupation.

Search for Madame Bois Lambert

We booked a room above a cafe opposite the Cathedral, as all hotel rooms were full, then went in search of Madame Bois Lambert at the Chateau Fief Pelloquin, at Berniere Sur Mere. On the way we stopped at Arromanches and saw the Mulberry—that incredible pier made to produce a safe harbour for our supply ships for the invasion of Europe. Great long sections of hollow blocks of concrete had been towed across the channel and dropped into place, then filled with more concrete. So the harbour remained, and provided an example of our constructive scientific effort in defeating the German overlords of Europe in 1945, so long ago.

On 4th June, 1969 Ann Marie and I visited the Chateau, where I knocked on the door and the housekeeper answered it. I asked if I could see Madame Bois Lambert's successor. "But Madame is alive Monsieur and having lunch 10 kilometres away with the French Canadian Army; Monsieur le Colonel est mort". There we went, and found them sitting down to lunch, Madame at the head of the table, very much alive and sparkling. I kissed her hand, and was welcomed with a warm embrace. She invited us to stay at the Chateau in one of its eleven bedrooms, and this we were very glad to do in view of the accommodation problem in the town.

Canadians Well Represented

We went to the colourful scene at the D Day ceremony. There

were two Canadian Mounties, resplendent in their scarlet uniforms; one was 6′ 5″ and the 'short one' was 6′ 2.″ All the Canadian Regiments were represented. General Allard, Commander In Chief of Canadian Forces, the Canadian Ambassador, General Chambers, and of course Madame Bois Lambert, as President of the Red Cross, was charming as ever. While we were standing in the packed crowd, Ann Marie heard a Welsh voice behind us and turned around to ask him what his badge of WG stood for. He said; "I am the representative of the War Graves Commission. I come over every year to inspect the graves. I'm from Maesteg". So we got together and I heard his story.

Taffy Lang of Maesteg (ex Assault Sapper)

He was Taffy Lang, one of that gallant group—the Assault Sappers whose job it was to clear a way through the beach minefields for our infantry. (I once walked through a minefield due to my own dull stupidity through lack of sleep, when I was lucky to get out alive by retracing my steps.) In Taffy Lang's case it was very different. One of his companions had put his foot on an anti-personnel mine in the sand, and was blown screaming to the ground. An officer shouted for someone to help him. So Taffy jumped the wire, picked up his friend, turned around to walk out with him, and put his own foot on a mine. He had both feet shattered and severe leg wounds. His friend he was carrying was killed outright, and so Taffy crawled the rest of the way to the wire. This must have been about D Day +4. He was admitted to the Canadian Casualty Clearing Station who had by then taken over from me. So on that Anniversary Day, I found Taffy Lang full of cheer but walking with a limp. What he had done was an act of great gallantry and cool courage. He paid for this with his legs, and nearly his life.

Brave Assault Sappers

As a Commanding Officer, I had copies of my personal records from my War Diaries of those officers and men I recommended for decorations, all of whom were awarded according to the merits of my reports. In Taffy Lang's his officer did not bother, possibly because the Assault Sappers advancing in front of the Assault Infantry accepted their extra risk as part of the job! Many men were killed in acts of great bravery, and their only reward was a white cross in a military cemetry and a letter from their officer to express his sympathy to his widow or parents.

Anti-British French Canadians

It was one long champagne party in Berniéres Sur Mer, Caen and Bayeux after the Anniversary ceremony. The Canadians were youngsters in the uniform of the Regimen Chaudière (The Bucket Handle of the St Lawrence River in Quebec); a company of these had landed after D Day. These youngsters then were very anti-British and made it very obvious. Madame Bois Lambert was so overjoyed to see us that she could not help talking about 'the wonderful British Army who had done so much for the town and its people'. The following day she arranged for a large party of women and a few men I had treated on D Day to come to the Chateau to meet me. I met them in the driveway; some of them still had their military wounded cards. Some had been wounded by our own shells but they did not resent this, as they realised that Freedom was coming. I felt pride at being remembered and thanked for my care.

French Praise for the British Medical Corps

Frequently as I was coming out of my room I heard Madame telling her French Canadian visitors how wonderful the British Medical Corps had been. She happily ignored their stoney silence. None of them would speak English, and pretended not to understand it. Monsieur Lepont, the Deputy Governor of Quebec in 1969 gave a toast "To the gallant Frenchmen who liberated France in 1944", and seeing me said; " We must not forget our Allies the British, who also helped". (As Captain Lepont he had arrived after D Day in command of his company.) All I said very slowly was; "Thank you sirs, I drink to the liberation of La Belle France". I thought of my previous happy experience with the brave Canadian Army throughout the Hitler War, which had been so very different to the antagonistic attitudes of these youngsters.

15. Hoogstraten, 1979

I had given up hope of finding Tilley again, until like a heaven-sent answer while I was still preparing this book, Ann Marie and I went to London on a shopping spree. We decided to lunch at Fortnum & Mason, but the place was crowded as usual. The Manageress asked if we would mind sharing with two other ladies. We said we would be happy to do so. I found myself listening to that particular Belgian-French accent I knew so well. I couldn't help but ask; "What part of Belgium do you two ladies come from?" Somewhat astonished, one answered; "Antwerp". Excitedly I said: "Do you know Tilly Brosens, the daughter of the Burgomaster of Hoogstraten". "But yes, she is married with grown-up children, living in Antwerp". I gave the ladies my card and asked them to contact Tilly for her to write to me. Later I got this eagerly awaited letter, and followed up by telephoning her. It was fantastic to speak to her again after so much fruitless searching. She was the bravest woman I have ever met. I decided to go to Belgium to see her again.

Antwerp and Tilley Brosens

Ann Marie my wife could not come with me, so my daughter Dr Geraldine Freeth, and I set forth for Antwerp. At our destination, there on the steps of the hotel was a grey-haired, charming and beautiful lady. It was almost unbelievable to meet her again. Geraldine and I booked a couple of rooms for the night and the three of us dined together that evening. Next morning Tilley came to show us around Antwerp, but prior to her arrival I had gone to the hotel desk and asked what my account was in English money up to date, and had the shock reply—£100. When Tilley arrived I told her that I had just £600 on me, and this would not last at £100 per night!

So, with her usual confidence, undiminished over the years she said: "Leave this to me, just give me your bill". She went over to the office manager and chatted away in Flemish, and came back saying; "I have reduced your overnight account, cancelled tonight, and pointed out that they have grossly overcharged you for telephone calls to Wales". Dear Tilley, you do not change! She then found us a motel just outside Antwerp—The Dennenhof—in very beautiful surroundings, very reasonable, with excellent cuisine. Tilley took us over old Antwerp, the home of Rembrandt with its wonderful history. Her husband had been in the Belgian Army and had taken a very active part also in the Resistance Movement. These days he is an art connisseur and has a wonderful collection of old books and antiques—and enjoys his Scotch whisky! Her daughter is growing up as lovely as her mother, and her son spends most of his time under a car, rebuilding it.

> (I recounted earlier in this narrative that Tilley received letters of appreciation for the work she did in the Resistance Movement in her area, saving twelve airman and sending them on their way to freedom, and home. These letters came from General Eisenhower, Montgomery, and Winston Churchill, and how well deserved they were).

Going to Breendonk, as well as meeting Tilley once more made me feel how worth while our fight had been from 1939 to 1945.

This episode in the life of Mad Gerry, Welsh Wartime Officer had been concluded.

Epilogue

AFTER THOUGHTS OF A DOCTOR ON DISEASE IN WAR AND PEACE

In view of the new drugs we use regularly in 1981 in any infective disease, I feel it is important to record the difference in treatments, resulting in speedy recovery rather than have the frequent or continued ill health of many years ago. Many young doctors today are unaware of the rapid, amazing changes in treatment since World War One (1914-18). These young doctors cannot imagine the problems we met daily fifty years ago as General Practitioners with a higher incidence of death. For instance, in those days 20,000 people died a year from Pulmonary Tuberculosis alone, which was called "The White Death". Now, thanks to drugs and modern treatment at home, the incidence has dropped to 300 each year.

Pain Relief

The public have changed too. Pain had become an evil thing and must be stopped at once, but pain is a life preserver. I remember particularly (when I attended a BMA Conference in Cyprus some years ago) a boy of eleven who could not feel pain. All his limbs showed bony lumps, due to his fearless jumping from heights and fracturing his limbs. No effort was made to splint these fractures because he could not feel pain and therefore did not complain. Today, the public demands' pain killers', but relief of pain without diagnosing the cause, leads to more frequent visits to the doctor's surgery.

The Killer Diphtheria

Diphtheria was a common disease years ago. My own mother had this shortly after marriage and was extremely ill. Her two babies (my sisters) were taken from her to the house next door and kept there until she recovered. Apparently she had asked my father, what would he have done had she died? He replied; "I would have cursed God and died too". Not a bad retort for a young parson!

The Klebs-Loeffler Bacillus is easily recognised by taking a swab of the tonsil area and putting it on a slide under the microscope. When a student, I attended the Poplar Fever Hospital (where we were given the vaccination against Smallpox) and saw a great many patients with Diphtheria, particularly infants and young children. A thick grey membrane appeared over the tosil area, and spread slowly down the throat to the larynx and bronchus. When it reached the larynx the two laryngeal cords, being covered with it, the air entry became so small that the patient choked and died. Babies and small children were carried into the operating theatre by the nurses, tightly wrapped around with towelling. The theatre sister would then hold the head firmly in both hands, lifting the head to the maximum by the chin. The surgeon then took a scalpel and made a vertical incision just below the chords to insert a curved tracheotomy tube, which was then tied in. The patient who was until then breathing with hoarse stentorous breathing, could take easy deep breaths. All this was done without anaesthetic, and the amount of pain in skilled hands was less than a tooth being extracted—also faster.

My Own Tonsilitis

Apart from breaking my neck on the football field at Bath, in my younger days, I used to get recurrent tonsillitis and necessitate having twenty-four hours off at a time. There was no treatment for this painful condition except salt and water, and antiseptic gargles. Finally, after the third or fourth attack I was told to have three weeks leave and then return to hospital where they would remove the offending tonsils but just as I was about to leave I was called back to have a swab taken of my throat. I went home to the vicarage at Torre, Torquay and the following day received a telegram: "KLB plus, culture virulent". This meant that I had diphtheria of a severe type, and that I was highly infectious. I wondered how many I had infected? The routine treatment was absolute rest (as it could affect the heart) and so I had a pleasant, capable nurse, the family doctor to take the routine swabs, as well as the local ENT surgeon, who gave me injections of anti-diphtheria injections. However I continued to get positive swabs. I tried everything possible—antiseptic gargles which only succeeded in irritating the mucous membrane without improvement. I then painted my throat with silver nitrate 1% solution, but after two days of this treatment we observed the diphtheria membrane coming back.

Swabs—All Those Swabs !

The Medical Officer of Health came to see me and said: "As soon as you get three negative swabs, you can have your tonsillectomy". My mother (not a particularly good tempered woman), used to come stamping up the stairs shouting; "Another positive swab, how much longer will this last?" When the Medical Officer of Health came to see me again, I suggested that, as I was a doctor, he could leave some swabs for me to take the necessary samples, instead of bothering other people. He agreed and told me to take three swabs, and send one every two days. I duly did this and surprisingly enough, I had three negative results. This surprised everyone except me, because I had merely waved the swab in the air, keeping it well away from my throat, and put it back in the test tube for despatch. (By this time I was confirmed as a carrier which meant that the bacilla were still present in the tonsil. The antigens in my blood kept the bacteria from multiplying but not producing symptoms in me; I was still highly infectious to anyone else).

Wire Snares and Scissors

However, I paid for my deceipt with these swabs (and I mean that literally) because when arrangements were made to take me into the nursing home for my tonsillectomy I was asked if I preferred a general or local anaesthetic for the operation. I chose the latter, and so I walked down to the operating table and my tonsils were injected with the local anaesthetic. My tonsils were big and very soggy. The surgeon dissected out the upper part of the left tonsil and then put the wire snare around the tonsil root, pulled it tight and then removed it. It bled the normal amount, as the wire snare crushed the blood vessels at the lower root. He then tackled the other side. Unfortunately for me, the wire snare became unhooked, and he had to use scissors to cut the remainder away and then cut into an artery near the base of the tongue. The tissues were so soggy from the chronic infection and inflammation, plus the local anaesthetic, that he had the greatest difficulty in getting the sutures to hold.

Long Time Recovery

I lost a great deal of blood, and swallowed plenty as well. Over two hours later, after finally sewing a swab into the gap where the tonsil had been uprooted, I was carried back to bed, exhausted and still bleeding. I felt dreadful and all I wanted to do was sleep. As they took my pulse they said; "I think he is going to vomit", which I promptly did, coughing up yet more blood over a long period of time. It took me a very long time to recover from this operation, as in those days blood transfusions were a rarity and not always safe, as the Rhesus factor had not then been discovered, and people sometimes died from transfusions.

Klebs Loeffler Bacillus

The staff at the hospital when I finally got back to work were very considerate. I got the full convalescent treatment of egg with milk and brandy on the wards, and a ten minute rest between operations in theatre with the same nourishment. All this was due to to the blasted little Klebs Loeffler bacillus. It is strange to think of disease and death from bacteria fifty years ago. When danger passes, how easily we forget! As a result of school children and babies being inoculated against diphtheria, it has virtually been wiped out.

The Blessing of Anaesthetics

A hundred years ago, anaesthetics had just become popular, after Queen Victoria agreed reluctantly to try it during the births of some of her children. With royal approval of anaesthesia for birth, minor and major operations became popular. Much later, Edward VII surrounded by his surgeons, when they had diagnosed appendicitis, were argueing whether operation or observation was the wisest course. Some said "Operate"; others said "No operation". The surgeon who was to perform the operation was nearest to the King, and he leaned over him (he was a bit deaf) and shouted "Operation". So the King closed his eyes and slept, and eventually recovered from his appendicectomy, making this a very sociable acceptable operation!

New Drugs Brought Benefits

Today, sanatoria are no longer in existence for tuberculosis, and Fever Hospitals have been closed for years. Lobar pneumonia is no longer the killer that it used to be. Because of new drugs the expectation of life has increased enormously. However, there is one exception to this, overweight people! If the height/weight ratio is adverse by 20% then insurance companies will charge a heavier premium. However with reduction of weight, the blood pressure will automatically reduce to normal and the expectation of life today has increased by 15 years.

Lock Jaw

A common cause of death years ago, was "Lock Jaw" or to give it the correct medical term 'Tetanus'. This was due to the tetanus bacillus infecting any cut or scratch. It is present in the soil, and particularly in cattle dung. Prevention by innoculation conveys complete protection and all our troops were inoculated against this. In 'Lock Jaw' the slightest movement caused the head and spine to be pulled backwards in dreadful spasm. The teeth are bared like a snarling dog, and this dreadful grin is called the "sardonic smile". The pain in the back is intensified with every muscle spasm, and eventually they die of cramp in all the muscles, which finally prevents breathing (the only other condition which produces the same symptoms is strychnine poisoning).

Suez Crisis

During the Suez crisis, President Eisenhower telephoned the British Prime Minister, Sir Anthony Eden and threatened to send in the 7th American Fleet unless we pulled out of Egypt. At that time Eden was a sick man with constant recurring pain from a chronically inflamed gall bladder, and doubled up with attacks of pain, he was in no position to fight back. So we failed in the Suez War due to a gall bladder! In the whole of history, more wars have been lost through disease than by gunshot wounds or sword thrusts. (General Sir Hugh Stockwell calculated that he needed only three more hours to finish the Suez War when he got telephone instructions to cease fire at once. All he said was "Yes, Sir, Yes, Sir!"

Typhoid The Killer

In the Boer War we lost over 100,000 officers and men through Typhoid, many more than were actually killed in action. Cholera took its toll in India. The British brought to India two things; one was Justice free from bribery and the other was Hygiene. Field hygiene was introduced by the Army particularly in eradicating fly borne disease. All medical units had equipment for testing the

purity of the water in a well, or if nothing else was available, a pool. The 'Horrocks Box' was the official means of testing quickly the percentage of foreign matter and estimating the amount of bleach powder to render it drinkable. (The only time I used this myself was on the Scilly Islands when checking out three of the smallest islands. We had no trouble, except the complaint that unless the pool was allowed to stand for 24 hours, the odour and taste of the chlorine made it unpalatable, although safe.)
The reader will recall that Queen Victoria's Consort, Prince Albert, died of Typhoid.

Death From Septicaemia

In World War One, every bullet wound, shrapnel or bayonet wound carried into the flesh a dirty piece of khaki which led to a foul smelling pus, with probable death from Septicaemia. For more than a hundred years the discharge from a wound was called 'laudable pus', and if this was thick, it meant that the man had some resistance against the infection and was therefore 'praiseworthy': if the discharge was runny, then the fever increased and expectation of survival was slim.

My Fifty Years as a Doctor

I am happy as a doctor to have lived through this last half century and seen the great miracles of medicine occur so suddenly and dramatically. Death from Septicaemia was so common. The wounded then, lay in bed with an arm or hand in hot salt water baths, had very little to look forward to, and the stench from such a ward was unbelievable. It was Bayers the chemists who produced Prontosil Rubrum which was injected to cure Septicaemia, Child Birth Fever and Erysipelas. This contained a red dye which was excreted through the kidneys, and many a patient as he got better was quite convinced that the bacteria were being shot out via the kidneys, which was very satisfactory to all concerned! Soon after this Bayers produced Prontosil Album, a white tablet with the same effect, and so the main cause of death from Septicaemia was wiped out.

Amputation at Sea

For hundreds of years, the treatment of a compound fracture of the leg at sea was amputation at the site of fracture. The unfortunate man was given a bottle of brandy to swallow (no heel taps) whilst three men held him down and gave him a piece of leather to bite on. The surgeon at great speed would then slash through the skin, and once the subcutaneous nerves had been cut, it was virtually painless to saw through the bone .The flap of skin was then pulled over the flesh and the stump dipped in hot pitch. This was exquisitely painful, but very antiseptic. Later on there would be a peg-leg strapped to the thigh. Aboard ship, particularly on the bridge and poop-deck, holes would be driven into the boards to take the peg-leg and steady the man in a rough sea.

Lung Cancer

Pneumonia has always been a common cause of death, although underlying many pneumonia cases years ago was an unsuspected lung cancer. I remember as a boy seeing hundreds of soldiers on route marches with a fag-end of Woodbine hanging on the lower lip. Looking back now, I wondered how many of these would suffer and die from pneumonia. When Winston Churchill developed pneumonia at the Yalta Conference, he was fortunate to be one of the early recipients of the new M&B 693 drug, which, for the first time in history, actually killed the bacteria, pneumonococcus. Up until that time the treatment had consisted of good nursing care kaolin poultices, morphia by injection to rest the gasping patient, and digitalis (the foxglove leaf) the keep the heart regular.

Pneumonia

Post-operative pneumonia was common when I was a student. The surgeon always blamed the anaesthetist if pneumonia occurred. When I was being taught at St Bart's Hospital by Geoffrey Keynes I remember seeing, on a ward-round, a man who had a simple hernia of the groin who was to be operated on the following day. The Great Man Keynes loudly announced that he would use on this man a local and not a general anaesthetic, and therefore his patient would not develop pneumonia as had happened before. The result was two days later, the patient developed pneumonia! Geoffrey Keynes had a great deal of embarassment passing this off, as medical students are a highly critical audience, and sadistically enjoy any failure attributable to their elders and betters!

Anaesthetics 'Rag and Bottle' Method

After qualifying at Bart's I did a Postgraduate course in Anaesthetics and was taught this by the famous 'Cocky' Boyle. Anaesthesia then was by the 'Rag and Bottle' method, this being a metal frame holding a layer of gauze which covered the nose and mouth. The Anaesthetist then with a dropper bottle moistened the gauze with chloroform, which was fairly quick, but occasionally fatal in inexperienced hands. Ether was then introduced as a mixture of one part chloroform and two of ether.

Nitrous Oxide (Laughing Gas) from a cylinder connected to a rubber bag and mask was put on the face for a short time, if it was just to extract a tooth or open and abscess. Reviving from this, the people would either weep or laugh, sometimes however they would come around fighting and struggling and had to be forcibly held down.

Time Gained for Longer Operations

Some years before, when the 'Rag and Bottle' method was being used, a surgeon was operating on an abscess in a limb with 'Cocky' Boyle giving him the gas. He asked Cocky to keep him going a bit longer as he had run into a bigger problem than anticipated. So he lifted off the mask until the patient drew a few breaths, replaced the mask before he regained consciousness, and kept this method up for half-an-hour more. He continued to practise this method for a while until he eventually connected up a cylinder of oxygen and another of nitrous oxide, with the gas bubbling through a vertical tube in a bottle of water. This mixture was then passed by a rubber tube to the mask over the patient's face, and the volume of mixture was regulated visibly. He then attached more bottles at a later stage, ether and chloroform—making a complete machine which kept the patient unconscious for as long a time as necessary, which improved th scope of surgery with ample time for the surgeon to work. This apparatus was used all over the world, and on a trip to America, he was asked to give anaesthetic to a wealthy American businessman with his new machine. The patient asked Cocky Boyle what his fee was, and was told; "A thousand dollars". The patient said; "That's a whole lot of money". Cocky replied: "You ship gold and diamonds, and pay heavily for safe delivery, you are *my* freight of gold and diamonds". The patient laughed and paid!

I remember how Cocky would generally chat through operations to the students and nurses who assisted him. More often than not if the girl sounded pleasant he would ask her out to dinner, only to find at times he had made an error of judgement when she took her mask off!

Excretia Inspection

Going back a century ago, purgatives and "blood letting" was the order of the day, often quite regardless of cause and effect. The results of each bedpan were thoroughly inspected. Dr Mathews Duncan, a famous physician and accoucheur at Bart's in the Victoria era, was noted to observe "she dungs like a sheep". Getting the bowels open was a "sine que non" for all patients. When travelling in Bruges I remember coming across an antique model made of wood, of a man with a large syringe giving an enema to a patient, whose bottom was sticking out of the open window!

Smallpox in Cardiff

Today, vaccination against Smallpox is still sometimes necessary. Only a few years ago in this country there was a gynaecologist who operated on a woman patient who was developing smallpox unsuspectingly. Both surgeon and anaesthetist caught smallpox and died. The first case noted in Cardiff was of a woman of easy virtue who travelled from London and the epidemic spread rapidly. A small hospital near Cardiff was opened for the treatment of smallpox, and Dr Jimmy Thomas of St David's Hospital who had had experience of smallpox in India was put in charge as RMO. There was panic amongst the public. At that time, as well as being a general practitioner, I was also Medical Officer to the departmental store of James Howells. I asked for the store to close early and for the whole staff to stand at the bottom of the stairs, where I explained to everyone what smallpox meant and how the innoculation would take effect in up to five days after the date of contact. I had already asked the Chairman and Managing Director to purchase the vaccine from abroad at a cost of £600 which they readily agreed to do, and this was delivered by plane. The Managing Director of Howells, Victor Thorpe was very familiar with this disease, because when he was in Italy awaiting his embarkation leave and routine discharge from the Army he contracted smallpox, and was put into the

Military Hospital in Rome. He was put on a wheeled stretcher overnight outside the ward (in spite of the pouring rain) with the protection of ground sheets only. The following day he was put into an isolated Nissen hut in the charge of a German prisoner of war medical orderly, who was the only person apart from a doctor to see him. He had smallpox severely, and was marked for life. Eventually he recovered and returned to Cardiff, to his job in the family store.

The Miracle of Penicillin

I referred earlier on in this book of our use of Penicillin on D Day. This was a new drug, where we saw the miracle of surgery combined with this new drug producing incredible healing. It was another step forward in ridding the civilised world of bacterial disease. We had two Field Surgical Units atached to each FDS with hospital trained orderlies capable of setting up the operation tents, with anaesthetists for each. I had also a Blood Transfusion Officer with his three ton truck and built-in refrigerator for whole blood and plasma for transfusions. He had, as well, the first Penicillin powder, which maintained its potency at room temperature for some years in its dry state (although we did not know this at that time).

Professor Fleming, a pathologist discovered it in 1929 on one of his agar bacteria plates in the incubator, a mould called 'Penicillin Notatum'. The bacteria had virtually continued to grow on the surface of the plate except, where the mould had grown, all the bacteria had disappeared. So he wrote his paper. All these years went by and no-one had the imagination or ability to grow the Penicillin Notatum with a view to treatment.

My Medical Student Days

I was then a medical student doing a course in the Pathology Laboratory at Bart's where we used to collect the samples of pus on a small dish to grow the bacteria in the incubator. So Professor Fleming, not being as clinically minded as a physician would have been— the world had to wait until the Americans decided to grow the mould on an enormous scale in their huge factories. We found it! They produced it!!

War Wounds Healed Quicker

Before the 6th June 1944, the treatment for shrapnel, bullet or bayonet wound was to clean out the wound, insert a drainage tube for the inevitable pus which would pour from the wound for many weeks. After, however, the surgeon opened up the bullet wound, swabbed it thoroughly, poured in a teaspoonful of Penicillin powder, closed the wound with sutures, and inevitably the wound healed.

1938 Meningitis in Cardiff

When I was Medical Officer to the 67th Searchlight Regiment in 1938/39 I took over a building in St Mellons Village for treatment of minor conditions, but which necessitated bed rest. It was at this time that an outbreak of Cerebro spinal fever occurred, otherwise colloquially known as "Spotted fever" because of the rash which occurred on the chest. This was an infective Meningitis which could prove fatal. Confirmation of the diagnosis was made by taking a swab from the back of the throat above the soft palate, this was then cultured in the laboratory in Cardiff. Some people without symptoms had this bacteria present. They were 'carriers' of the infection and did not develop meningtis themselves. Treatment was effective by the use of Sulphonamide tablets. All soldiers admitted had swabs taken and if the findings were positive, thy had treatment and all their contacts examined. Positive swabs were normally found in 5% of the population whether they were fit or not, and so I started taking swabs of all soldiers whether ill or healthy. In the 5% of carriers, they had just enough resistance from the antibodies in their blood to prevent development of the disease. After taking swabs I found that if the percentage of 'carriers' rose above the 5% to 15%, then an outbreak of meningitis would occur. When this happened I had close co-operation with Professor Duguid's laboratory in Cardiff, and I continued to carry on with this research work. (In pre-war days, infants under the age of two years had a high mortality rate from meningitis.)

When Medical Officers inspected troops their chests were bared to look for the spotted rash.